THE TAMING OF THE GORILLAS

Bob Campbell

MINERVA PRESS

LONDON

MIAMI   DELHI   SYDNEY

THE TAMING OF THE GORILLAS
Copyright © Bob Campbell 2000

ISBN 0 75410 963 1

First Published 2000 by
MINERVA PRESS
315–317 Regent Street
London W1R 7YB

Printed in Great Britain for Minerva Press

THE TAMING OF THE
GORILLAS

Foreword

This is the story of what really happened in the initial years of the late Dian Fossey's field observations of the mountain gorillas in the Eastern Congo and Rwanda. It is a remarkable, sensitive account of various incidents that took place. Anyone with even a passing interest in the gorillas will know of Dian's work, but only a handful of people have ever known what actually lay behind her success. Bob Campbell was there and it was he who in fact 'broke the barrier' as it were, with these magnificent apes. This is an eyewitness account.

It was not too many years ago that rich, big-game hunters set off from Europe and America to shoot the great silverback mountain gorilla. Success was considered to be a feat of great daring and prowess. Fortunately these times have passed, but it is all the more remarkable to read the story of the first man to be physically and perhaps affectionately handled by a wild, free-living gorilla on the mist-shrouded slopes of a Virunga volcano in Rwanda.

The gorillas, particularly the mountain gorillas, have never faced such an uncertain future as now. With the tragedy of the massacres in Rwanda and continuing civil war in the region, the chances of saving the national parks and refuge for the gorillas are slim at best. Dian's main legacy is the ongoing international efforts to raise support for the wild gorillas, and I believe that this sensitive narrative will do a great deal to rekindle and reaffirm our concerns. Bob Campbell, a close personal friend of mine for many years, has written a very intimate account of his time with the gorillas and with Dian. It is a memorable account in all respects.

Richard Leakey

Preface

As though the sun had already set, thick cloud spreading low and grey had darkened the surrounding forest. Gentle currents of cold air lifted the smell of freshly crushed foliage and stirred long pendants of lichen in the trees. In the fading light I wrote notes on a small pad, trying to recall clearly all that had happened during the day. Subconsciously my mind monitored small sounds coming from the animals scattered in the dense undergrowth nearby, and registered also the ominous rumbles of thunder far off to the east. Otherwise the forest was remarkably silent: a brooding, expectant silence, as if awaiting the turbulence a storm would bring.

The morning's work had been hard but very satisfying. Lying on a bed of crushed stems and leaves, almost warm in spite of wet clothing and the wafts of chilly air, I felt comfortably relaxed and reluctant to stir. After two hours of rest, one by one my subjects were starting to feed again. With light levels plummeting there was no pressing need to keep in close contact, so I waited for a while, lazily tracking their quiet movements with my ears and contemplating which route I would take for the long walk back to camp.

The breeze freshened, rustling the leaves of the gnarled old hagenia trees, then strengthened sharply and brought the smell and promise of rain. The wind drew icy fingers across my damp clothes and carried away the receding sounds of movement. I listened carefully for a minute, trying to confirm I had correctly judged the direction the animals were taking, but the wind was too strong. On an impulse I left my heavy pack in the undergrowth and went forward on hands and knees.

Aware my own progress would be noted, slowly and cautiously I crawled along freshly trampled trails, until the sharp snap of a dry twig brought me to a stop. Peering in the dim light, I could see a vague black shape behind a screen of leaves; two other animals moved on my right, but they ambled on quietly and were quickly swallowed up in the tangled greenery. Ahead, I could hear the distinctive sound of thistle plants being broken and stripped for eating, then the crackle of twigs and protesting plants as a heavy body forced through a thicket.

Suddenly, with a bare instant of warning, the foliage on my left parted; there came a double beat of hands against chest and two arms thumped down solidly on the middle of my back. Unprepared and astonished by the action I remained perfectly still, a feeling of indescribable exhilaration flooding over me. It was the young male gorilla who had been my close companion for several hours during the morning. With this first, unrestrained demonstration of complete trust, months of painstaking work were paying off in a totally unexpected way. The two arms continued to press down as the gorilla supported the full weight of his upper body on my back. He swayed gently; I felt his fingers begin to explore the collar of my jacket – then the hair on the back of my neck. In a poor position to respond, I resorted to my best rendition of the low-pitched, rumbling growl gorillas use as an apparent sign of pleasure or contentment. This caused him to pound me firmly on the shoulder with a big fist and roll away on to his back. Looking at me calmly with soft brown eyes, he extended a long arm across the gap between us. The invitation to continue the playful encounter seemed very clear, but I did not dare. I had been walking, climbing and crawling over the Virunga volcanoes of Rwanda and Zaire for over three years, and was more than content to stay still and savour the lingering pleasure brought on by the brief moments of contact.

As I gazed at the gorilla, sprawled on his back, relaxed and unafraid – inviting response – I knew some sort of pinnacle had been reached. In a very tenuous way, this formerly shy creature had suddenly become a new partner to my efforts and I could not have wished for a better reward for hundreds of hours of patient work.

When I first came to the Virunga mountains in 1968, there had been no reason to believe I would develop any sort of close affinity with gorillas, nor had there been any intention to do so. But time and changing circumstances had dictated otherwise. After months of slow progress, a new habituation technique had allowed me to break down the gorillas' strong resistance to close approaches. Now, in just a few carefree seconds, this powerful creature at my side had caused a major shift in my thinking. While I remained unmoving on hands and knees he began to sway his head from side to side in a playful gesture, then regained his feet, plunged into the foliage and was gone.

The short, unexpected encounter held great significance: a wild gorilla had chosen of its own free will to give a spontaneous and uninhibited display of trust in a human being. For a fleeting period of time two very different primates shared the electrifying thrill of strong physical contact. There was no way to tell what passed through the gorilla's mind, but the message in his eyes and motions of his body were very expressive and clear to me. The experience gave such immense pleasure and meaning because it forecast a reversal in the nature of the relationship that had developed between us. All previous physical contacts initiated by this shy creature had been tentative touches and gentle examination of my clothing and equipment. In analysing the courageous action he had just taken, I felt sure a new and significant level of confidence had been reached.

I can recall the day and the feelings generated by that trusting demonstration with exceptional clarity. It took place during the afternoon of 10 February 1972 and dominates the memories of an eventful and ultimately very rewarding period in my life. With the advantage of hindsight, I know the habituating process that enabled me to penetrate the secretive world of mountain gorillas was excessively drawn out. I know also that the encounter that led me to become the first human playmate of a wild gorilla was merely the beginning of a new and fruitful association between humans and the giants of the forest. At the time, I was simply delighted the way was opening for me to move more freely with and within a gorilla family group – accepted almost as a member – able to film at last some of their more intimate behaviour with a clearer view. In the months that followed many more extraordinary interactions took place. The young male grew bolder, regularly seeking me out to indulge in sessions of play that can only be described as exquisite. Other members of his family became more relaxed and friendly, allowing many fine openings for close observation. I should have spent many more months taking advantage of the hard-won ability to manoeuvre within a few feet of them. But pressures of a personal nature intervened – ultimately breaking my unique relationship with the fabulous creatures.

It is common knowledge that history records a mixture of fact and fiction, but the period covering what is known about gorillas carries more than a fair share of myth and sensational fiction. It must be admitted, however, that few animals have stimulated the human powers of imagination as strongly as the gorilla. For over two thousand years, ever since European explorers first recorded their meetings with them, the gorilla has been saddled with an undeserved reputation: that of a huge, brutish and ferocious human-like beast, said to be endowed with many human characteristics and unbelievable strength. In all fairness, the first contacts made by explorers must have been astonishing experiences; even in this enlightened age, few people are not awed by their first sighting of a wild adult male gorilla – especially if an approach elicits a fearsome, noisy demonstration. In recent times, a combination of popular books, documentary films, and many long-term behavioural studies have stripped away old conceptions and helped immeasurably to clear the gorilla's tarnished image. Nevertheless, misconceptions still abound. A surprising number of people still hold to beliefs based on old adventurers' tales.

The most widely seen film to feature gorillas is the highly successful Hollywood production, *Gorillas in the Mist*, the dramatic screen version of Dian Fossey's long association with mountain gorillas. With a significant part of the film designed to reveal the role I had played in her African adventure, it was inevitable that I became involved in the production. Much of the filming was carried out in Rwanda at locations very familiar to me, and watching the screenplay unfold in front of the cameras – especially my part being played by a professional actor – evoked some very strange feelings.

Not many people see a special and rewarding period of their life exposed on the big screens of the world, but in my case, the drive to create box-office appeal and the limitations inherent in feature film production resulted in a portrayal of events that had only a tenuous connection with reality. I found the experience quite extraordinary, sometimes disturbing, but it helped reinforce a long-delayed intention to write about my adventures with gorillas. The strongest influence in this respect came before the filming even started – on the day I climbed with members of the film unit to visit Karisoke, the small research station Dian Fossey had established in 1967, and where she was brutally murdered in 1985. Important sequences were to be filmed in the vicinity and the director, Michael Apted, wanted me to help select some good locations. I had by this time been in Rwanda for a week, accompanying Michael and his unit managers on several excursions into the mountains. We had examined some prime and beautiful locations, all for one reason or another reminding me of events long past, but I knew the imminent climb to Karisoke would revive particularly strong memories.

By pure coincidence the date set for the visit was 29 May, so that on the same day and month, almost to the hour, I found myself once more at the base of Mount Visoke, standing on the very spot from whence I had departed exactly fifteen years before. With a recollection of that day occupying my thoughts, I had looked over the familiar slopes of the volcano. As though it were yesterday the scene returned to mind with easy clarity; at this place, on 29 May 1972, thirty-five porters had deposited their heavy loads. Aware that I had cleared out my cabin, the men knew this was no routine departure. They had stood patiently and unusually silent while I said goodbye and paid their wages. Guamhogasi and Guihandagaza, two long-serving porters who made the twice-weekly mail and supply run between camp and the town of Ruhengeri, were especially downcast; only wan smiles acknowledged the bonus payments I gave them. The day had begun at dawn with the full realisation that my term in the mountains had finally come to an end. A restrained and difficult farewell to Dian Fossey had left me with conflicting emotions – and a mind that still refused to accept there would be no return.

Over a period of three and a half years I had become thoroughly adjusted to the lofty mountain environment: the wet, the cold, the long daily hikes to search out the gorillas. The strange way of life amongst the ancient volcanic peaks had become almost normal, and successes during recent months were still vivid and cause for much personal satisfaction.

The finality of my departure had been brought about by a determination to rejoin Richard Leakey in his hunt for the fossils of prehistoric man. Within twenty days I would be back in the rugged country that lay to the east of Lake Turkana, in Kenya, adapting once more to the searing heat and powerful, dust-laden winds of an arid semi-desert. Unaware that a decade and a half would pass before I set eyes on Mount Visoke again, I had crammed the great pile of equipment into my old Land Rover, until it sagged under the weight, then drove off down the rocky, rutted track towards Uganda and my home in Kenya.

During the two-day journey there was ample time to reflect on the reasons for exchanging one prime assignment for another: the study of the world's most dramatic primate for the search amongst prehistoric sediments for the roots of human ancestry; totally different occupations, yet both firmly linked by strong lines of scientific enquiry. I had already been associated with Richard Leakey's first three major palaeontological expeditions. They had all been carried out in remote, exciting areas, and combined with many varied photographic tasks for his parents, Louis and Mary Leakey, had generated a strong personal interest in the study of human origins. In taking on an assignment to cover research on mountain gorillas, I had been given a mar- vellous chance to observe and film the little-known behaviour of a closely related primate – one that was being studied, in part, to help throw some light on the complexities of hominid evolution – but at the same time, much to my regret, I had forfeited the opportunity to record the discovery of several outstanding hominid fossils by Richard Leakey at Lake Turkana.

By the end of 1971, in spite of a close relationship with Dian Fossey and mounting achievements with the gorillas, I had been torn between the powerful urge not to miss another season by the shores of that ancient lake, and the equally strong desire to build on the tolerance and trust of a family of great apes. As it happened, I had chosen a wonderful year for a return to the hunt for hominid bones, but in so doing had unintentionally brought my long association with Dian and mountain gorillas to an abrupt end.

The day that I returned to Karisoke in May 1987 is one I shall not forget; it was truly a journey into the past. In recounting what happened I can think of no better way to set the scene for my personal story of *The Taming of the Gorillas*.

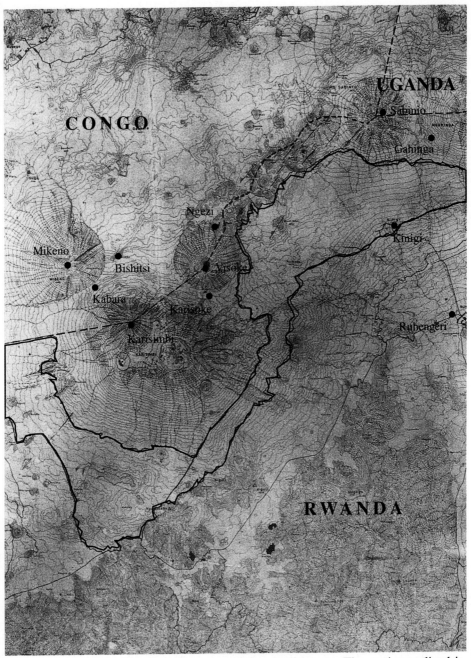

A contourmap of the Virunga volcanoes and surrounding area. The section outlined in heavy line defines the area excised from the Parc des Volcans for settlement and cultivation.

Contents

Karisoke

29 May 1987

I stood below the looming bulk of the volcano and looked over the steeply rising slopes. Dull veils of mist drifted in the deep erosion gullies and shrouded the upper reaches of the mountain; the scene seemed so familiar I experienced a fleeting sensation that time had turned back. Mount Visoke – now named Bisoke in deference to the correct Rwandese pronunciation – looked much the same as the day I had first set eyes on it. But behind me, the long stretch of freshly cultivated land I had traversed to reach its base nearly twenty years before now had the look of permanence and age. Buildings and shacks crowded the road to the mountain and a great many more huts littered the undulating landscape. Alien trees of eucalyptus and cypress had grown to maturity and not a vestige remained of the forest that had once flourished here.

But this was no time for reflection and the noisy activity all around me brought a swift return to reality. While some members of the film unit looked with transparent dismay at the high slopes, others had shouldered their packs and were impatient to be off. Greetings were being shouted at me from men who crowded the roadhead parking area. Boys had become men and men had grown older; I looked them over, struggling to identify faces and remember names. I became conscious also of the sly interest with which many were studying me: the eyes that would not meet mine, the murmur of quiet voices obviously discussing my presence. I guessed word had already spread that I had been asking questions about the murder of Dian Fossey. Having confirmed that at least three of the men who had worked with Dian and myself were still employed at Karisoke, I fully intended to ask plenty more. During one of the early casting sessions held by Michael Apted, I had met Sebucha, one of several men who had worked for me on the mountain. He had been selected to act as porter in the film, but until the time came for him to play the part he had become my personal assistant. When I asked what the men were talking about, in halting Kiswahili he confirmed rumours were indeed circulating that I might be here to enquire about the murder.

Putting aside a rush of unpleasant thoughts, I headed for the narrow cleft in a ridge of ancient pumice that marked the start of the ascent to Karisoke. Water seeped and dripped from the dark walls of pumice and the well-remembered trail rose steeply ahead. As I set foot on it and began the climb, past and present seemed to merge. Automatically breathing deeply to compensate for the oxygen-depleted air, I settled to a rhythmic climbing gait.

While the energetic members of our team surged ahead, I climbed slowly in the company of the group who professed to be out of condition and wanted to be paced. Although most had already laboured their way to several locations above nine thousand feet, they had suffered in the foolish attempt to keep up with the macho youngsters and hardy porters. From past experience I knew the climb to Karisoke exerted some sort of psychological influence on many people, leading them to expect and believe it to be a taxing one. That the trail began with a slope of nearly forty-five degrees did not help. But in reality, aside from a few short, steep sections, the average gradient was moderate: a rise of two thousand feet over a distance of roughly three miles. For mountaineers, the trail to Karisoke would rate as a mere stroll, but many people who walked up were unfit and unfamiliar with the effects of a reduced oxygen supply and suffered accordingly.

I had climbed to the Karisoke research camp along this winding path countless times, and in doing so once again was astonished to note the passage of time had done nothing to alter the old track. Familiar tree trunks lay where they had fallen decades ago; treacherous patches of aqueous mud lay in wait for the unwary, exactly as before; and the sight of sections of old logs, laid like stepping stones across many of them, recalled the effort I had made to have them set down so many years ago. My companions paused frequently to rest, a few red in the face and gasping for breath in the thin air. Their predicament reminded me strongly of Dian, who was seldom able to complete the climb in less than two hours. I remembered how often I had resigned myself to match her painfully slow pace.

Light rain began to fall gently, adding more moisture to the already slippery soil. From long habit my eyes wandered over the lush green of the heavy foliage, instinctively searching for signs left by the passage of animals. Concentrating on their physical stress, my group struggled on under the weeping pall of cloud. We climbed slowly into a woodland of ancient hagenia trees, then on across the more gentle rises.

Plodding along, my mind occupied by times long past, I was taken by surprise as we approached some buildings. The trail no longer crossed the open glade where in September 1968 I had first set eyes on Dian Fossey. Instead, it led us directly in front of the African staff quarters, expanded now with additional buildings new to me. We moved on along a muddy walkway of cut branches and logs; I caught sight of Dian's second cabin, and forty yards beyond it the one I had built for myself in 1971. A little further away, beside the path that led out to the high meadow on the saddle between Visoke and Karisimbi, was the large building that had been Dian's third and last residence. It was huge by Karisoke standards. Clad and roofed in green-painted corrugated iron, like all the rest she had built, it was now visually decrepit and displaying signs of neglect and slow decay. Generally strapped for adequate funds, Dian had constructed the cabins with saplings cut from the forest, and had used the cheapest, thin gauge corrugated iron sheets for the roofs and outer walls. Although they came free, the forest poles were not always straight, and the thin metal sheets were easily buckled and dented, making it difficult to achieve a neat final appearance. My old cabin had been built with lengths of Dexion angle-iron, but had been destroyed in a fire long ago and then re-constructed; now it looked just as tired and shabby as the others.

While the team rested, sampling the tea and coffee brought along to sustain us, one of the men I wanted to see appeared. In traditional African fashion we exchanged long and warm greetings. For two and a half years Kanyarugano had taken care of my simple camp requirements, bringing hot water when it was needed, washing through the never-ending piles of muddy, wet clothing, keeping the floor of my tent and later my cabin brushed and clean. He had heard I was in Rwanda and seemed genuinely pleased to see me, but his eyes slid away from mine and he appeared tense and nervous. Although we both knew they were hanging in the air I did not press any questions on him – there would be plenty of time later to discuss unpleasant matters.

Curiosity drew me to Dian's large building, and I saw at once where her murderers were said to have cut their way in through the iron sheeting. Looking at the jagged cut marks, it seemed very strange to me that they had selected such a noisy method of entry. Under orders from the police the cabin was still firmly locked, but by peering through the dirty panes of a window near the front door I could see a little of the interior. As my eyes adjusted to the gloom of the room, I picked out a large montage of photographs on a facing wall – the sight of them was a surprise and instantly revived a surge of vivid memories. The pictures were all black and white prints of gorillas: old enlargements specially prepared by the *National Geographic* photo lab from my early colour slides, pictures that Dian and I had used for reference and identification purposes. Familiar gorilla faces stared at me through the dusty glass: Old Goat, Bravado, Petula, Tiger, Augustus, Simba, Rafiki, Peanuts… the names came back readily as I looked from face to face. It struck me forcibly that the whole montage consisted entirely of my old prints, most made over seventeen years earlier. Right at the centre, the face of Digit when he was a young blackback, looked calmly at me. Digit was one of the few gorillas I had been able to give a name, and the shy youngster had later dramatically changed character to become a very unusual and very special anthropoid friend.

Why were there were no pictures from more recent years, I wondered. When I had left this remote camp a decade and a half ago, the way had been open for Dian to continue her research with an entirely new approach – one I had developed specifically to defeat the vegetation barriers and overcome some serious filming problems. In July 1970 I had persuaded Dian that I should break from her non-intrusive observation rules and purposely move in on the animals. Then, unfettered by the restraints she had established to protect the gorillas from harassment or stress, I had evolved a technique that quickly broke down their strong resistance to close approaches. Though circumstances had then intervened to halt the habituation process, a few months later I became the first human privileged to be accepted within a gorilla family. There were surely other collections of photos elsewhere in the house, but for the moment all that were visible were my own. The sight of Digit's young face brought to mind some fabulous interactions with the gentle animal. In all my encounters and work with a variety of wild animals, nothing could match the exquisite pleasure I had gained from the gorillas that looked at me through the dusty glass. Knowing that nearly all of them were now dead, I stared at the photographs for many minutes, a growing and uncomfortable sense of depression washing away much of the unexpected enjoyment at seeing old friends.

A short distance beyond the front of the cabin lay Dian's gorilla graveyard. Like a magnet, it exerted an invisible attractive force on me. Many recent articles I had read were accompanied by pictures of this place, but looking at it closely for the first time I became aware of an almost tangible aura of tragedy: tragedy born of sympathy and concern that one particular person had felt for the misanthropic mountain giants. Someone had very recently taken the trouble to cut down foliage that had overgrown and obscured the simple grave markers. Faded letters on small, metal-faced boards spelled out the names of long-dead creatures. Many had been my firm friends, and several, I knew, had died violently at the hands of humans identified as poachers. Beyond them, close by a board that carried Digit's name, a large mound outlined by a simple oval of stones marked the final resting place of Dian Fossey.

A few members of the film unit strolled over to join me, breaking my preoccupation with grim thoughts. I set about taking photographs of the depressing scene, but then without warning was engulfed by a great wave of sadness. I had to turn away and move off into the thickets beyond to hide my emotions. My association with Dian, with the great apes, with nearly everything to do with this isolated research camp, had been cut off at a stroke fifteen years before. Although I knew much of what had happened throughout the following years, my personal recollections centred firmly and selectively on some wonderful moments – all locked away at the time I had left this place so long ago. I felt as if I had walked out in the middle of an enthralling play, missing the many eventful and sometimes tragic acts that followed, and had returned now to observe the final closing scenes.

It took a while to submerge the welling up of old memories and recover my composure. When I caught up with the team, they were viewing the site at which sequences would be filmed to describe where Dian's research work had begun at Kabara, in Zaire. A dingy shack was under construction to represent the old wooden cabin she had utilised, and beyond it stretched the large, waterlogged meadow where my boots had been soaked on the very first walk to see gorillas.

A pale sun broke briefly through the drifting ceiling of dull cloud, illuminating the scattered, moss-laden hagenia trees and bringing some colour to the mountain foliage. Leaving my companions to examine the cabin and discuss the scenes to be shot around it, I walked along the edge of the meadow to sit on an outcrop of lava rocks. From them I could see the full sweep of Visoke's south-western flank. The outlines of sharp ridges and deep gullies were softened by the weak light and lowering clouds concealed the peak. I let my eyes wander over the familiar features, thoughts slipping back effortlessly to many exciting contacts with gorillas on the misty slopes. I wondered if the numerous little access paths I had cut still existed, and how many gorillas now utilised this segment of the volcano.

I had so often sat on this rocky outcrop at the edge of the meadow – listening intently and patiently for any sounds that would give away the position of a gorilla family, but now the slopes were silent, only the faint voices of the film-makers carried to my ears. In my mind's eye I could visualise the first sight of this large open patch in the forest: the brilliant day that had etched the mountain peaks with startling clarity; Dian, preceded by her tracker and followed by her dog, walking slowly towards the rise that marked the boundary with Zaire. I wondered again what would have happened had I not left to rejoin the hominid hunters. For five months I had enjoyed an unbelievably exciting and unique position within a gorilla group; a whole new era for research and filming was opening up. Dian had wanted me to give up my life in Kenya and work with her on a long-term partnership in the study of mountain gorillas. But that had not been possible. We had parted company on stressed but friendly terms, and save for one brief meeting had never seen each other again.

In the aftermath of Dian's violent murder, journalists and professional writers had taken advantage of the tragic event to focus worldwide interest on her eighteen years in Africa. Some praised her and others were somewhat disparaging, but most agreed she stood above all in her dedicated efforts to ensure the remnant population of mountain gorillas on the Virunga volcanoes would be allowed to survive. Now the film-makers were working to create an epic that would dramatically romanticise those efforts. I knew the feature about to be put together was bound to establish new myths and beliefs about Dian. Only the many who had actually lived at Karisoke, working with and for her, knew exactly what had taken place. It seemed most unlikely that the full story would ever be told. Though I had a wonderful tale to tell, before leaving I had promised Dian I would not write anything until she had published an account of her work. But it had taken her twelve years to complete a book, by which time the freshness of my own experiences had long since faded. When Dian's book was published, *National Geographic* finally released their long hold on my pictures. I had reviewed the large collection and once more felt compelled to write about the hard-won images, but so far had only assembled a mountain of old correspondence, dairies and film logs and set out a simple outline. I knew a biography on Dian was to be published shortly, and wondered if it would have anything to say about all the hard work and painstaking care devoted to the taming of the giant apes.

Clouds were darkening and dropping a shroud over the distinctive scenery. Soon it would rain. I walked back to join my companions, promising myself I would one day describe how I had made friends with the once feared and unapproachable gorillas.

Gorillas by Chance

It was a bite by one of Africa's most venomous snakes that brought about my first visit to the realm of mountain gorillas. The near-fatal strike changed the course of my life, and I have often wondered what history would have recorded had that reptile not found its mark.

In August 1968 Alan Root, a naturalist and wildlife cameraman of some repute, made an uncharacteristic error while handling a puff-adder and was bitten on his right hand. The accident occurred in Kenya's remote Meru National Park, where he was given hasty emergency treatment before being flown to Nairobi. By the time he reached the hospital, the spreading effects of the snake's venom were clearly serious. Uncertain how to handle the situation, the doctor on duty administered an intravenous dose of antivenom that caused Alan to go into anaphylactic shock. He came perilously close to losing his life; only his strong constitution and sheer will-power enabled him to survive the traumatic experience. He began to recover remarkably quickly – but not without severe damage. He would eventually lose a finger and be left with a hand that would never again function normally.

Recently assigned by the National Geographic Society to document Dian Fossey's research on mountain gorillas, Alan was bitten only days after returning from a visit to make a start on the work. The accident immediately placed further filming with the gorillas and two other major projects out of the question. By the time I saw him early in September he was already on his feet, fighting to overcome the lingering damage to his hand and worrying about the immediate future.

For Dian Fossey, news of the disaster was doubly distressing. It was Alan who had introduced her to gorillas in 1963, helped her establish her first research camp in Zaire four years later, and who was now set to handle the photographic coverage of her work. She was not only deeply concerned for his well-being, but happened to be preparing to leave Africa for the first time in two very hard and eventful years. Alan had promised to find someone who would act as caretaker in her absence, and, if that was not possible, he would return himself and continue work with the gorillas. But now he was unable even to think of filming for weeks, possibly months. It had become urgent that someone be found to take his place and he came to ask if I could help.

Having just completed a three-month assignment for *National Geographic* in the hot, semi-deserts of Kenya's northern frontier district, I was in a very contented frame of mind. I had been filming and hunting for fossils with Richard Leakey's first expedition to the east side of Lake Rudolf, where a wide-ranging survey of vast deposits of prehistoric sediments had been very successful. The discovery of some hominid fragments amongst the wealth of fossil material in the area had made the possibility of a second expedition look extremely promising, virtually ensuring a further period of work for me in the coming year.

The mere thought of seeing mountain gorillas instantly fired my interest. Gorillas seem to precipitate strong emotions in people and exert a powerful influence on the imagination, and they did so now on mine. In spite of what I had read that fully countered the traditional image, unrealistic visions of aggressive, enormously powerful, six-foot creatures passed momentarily through my mind. The quick anticipation of a new and stimulating adventure induced a pleasant tingling of the nerves; I felt an immediate urge to jump at the chance, but at the same time reality and responsibilities intruded, and I hesitated. The timing could not be more awkward. A new house my wife Heather and I were building on the outskirts of Nairobi had reached a critical stage. Accumulated piles of correspondence, accounts and many other matters awaited attention. Also, I had seriously damaged the transmission of my safari Land Rover during the expedition, and already the gearbox was in pieces in my makeshift, open-air workshop. Letting the heady images of gorillas fade, I cut off an instant affirmative and promised to let Alan have a response in a few days.

But then Dr Louis Leakey, Dian Fossey's sponsor and general supervisor, quickly sought me out and put his weight behind Alan's proposal. He insisted that he must have a person he knew and trusted to watch over the camp; someone he could rely on to behave responsibly with the gorillas. In fact, very little persuasion was needed; the opportunity to climb the Virunga volcanoes and visit the gorillas was in itself irresistible. Rushing repairs on my car to completion, I abandoned all commitments at home. On 17 September I headed for Kampala, in Uganda, on the first stage of the eight hundred miles to Rwanda.

A day later, leaving early from the small Ugandan town of Kabale where I had spent the night, I began the final lap of the journey with growing and pleasant anticipation of what was to come. The road was soon engulfed in a thick mist that filled the narrow valleys of the hilly countryside. Not until I skirted the tip of Lake Bunyoni to begin a stiff climb through the Echuya forest did the white veils fall away. The narrow earth road unwound ahead in a long series of sharp bends and gentle curves, first through thick forest, then dense stands of bamboo. My old vehicle laboured up the steep inclines, until at nearly eight thousand feet the bamboo gave way to open grassland and I could see for miles across the seemingly endless hills of southern Uganda. Then abruptly the road changed course and a marvellous view opened up to the west. I had reached the high mountain pass called the Kanaba Gap, and my first sight of the Virunga volcanoes was unexpected and breathtaking.

Drawing to the side of the road, I stopped for a while to enjoy the scenery. I was at the edge of the western arm of the Great Rift Valley. At my feet lay a vista of green, heavily cultivated hills and valleys that fell away sharply. On the horizon, softened and partly obscured by a light-blue haze, stood a cluster of high volcanoes. Unearthing binoculars, I gazed at the lofty peaks for a long time. While on a lengthy safari for *National Geographic* three years earlier I had passed very close to the south of these mountains, but had seen nothing of them. Haze in the atmosphere had been so dense even their foothills had been obscured. Now the outlines of the individual volcanoes were clearly defined and I took time to sort out their names from my map.

First in line stood the bulging cone of Mount Muhavura, then smaller Gahinga. The deeply eroded bulk of Mount Sabinio marked the junction of the boundaries that separated Uganda, Rwanda and Zaire, but blocked the view to my destination – Mount Visoke. The sharp peak of Karisimbi, highest of the group, was barely visible, but the pale outline of Mikeno stood on its own and drew my interest. It was on this mountain that George Schaller had based himself in 1959 for an intensive, year-long study of the Virunga gorillas, and had been followed six years later by Dian Fossey. From the high position at the Kanaba Gap, this first clear sight of the volcanoes reinforced a nebulous sense of mystery about gorilla country, sharpening my desire to set eyes on the legendary apes. But as I examined the cratered land below the steep slopes, the feeling was moderated. It was clear the volcanoes were isolated in a great sea of cultivation: an aspect that had the disturbing effect of reducing their dominant position in the landscape.

Within three hours I was in Rwanda and ascending with some care a rough, rock-strewn track leading from the town of Ruhengeri to the small village of Kinigi. Healthy plantations of banana trees and row upon row of beans and potatoes stretched on either side as far as the eye could see. The gaunt and vaguely menacing bulk of Mount Sabinio rose up ahead, and on approaching Kinigi, at last I could discern the full outline of Mount Visoke. I called in briefly to see Monsieur Descamps, Dian Fossey's nearest white neighbour, then picked up Demaret, the driver who was to guide me to the roadhead and look after my vehicle.

Skidding and sliding along a recently improved track still wet from showers of night rain, gradually we closed on Mount Visoke, our progress painfully slow over many sections where jagged lava boulders protruded through a new, soft soil capping. Visoke grew in size until it dominated the view, but we were still a good way off when a large crowd of people appeared ahead. They surged forward as the car approached and Demaret explained these were the men who would carry my belongings up the mountain. Dian Fossey had sent word that I was due and all were eager to earn a porter's wage. Dressed in a wild assortment of ragged but modern clothes, the men were cheerful and vociferous, crowding impatiently around the vehicle until I insisted they stand back and form up along the road.

I lined up boxes of supplies and equipment and twenty men were soon selected, leaving at least thirty others disappointed. The last load allocated was a battered metal box I did not want to risk leaving in the vehicle; it was fairly small, but packed solid with a large variety of spanners and various hand tools. I clearly remember the man who stepped forward – grinning – thinking he was on to a good thing with such an insignificant box to carry. On picking it up his face registered instant disbelief at the weight. There were shouts of laughter from others who had been clamouring to be chosen for the load and several came forward to try lifting it. Small though it was, the tin weighed at least fifty pounds.

As I stepped out with my long line of porters towards the still distant base of Visoke, dark clouds were rolling in from the east. The men cheerfully assured me we would soon be wet. It took half an hour to walk through the cultivated fields on the gentle lower slopes of the volcano. All around the land showed obvious signs of recent clearing; the whole countryside was littered with the hacked up remains of great trunks and thick branches, and the thatched huts scattered all about were recently built. A few ragged and forlorn trees still stood as silent witnesses to a vanished woodland. I wondered what the area had looked like only a year or so before. Though broken everywhere by great outcrops and clumps of lava rock, the soil was dark and rich. Neat patches of new pyrethrum plants stood out, flanked by luxuriantly sprouting crops of beans, potatoes, corn and tobacco. Clearly the Rwandans now settled on this land were very happy with their lot. There were smiles and greetings from all we passed on the path, and much laughter and joking from those who paused in their work to watch us walk by.

Halting where cultivation stopped abruptly and the huge bulk of Visoke rose sharply, my porters grounded their loads for a brief rest and a quick smoke. Feeling disturbed and sad that yet another huge swath of African forest had disappeared for ever, I sat and looked back over the stretch of newly cleared land. Clouds cast darkening shadows over the patchwork of fields and I watched them with a touch of apprehension; with nothing to cover the cases and cardboard cartons I worried over the damage that might be done by a heavy downpour.

Cigarettes drawn to the last centimetre, the men hoisted their loads and headed for a narrow trail. The transition from freshly dug fields to dense foliage was abrupt and we were immediately swallowed up in towering stands of rich green plants. In spite of their slight build and the heavy loads, the men began to climb a steep, slippery path with considerable speed and agility. Carrying only a light pack, I matched their pace, but it was not long before I had to concede they were much fitter than me. My shoes were soon wet and muddy and my lungs pumped hard to compensate for thinner air. But the prolific vegetation held my attention, reminding me strongly of the higher slopes of Mount Kenya and the Aberdare mountains back home.

Amid a constant lively chatter, we climbed sharply rising ground. Up and up we went at a relentless rate, the porters sure-footed and breathing easily. Looking for chances to enjoy occasional views of the landscape, I considered suggesting there was no need for such haste, but instead called out extra reserves of energy and concentrated on avoiding the deeper patches of mud in the path.

Half an hour later we reached a small strip of grass bisected by a narrow stream. Clear, cool water was tumbling off the mountain down a narrow earth chute. Here the men stopped for another rest and a second smoke. A few of them had pipes and the tobacco they were using produced a sharp, pungent odour quite unlike any pipe smoke I had smelled before. I chatted with the men, discovering only a few could speak the Kiswahili language. I learned that a narrow track followed the stream directly to the peak of Visoke and was the main route for a few occasional climbers. I asked about gorillas, but on listening to the vague answers realised few in the group had any real knowledge of them.

Now the clouds were closer, racing overhead to collide against the towering flank of the mountain. Hot and sweating from the effort of the climb, all of us welcomed the chill wind thrusting them along. As we set off once more, climbing steadily, spatters of heavy raindrops heralded the promised wetting. We passed through a thickening woodland of hagenia and hypericum trees, the undergrowth studded everywhere with distinctive, tall lobelias. We marched on across occasional open grassy glades, where many boggy patches caused the men to tread warily to avoid sinking deeply in glutinous black mud. The scenery was fascinating, shortly made all the more dramatic by several brilliant flashes of lightning and ear-splitting cracks of thunder. Silent now, my porters hurried on through the deepening gloom. The ancient, gnarled hagenia trees, their heavy branches covered with thick sheaths of moss and festooned with waving lengths of pale lichen, took on a surreal look. Wisps of low cloud scudded through the crowns of the trees and I was thankful the rain still held off.

Minutes later the trail began to level out. In trees beyond an open glade of grass I caught sight of a thin wisp of smoke; below it stood a single, green-painted cabin, flanked on one side by some faded canvas tents. As I walked across the glade, the tall figure of Dian Fossey appeared and watched me approach. We met and shook hands, exchanged formal greetings and politely eyed one another. Clearly interested to know what kind of person her establishment was being entrusted to, Dian's greeting was cool and reserved. I was curious to know what sort of woman was prepared to live alone in this remote, isolated camp and matched her frank examination. She was dressed in a blue shirt and blue jeans that were wet and stained from the knees down; a jacket tied by its sleeves hung loosely from her waist. On her feet were heavy, brown leather boots, wet and muddy and capped by white socks with an eye-catching red band. A plait of dark-brown hair lay across one shoulder and her angular face looked tired and drawn. It was two o'clock and she had just returned from a contact with some gorillas.

The wind had died to a gentle breeze, and in my light cotton shirt I was suddenly acutely aware that the air had turned very cold. Mist was drifting silently through the trees and it became quite dark. The porters were champing to be paid off so that they could return swiftly to their warm huts far below. While I handed out money, then hastily stacked my belongings in a small tent that had clearly seen better days, Dian retired to her kitchen to make lunch. The wind began to blow again, strong gusts setting the trees in motion and snatching dried leaves from their branches. As we sat down to eat in the comfortable warmth of the cabin, the heavens opened and heavy rain came thundering down on the sheet metal roof.

That night, lying on a canvas cot in the damp and musty old tent, uncomfortably cold in spite of several blankets, I listened to squalls of rain and wind beating at the canvas and wondered what I'd got myself into. Recently accustomed to a hot, arid environment only twelve hundred feet above sea level, my body was objecting to the high altitude and the bone-chilling mountain air. I had considered myself to be reasonably fit, but the swift climb with the porters had shown that was not quite the case; my limbs would surely be stiff and sore in the morning. I fell asleep wondering about gorillas, the anticipation of meeting them face to face the next day balancing then erasing the slight sense of unease.

Coming all too soon it seemed, the dawn was clear and not a vestige of cloud marked the sky. The air was still and icy cold. I admired the immediate scenery, but shivered as I shaved hastily under the tent flysheet. With only two days to go before her departure, Dian had very little time to introduce me to the basic routine of her daily work. As soon as we had downed an early breakfast at a little table outside her cabin, she called her assistant, a short, heavy-set man called Nemeye. He took her rucksack and we set off to search for gorillas.

The trees and undergrowth still dripped from the deluge in the night, and bright rays from a rising sun reflected off millions of droplets caught in the lush foliage. The high contrast between sunlight and shadow gave the scene a stark brilliance that seemed to accentuate the icy chill in the air.

We walked out west from the camp through open woodland, accompanied by Cindy, Dian's part boxer dog, and followed by the camp woodcutter who would take her back after a brief run. We came first to a large grassy meadow dotted with lobelia plants and a few giant senecio trees in full flower. However, the broad expanse was more like a bog than anything else. Deceptively solid-looking bunches of grass and pads of sphagnum moss sank into clear water underfoot. Within minutes my light canvas 'jungle boots' were soaked through. But the views from the meadow were breathtaking.

To our right lay the steep, thickly vegetated slopes of Mount Visoke, the angled sunlight accentuating narrow ridges and deep gullies created by ages of erosion. Ahead, fringed with a thin belt of cloud, the massive and barren lava plug of Mount Mikeno reared against a hard blue sky. Across the meadow to our left stood the symmetrical cone of Mount Karisimbi. Rising to close on fifteen thousand feet and sharply defined in the clear air, the summit was covered with a pale flush of snow or hail. We came to a second, narrower meadow and Dian pointed out we were crossing the invisible border that ran in a direct line between the peaks of Visoke and Karisimbi. Here the dog was put on a lead and sent back. We walked on slowly, out of Rwanda's Parc des Volcans and into the Parc des Virungas of Zaire. Aware that Dian was a *persona non grata* in Zaire, I asked the obvious question. But she shrugged it off with the answer that this portion of Visoke was virtually out of reach of Zairian authorities; she had no respect for them – and no compunction about breaching the border for the purposes of her research.

Beyond the second meadow the ground fell away to reveal a great sweep of widely-spaced hagenia and hypericum trees. Below the trees the undergrowth was heavy and dotted everywhere with the tall lobelias. Hugging the base of Visoke, we followed a descending path that threaded through increasingly dense stands of giant stinging nettles. Already resigned to a day with wet feet, now I discovered my lightweight trousers were not the best for the task in hand either – they were certainly no protection against the potent hairs of the nettles. I was soon suffering from a multitude of stings on legs and hands. We were heading directly for the area where Dian had contacted gorillas the day before. As we descended slowly from the saddle, Nemeye's sharp eyes picked out a gorilla high on a distant ridge. For a brief moment an indistinct black shape remained visible, then abruptly vanished in the surrounding greenery. We pushed on quietly along the narrow pathway through more acres of shoulder-high nettles. Already visualising a meeting with gorillas, my eyes kept returning to examine the high ridge.

Minutes later we were brought to an abrupt stop by a sudden thrashing in the undergrowth – followed by an explosive roar that lifted the hair on my neck. Dian crouched down immediately, motioning to me to do the same. Nemeye backed silently away behind us to slide out of sight behind a tree. We had nearly walked into a gorilla and I felt an intense surge of excitement. This is all too easy, I thought, and waited expectantly for one or more of the creatures to show themselves. But though close, the gorillas remained invisible. Minutes passed, then tens of minutes. Crouched down at the base of a tree, surrounded by tall nettle plants and tangled vegetation, we were clearly in a poor position to see anything. At first we listened to the slight sounds the creatures were making; they were perhaps forty feet away and I strained in vain to get a sighting. Now and then part of a black body could be seen through the thickets; I thought a face peered from behind a screen of leaves, but it was gone before I could determine the full outline. Group 8, Dian assured me – a small family consisting of only five males with whom she had apparently had some exciting contacts recently. If we remained very still and quiet she thought they might become curious and move closer.

As time went by without any change in our relative positions, the tension generated by the first moments of excitement gradually dissipated. In her quiet, almost girlish voice, Dian began whispering to me, passing on advice about gorilla habits and information on the ranges of the groups she had under observation. I listened with keen interest, wondering all the while how quickly I could learn the lie of the land and make the best use of my stay. Part of my mind remained diverted and tantalised by the proximity of the gorillas, making me increasingly impatient to creep closer to them. When eventually I voiced my thoughts, Dian quickly dismissed the idea. Explaining that her methods of observation were purposely non-intrusive, she stressed that her subjects were not to be subjected to any pressure, going on to describe in detail how she worked and how I must behave while trying to make contact with them. I was the novice and she seemed to be enjoying her position as an old hand.

Forced against her will to abandon her original study area centred around Kabara, a high meadow on the slopes of Mount Mikeno lying a mere two or three miles to our west, after traumatic difficulties and against the advice of American State Department officials, Dian had restarted her work on the Rwandan side of the mountains. She told me how she had soon discovered that her new subjects were much shyer and considerably more nervous than the Kabara gorillas. But now, after a full year of work from the new base, she had identified and named a good many of the animals in four separate families: some fifty-four individuals in all. A fifth group with fourteen members ranged to the south of her camp, but she had met up with them only six times at the end of 1967, then never seen them again. She knew a sixth group inhabited the eastern face of Visoke, but received only occasional reports of its presence from the people living below. She took care to explain her main object was to observe truly uninhibited behaviour. She was fully aware it was possible to stalk quite near to the gorillas by being very careful and quiet, but all too often they hastily moved away from these close approaches, becoming alarmed and retreating quickly if followed.

The technique she had adopted for most of her study was simple and sometimes very effective. She would locate a group, then, trying not to cause any disturbance that would make the animals react and move away, attempt to find a reasonable position from which to watch. The gorillas were often evasive, but sometimes curious enough to remain static or even move closer – especially the youngsters. Occasionally, if conditions were right, she might be rewarded with a good view and witness some interesting activities. Most of her best observations had been made from up trees, or the opposite side of ravines: positions that allowed sightings from above the dense foliage. She made sure I understood she was very concerned that some professional photographers would want to record dramatic situations in the 'King Kong' image. She made it very plain that such people were not welcome to take advantage of the partial habituation she had achieved. Although she spoke quietly, her voice clearly conveyed an inner glow of enthusiasm for her work. I felt she was genuinely keen that I should benefit from her knowledge. Some of the reserve she had maintained until now slipped away and I listened carefully to all she had to tell me, trying to guess from her explanations what excitements lay in store.

Although Louis Leakey had occasionally mentioned Dian's work to me, watching her animated face while she talked I realised how little I knew about her. In June 1967, when she had run into serious trouble as civil war flared again in the Congo, I had been in southern Ethiopia, occupied with the photographic coverage of Richard Leakey's contributions to an international expedition in the vast fossil fields of the Omo River valley. During a brief visit to our Ethiopian camp, in his usual spirited way Louis had described Dian's dramatic escape from detention. Now I wanted to know more about what had happened, but felt this was not the right time to ask.

We had been in position for nearly an hour. To me, the forest seemed un-usually quiet: the clear, ringing call of a bird I took to be a turaco echoed down from Visoke several times, and for a while a pair of ravens had wheeled and swooped overhead, cawing harshly. Disappointment at failing to get a good view of the gorillas combined to aggravate the discomfort of wet feet and some throbbing welts from the nettles. Expecting much more of this first encounter, I found it difficult to simply wait and hope for something to happen. The gorillas had fed for a while, remaining almost totally obscured behind the wall of foliage. Now and then one could be heard moving, but overall they were so quiet, at times I thought they had actually moved stealthily away.

When some mild breaking of foliage raised interest momentarily, Dian said the gorillas were constructing 'day nests' for their usual rest at this time. We continued to converse in whispers about the camp, the staff, the daily chores to be attended to, until about half an hour later quiet sounds indicated the gorillas were again active. We waited, Dian still hoping they might come closer, or at least cross over the path ahead and show themselves. But instead they chose to head directly away – the faint sounds of their departure fading rapidly. Dian judged it to be too late to start the search for the animals seen earlier, so we retraced our steps and returned to the camp.

While she disappeared to work in her cabin, I went for an exploratory walk in the woodlands nearby and thought about the events of the day. It was clear that if I was to respect and adhere to Dian's methods, it would be essential to cultivate a considerable degree of patience. Dian had effectively used the waiting hours to pass on much of her basic knowledge about the gorillas, also making it plain she trusted me to conform to her technique for making contacts; she did not want to return from her holiday to 'a bunch of screwed up gorillas' as she had bluntly put it. Thinking about the disappointing contact, I decided she had been testing me as much as anything else, for we could surely have abandoned the first group and gone on to find the gorillas sighted on the mountain.

In soft afternoon sunlight I wandered through some boggy but beautiful glades south of the camp, surprising several forest antelopes: little russet-red duikers, and a bushbuck male that bounded away giving hoarse, dog-like alarm barks. Apparently a large gorilla group sometimes utilised this area, but though I looked hard could see no trace of their activities. I noticed countless hoof prints of what appeared to be buffalo, but then quickly realised they were the smaller, narrower prints made by cattle.

The following day dawned crisp and brilliant. Traces of frost lay on the grass of the glade by the camp. I walked out to enjoy the scene, the clear air quickly chilling my nose and ears. I had slept fitfully, nettle stings aching gently, legs as expected still stiff from the rapid climb with the porters. With a change to corduroy trousers and a borrowed pair of gloves I was better prepared to deal with the nettles. It was Dian's last full day, and over our simple breakfast she expressed a determination to produce a good contact.

We returned directly to the position where we had sat for so long. Then, with Nemeye leading, we followed the gorilla spoor some distance through a forest of nettles to a 'night nest' site. Five scattered and simple foliage beds confirmed that we were on to Group 8. I looked with interest at the shallow, round 'nests', noting that each contained large amounts of flattened faeces that had already attracted a multitude of dung-flies. Dian made a note of the site on a little pad. Then we crept on carefully along freshly broken trails until a rapid but muted, thump-thump, thump-thump of a gorilla beating its chest told us the family was aware of our approach. Intrigued by the curious sound, expecting it to be louder and much more impressive, I was soon to learn there were many variations to chest beating. Again I felt the rise of internal tension, but the small group was on the move and as on the previous day remained hidden from view in the luxuriant nettles. Dian explained it was unwise to follow, so we turned away and for the first time began to climb Mount Visoke.

Progress up the sharply angled side of the mountain was painfully slow: a tangled mass of interlaced vegetation constantly impeded movement. Nemeye led, slicing with remarkable lack of noise through the soft barriers with a deadly looking, hook-shaped Rwandan weapon called a muhoro. Dian paused frequently to look all around and listen carefully, but save for the sounds of a few invisible birds, the slopes remained silent. As we gained a little height some magnificent views opened up. Beyond the broad expanse of hagenia forest below us, Mikeno reared dramatically in the haze-free air, its profile now changed to show what looked like two peaks. I was enthralled by the wild, unspoiled look of the terrain; it looked mysterious and intriguing, creating for me an impression of ageless, untamed beauty that fully matched my inner visions of gorilla country. The morning was still remarkably clear. The bright sun warmed the vegetation, strengthening the smells of moist soil and crushed plants. We advanced steadily, looking for fresh signs of gorilla, a pleasant breeze helping to keep us cool.

Old traces of gorilla trails were everywhere, and before long we came upon several that were obviously fresh. They led directly to the north and Dian confidently predicted we were heading for Group 9; she had previously explained how each family had been numbered in sequence as she first located them. Groups 1, 2 and 3 were those she had followed in the Kabara area, and on restarting her research in Rwanda she had simply continued the sequence. The tracks took us to a sharp ridge lined with a stand of giant heath. As we edged over the brow a very loud roar combined with chest beating instantly drew our eyes to the source. While Nemeye crouched to keep himself out of sight, we moved cautiously forward to get a clearer view.

Across a deep ravine, spread out in the dense foliage where they had been feeding, were many gorillas. The chest beats had come from the family leader, a huge silverback male. At last I had clear sight of a wild mountain gorilla and quickly brought binoculars to bear. I was immediately impressed. The gorilla was sitting on his haunches, glaring at us and almost fully exposed to view. As I watched, he rose on stocky hind legs to beat his chest once more. The strange, powerful sound echoed marvellously in the narrow confines of the ravine. Dian had named this animal Geronimo; he had a rusty red triangular patch of hair in the middle of his forehead and seemed to me to be in the prime of life. The muscles on his black, hairless chest bulged like those of a heavyweight wrestler. He filled the field of my binoculars as he smacked them with open palms and the display was magnificent. The big male riveted my attention for long moments, and all the while other members of his family were quickly seeking deeper cover and making their way through the heavy undergrowth to vanish over the next ridge. Dian was trying to count individuals and by the time I dragged my attention away from Geronimo most had already slipped out of sight.

We were in a superior position looking down on the group, which, combined with the sight of a stranger, had apparently made them nervous. The great silverback gave us a long baleful stare, then pushed through concealing bushes to follow his family over the ridge. The show was over, but I was content with the brief sighting; it was also dawning that the filming of these creatures was not going to be easy. I had expected the gorillas Dian was studying to be more approachable, but so far they were proving to be very elusive. I had also seen how well their coal-black bodies and long black hair helped them merge with the dark green of the rank vegetation.

Although we had enjoyed two sun-filled days in a row, I knew that the mountains were more usually shrouded in cloud and subjected to frequent rain. Filming in dark, wet conditions would undoubtedly be very difficult indeed. Mindful of his position as the assigned photographer for what was a prime subject, Alan had asked me not to bring my still cameras. But since *National Geographic* had agreed to finance my stay and expected me to continue the coverage he had already started, we agreed I would work with cine only. Dian had been upset by this arrangement, insisting that I use her camera and film until she left. I had taken a few shots of her at the camp, but out in the field, at first hand it was obvious that obtaining good pictures of gorillas was going to be a real challenge.

Dian was transparently pleased to see that I had been greatly impressed by

Geronimo. It was already late morning and she ruled out any attempt at following the group. Instead, so as to sample some different terrain, we began a traverse across the western flank of Visoke several hundred feet above the nettle fields. We travelled very slowly, crossing gullies and ridges, passing many signs showing that gorillas used this area extensively: old nesting sites, chewed up thistle and wild celery plants, broken branches in the small and scattered stands of vernonia trees, and countless old trails slowly being obscured by fresh foliage growth. I was inwardly pleased to see that gorillas left ample evidence in their wake that made tracking them relatively easy.

The excitements of the day were not over by any means. On a wide, almost treeless section of slope we ran into yet another family that Dian thought would be Group 4. The animals were some distance below, and as with Geronimo's family, not at all happy with our position above them. After an initial sighting that elicited a few staccato barks of alarm, all remained quiet and totally concealed. We crouched down, waiting patiently to see what would happen. After a short while, Dian came out with the old American expression, 'I have to go to the bathroom', so while Nemeye and I sat tight she crept away across the slope.

Within minutes the gorillas began to move, seemingly confident the small sounds of her departure meant the humans had moved on. Quite unexpectedly they started climbing, their passage through the tall vegetation marked only by the silent shaking of stems and leaves at various points across the slope. I glanced at Nemeye, but he said nothing and turned to burrow quietly but quickly out of sight into the thickets behind me. Moments later I heard movement and saw the foliage quiver directly below. Not willing to let the unsuspecting creature get a fright, I gave a suppressed cough. Silence reigned for a few seconds, then a sharp, explosive roar came from our right, conveniently locating the position of the family leader. But the gorilla below me simply stopped in its tracks – only feet away yet still fully hidden.

While adrenalin pumped in my blood from the excitement of not knowing what to expect, tense moments passed. The foliage shifted, a shiny black face rose above the leafy screen and I received a direct stare from a pair of brown eyes. The gorilla's lips were pursed tightly, eyes wide and inscrutable; I remember registering that the scleries of its eyes were almost black, accentuating the soft brown irises locked on to me. Time stood still it seemed, then the face vanished abruptly, followed by the crashing sounds of rapid descent. This caused several nearby gorillas to scream with alarm, then more loud crushing and breaking of foliage indicated the whole family was descending and leaving the site in a hurry.

In the quiet that followed I became aware of a plaintive whistle. Nemeye explained that it was Dian's signal, meaning that we should go to her. She was some distance away and now obviously furious. She directed her wrath at Nemeye, but her broken Kiswahili failed to convey her meaning and she turned on me. Her previously soft, girlish voice had become clipped and harsh, her face flushed and angry. I was taken aback by the abrupt change in manner. Apparently she had begun whistling to Nemeye as the gorillas started up the slope. He confessed to hearing the signal, but had failed to respond or mention it to me. Dian was very cross, thinking I had deliberately made an approach to the gorillas while she was out of sight, so causing the commotion that followed. It took a while to explain and convince her of what had actually happened, but the misunderstanding put a damper on what had otherwise been a very satisfactory day.

On the walk home we came across fresh signs of cattle and saw several of them grazing on the grasses of the big meadow. This served to darken Dian's mood further, but there was far worse to come. At the camp a porter was waiting with a package of mail carried up from the post office in Ruhengeri. Dian went into her cabin to go through it all. She came out later, red-eyed and obviously very upset, but it was some time before she chose to explain what was wrong. A cable had come through Dr Leakey to say that her father had died; in fact it stated all too baldly that he had committed suicide and the news distressed her considerably. She had been looking forward to her holiday away from the mountains with unrestrained eagerness; now much of the pleasure would be taken from it.

The next morning was again clear and sunny. Though Dian had arranged for porters to be ready at the camp by mid-morning, she insisted on going out to find gorillas once more. I had to admire her persistence; she had a long way to travel and could have well done without the additional walk. As it turned out, the time spent on the effort was wasted. We saw cattle again and heard the distant shouting of their owners. An outbreak of screams from a gorilla family high on Visoke came to our ears – probably Group 4 – but there was not enough time left to complete a climb to reach them. On the way back, the faint sound of jangling bells carried to us on a light southerly breeze. Beyond a line of hills extending away from the camp, poachers were obviously out hunting with dogs carrying locating bells. Dian had told me how often cattle herders and game poachers interrupted her work. She had some bitter comments to make about the park authorities, whom she had long since discovered were totally ineffective in maintaining any sort of control in these parts. For many years illegal intruders had enjoyed almost free rein to do as they pleased within the confines of the park.

Back at camp the porters were waiting, and within the hour Dian was ready to go. She emerged from her cabin and was no longer the somewhat unkempt researcher I had known for the past two days; dressed now in clean and smarter clothes, long hair brushed out and loosely secured with a clip at her neck, she had carefully applied make-up that transformed her face. Only dark smudges under her eyes gave any hint of the distress caused by the news of her father. I received final instructions and requests, then, with some misgivings, I am sure, Dian Fossey went on her way, leaving her research camp and the gorilla groups under the care of a complete stranger. Holding Cindy at my side, I watched her cross the glade and disappear into the hagenia forest. Aside from the apparently numerous cattle, their herders, the poachers and other intruders, for a few weeks I would have the mountains to myself and firmly intended to make the most of it.

As we had arranged, I transferred my possessions from the musty old tent into the comfortable cabin, and immediately felt more relaxed and at home. The cabin was a simple but sturdy framework of stout poles, with corrugated iron sheeting nailed to the outside and painted a dark green. The floor was made of heavy wooden planks set two feet above ground level. The interior was nicely lined with thick, patterned matting woven by local Rwandan women. A table, chairs, a bed and a few simple shelves for clothing, books and ornaments were the only furnishings, but colourful cloth prints, pictures on the walls and curtains over the three windows gave the room a homely look. The focal point was the fireplace, an inverted half of an old fuel drum supported and surrounded by large stones. Maintained by Nezarwanda, the man who did the chores around camp, a fire burned in it night and day, drying clothing and boots, generally giving out a pleasant glow and successfully keeping the cold at bay.

Although sometimes muddied by buffalo and the occasional elephant, a plentiful supply of water came from the stream that tumbled past only yards away. Hot water was constantly available from tins stacked in an open pit fire in front of the cabin. The kitchen was more basic: a rickety structure set up some thirty feet from the cabin. Matting nailed to poles formed the walls and the roof was an old but still waterproof tent flysheet. Inside, packed gravel on the soft soil gave a firm though constantly moist surface. Rough board workbenches and shelves carried a moderate selection of cooking utensils, crockery, tableware and kerosene lamps. There was a small cast-iron, wood-burning stove in one corner, but most of the cooking was done on a compact, double-burner kerosene unit. There could be no doubt about it, with the minimum of expenditure from her meagre funds, Dian had built up a functional and comfortable base for her research project.

After the move, I set about preparing camera equipment and making ready for the first day of filming. Dian had left me a sheaf of notes giving basic details of her four study groups. With Nemeye's help I hoped to track them all down before long, but first I would return to the west side of Visoke and search for Geronimo. At least I had seen him clearly and would recognise the distinctive red patch on his forehead. The weeks ahead were going to be a rare experience and I felt very content with my luck. If time allowed, I intended to explore the interesting-looking territory on the slopes of Karisimbi – perhaps even penetrate the forest towards Mount Mikeno and the Kabara meadow.

Normally a very early riser, in the cosy comfort of the cabin I awoke with a start the next morning and realised the sun was nearly up. Hastily downing a light breakfast, I called Nemeye. Encumbered now with camera gear and tripod, we set out at a swift pace to make up for lost time. The brilliant sun was rising above the trees and had already shifted some of the night's chill; all too soon I was sweating and discarding layers of clothing. We squelched over the waterlogged meadow, made our way through the zone of nettles, then climbed directly to the ridge where I had first seen Geronimo.

The nearly two-day-old traces left by the gorillas were still clearly defined and we began to follow them. We had covered less than a hundred yards when several gorilla screams echoed eerily across the slopes. *Kike wanakombana* (the females are arguing) was Nemeye's brief comment. The cries had come from a good distance away, but at this point Nemeye handed over the tripod and left me to go on alone. It was Dian's policy to keep her African assistants out of sight of the gorillas as much as possible; she had found early on that the gorillas became very agitated when they happened to see any of her men, and realised the creatures had previously only encountered men who were invading hunters, honey gatherers or cattle herders – people who had probably harassed them, if nothing else. As soon as the position of a group was known, preferably before any visual contact, the assistant would fade away and conceal himself, waiting until the day's work was over. Dian's whistle signal actually required an answer, as quite often it was necessary for him to move off a considerable distance. She had told me of several occasions when she had failed to find her man – more than once because he had fallen into a deep sleep. Now I followed the rule, going on to make contact while Nemeye retired to seek a comfortable hideaway.

Once alone, an energising tingle of excitement flowed in my veins. I moved on along the obvious tracks left by the gorillas; their large bodies had crushed the soft foliage, leaving ample evidence of their passage and direction of travel. A steep, curving slope lay ahead, and, somewhat destabilised by the awkwardness of the camera tripod and heavy pack, I began to cross it. A thunderous crashing of bushes erupted suddenly from the thickets above; my mind switched instantly from interest in the trail to churn with snatches of advice on what to do in the face of a gorilla charge, but before there was time to collect shattered wits, the grey bulk of an elephant smashed through a tangle of bushes and trees thirty feet ahead. The loud sounds of the elephant's hasty descent seemed to continue for minutes. Motionless and distinctly tense, I spent long moments scanning the slope, wondering if other elephants were still waiting silently above. A whistle came from the ridge behind, so I retreated until I could see and signal to Nemeye that all was well.

With all senses considerably more alert, I began to follow the gorilla trails again. While examining the great gouges the elephant had left in the soft earth, several abrupt screams confirmed the gorillas were still well ahead. Though impatient to see what was causing the screaming, I crept on quietly, determined to make a stealthy approach. I crested a ridge, expecting a good view, but a screen of bushes effectively obscured everything ahead. The gorillas had already detected me – a loud alarm bark and a flabby chest beat told me that – but I could see nothing. I found a break in the barrier, only to see a view of an empty valley. That the gorillas had been nicely exposed was obvious from expanses of crushed foliage, but now they were well concealed on the far side of the valley. Carefully, I set up tripod and camera, many of my slow actions eliciting further chest beating and shouts of alarm. Individual movements made it clear the group was melting away. With lens apertures nearly wide open, in spite of the sunlight, I managed to shoot a few scenes of faces peering at me. Then it was all over – the family had vanished.

Easing slowly down the ridge, hoping for more sightings of Geronimo's band, instead I spotted other gorillas far below. They were moving too, drifting slowly on a parallel course to the group above. I watched for a long time, hoping all the while that one would expose itself clearly, but saw only tantalising glimpses of dark bodies. Eventually my binoculars settled on a grand old male. His head carried a huge sagittal crest and the silver hairs on his back extended right up and over his shoulders. On checking Dian's notes I guessed this had to be the leader of Group 8 named Rafiki – the Kiswahili word for friend. He strode majestically across another small opening and was gone before I could even begin to line up the camera. I contemplated following the animals, but the words 'screwed up gorillas' came strongly to mind.

The day was mildly warm. I sat for a while to scan the territory that fell away to the west. Across a wide expanse of seemingly dense forest, the edge of the scarp called the Bishitsi bluff stood out clearly. Beyond that the forest appeared to be more open and I wondered if many other gorilla groups lived there. Towards the northern horizon a few scattered huts and the vague line of a road could be discerned. In contrast to the intensely cultivated Rwandan countryside, the area appeared almost uninhabited, but my vision was limited by haze and I knew many people lived beyond the distant forest fringe.

Hours had passed since the elephant had so effectively activated my nerves. With the sun already dipping towards Mount Mikeno, reluctantly I turned away to retrace my steps and find Nemeye. On the long walk home I tried to draw him out about the work he was doing with the gorillas, but his grasp of the Kiswahili language was poor, making it difficult to converse easily. At the camp he shared a rather small tent with two others, the woodman and Nezarwanda. The three huddled together for warmth at night, covered with a few blankets and coats, but they seemed quite content with their accommodation. Nemeye acknowledged it was the wage he received that most attracted him to the work – much more than he could ever hope to earn elsewhere, and certainly enough to make all the discomforts of life up the mountain worthwhile. As an uneducated peasant farmer he obviously enjoyed what was to him fairly undemanding work, but as I questioned him further about the gorillas, he revealed a total lack of understanding over what Dian was trying to achieve. His work was basic: to carry Dian's pack and to clear clogged paths and track down the gorillas for her. Why she was spending so much time and money simply following and watching them mystified him. I tried to explain in the most simple of terms, but he did not know enough Kiswahili. Though he nodded and grunted, I could tell the language barrier and his limited knowledge did not allow him to grasp what I was saying. How could I possibly explain to this simple man that, apart from discovering everything about the way gorillas lived, Dian's work was related to the study of mankind and the associated search for human origins.

Nemeye told me that Dian often sent him out with the woodman to locate gorillas, but admitted he had not seen much of them. Confirming they became very nervous if he happened to reveal himself, he laughed as he recalled at least two incidents when he had been out with Dian and the gorillas had come across his hiding place. 'They make me very afraid,' he said, 'screaming, beating their chests and getting very angry.' They made him want to break and run, but knew he had to lie perfectly still and wait for them to back off. He laughed again. 'They make my heart run very fast,' was his final comment. I could sympathise with him in that respect; the mere action of trying to approach them had already caused my pulse rate to increase – and I had yet to see or experience any aggressive behaviour. But it was early days and so far the fabulous creatures were proving to be very evasive. As we threaded our way along the narrow pathway, the setting sun bathed the woodlands and mountain peaks in a soft, golden glow. Four full days of sunshine had nearly dried out the undergrowth and the walk home was very pleasant.

It could not last, and indeed it did not. The very next day I received a thorough soaking and experienced the acute discomfort of facing the elements with inadequate protective clothing. While bent on the task of closing with Group 9 once more, the brilliant sunlight suddenly faded. I looked up to see a great bank of cloud sweeping in from the south-east, then a strong wind began to thrash noisily across the slopes. As if to make up for lost days, within seconds the darkening clouds had opened and torrents of rain streamed down.

Minutes passed; the wind blew harder and the temperature dropped rapidly. While the storm continued unabated, I hunched protectively over my backpack, cold water entering every weak point in my lightweight, supposedly waterproof nylon wind jacket. Rapidly losing warmth in the extremities, I contemplated getting up and heading for a tree, but there were none close by and I knew my pack was not sufficiently waterproof to give adequate protection to the camera gear. The rain battering my back suddenly became quite painful. I lifted my eyes to see large hailstones bouncing off the streaming leaves. The ice stones slowly collected into little heaps under the foliage and the temperature dropped lower, adding to my misery.

This was certainly an abrupt return to some of the less attractive aspects of wild nature. While my body cooled further, I felt thankful at least that a snug refuge was not far off. The warm cabin lay only an hour's walk away and I longed to get up, at least to start moving and generate some heat. The hail eased at last, changing to a steady beat of rain that gradually faded to a thin drizzle suspiciously like sleet. Uncurling my frozen body, quivering from the cold, I abandoned the pursuit of gorillas and set out to look for Nemeye.

Thick grey fog now replaced the drizzle, effectively cutting visibility to a few gloomy yards. Under the weight of water the heavy vegetation sagged over the narrow gorilla trails, almost obscuring them. Slipping frequently on wet tangles of plants and the saturated soil, it took a while to backtrack and then home in on Nemeye's responses to my whistles. Eventually I found him. He grinned hugely at my sodden appearance: hidden away from the storm in the hollow bole of a massive hagenia tree, he had remained quite warm and dry.

That storm marked the end of the fine weather. As the days passed I became progressively more used to hours of mist, cloud and frequent squalls of rain. I knew that out in the vast reaches of the Indian Ocean the monsoon winds were changing direction; the unstable conditions during the change would now bring about a period of wet weather that could last two or three months. There were many times when I wished the gorillas lived in a less hostile environment. But if getting wet and cold, stung by nettles, scratched by thorns and pricked by thistles was part of the price one had to pay for the privilege of watching the great apes – then I was happy to pay. My muscles and lungs had gradually adapted to the effort of clambering about two miles above sea level, and the multiple discomforts only moderated the level of pleasure I was drawing from the experience.

For the first time in years, the almost indispensable safari vehicle that was my transport, mobile home and camera platform, was miles away. I was on the same level as other animals of the forest, and since some, in the shape of elephants, buffalo and gorillas were large, powerful and potentially dangerous, an element of expectant excitement coloured the adventure. Geared to the slower pace of leg power and a more personal contact with the earth, my senses seemed to expand and take in the sights and sounds with greater awareness. I particularly enjoyed the ability to sample the flow of natural odours from the environment, untainted by any smells of fuel and oil and hot metal.

To make contact with the gorillas every day was demanding yet exhilarating work. Their reluctance to be seen was a challenge to one's skill at making an approach that would not cause alarm: a process I consistently found exciting and stimulating. On the outward journey, long walks and climbs generated much heat and sweat. Then, with the wary creatures located, almost invariably, several hours of near-static inactivity allowed clammy cold to displace the warmth of physical effort. But somehow, all the difficulties seemed only to enhance the hours spent near the gorillas.

At first, mainly because at least three families ranged there, I continued to select the western segment of Visoke. During her year of work from the Rwandan base, Dian and her men had opened up a few narrow paths on Mount Visoke; they connected with the natural game trails on the mountain ridges and helped to reduce the time taken to reach specific areas. Many of the game trails were kept reasonably open by buffalo, the gorillas, antelopes and sometimes elephants, but plant growth was so swift that large sections not used for a while were soon overgrown.

With plenty of distinctive landmarks and the help of the access paths, I quickly became familiar with the terrain. After taking the shortest route to where contact had been broken off the previous day, it was then only a matter of following up the meandering trails to find where the group had slept the night. Dian had asked me to try to keep a check on numbers, so a careful count and examination of scattered foliage beds followed. Because individual gorillas slept anything up to twenty or more yards from the central cluster, it sometimes took quite a while to find them all. The two days spent with Dian had not prepared me for the placid pace of gorilla life. I discovered that they were not early risers and seldom far from their beds at seven or eight in the morning. They could be remarkably quiet too. At the sleeping site it paid to determine the rough direction the family had taken, then select a vantage point from which to watch and listen carefully. Depending on the drift and strength of the wind, sometimes it was possible to detect sounds of feeding or move- ment from a considerable distance; it was also quite likely the creatures had not gone far, and were sitting silent and unmoving until they could ascertain who or what was approaching.

As the gorillas generally spread out while feeding, the density of the vege- tation ensured that only a few were in visual contact with one another; without an actual sighting they could not know for sure if any faint sounds heard were from another gorilla, an antelope or perhaps a buffalo. I found it strange that, unless really worried by a noise, they rarely bothered to stand or climb above the undergrowth to make a visual check. Occasionally this trait made a stealthy approach turn into a surprise for both parties. While concen- trating hard on following tracks, several times my composure was destroyed by a shriek of alarm at close range: some poor gorilla had been waiting silently to find out who was coming, only to see a most unwelcome human! This sort of meeting was definitely not the best. Alarm barks or roars instantly alerted the whole family and set them on edge. But screams, especially, could provoke an unpleasant situation, as I was to find out before long.

The final approach to visual contact – the last act of each day's tracking – created a sort of dynamic tension. Tiring limbs and soggy clothing would be forgotten. Eyes, ears and nose came up to full and expectant alert. It was like an enthralling game, and one that never failed to give me a physical and mental lift. Every day the approach was different, as the terrain, the weather, even the mood of a group, combined to guarantee an endless variety of situations. Generally the creatures reacted warily by keeping a sharp watch or seeking better concealment. It was absorbing to try to remain fully concealed and undetected, then watch through binoculars. But my camera was there to be put to work and the urge to record the sights ahead quickly surfaced.

Trying to stay reasonably obscured while setting up the camera was a time- consuming business. No matter how carefully it was done the movements invariably gave my position away. Even though the gorillas were usually at some distance, sharp eyes easily picked me out – often causing a retreat to full cover. The gorillas were clearly made anxious, if not alarmed, by my activities with the camera. Fixing the tripod firmly on a sharply angled, foliage-covered slope sometimes taxed my patience, especially when the legs caught in the tangle of stems, or sank deeply into the soft, moist soil. It was seldom possible to set the awkward thing in a good position and make it really stable.

My film stock and lenses were perfect for filming animals on sun-bleached African savannahs; pitifully inadequate to record jet-black animals in the dense vegetation of a mainly clouded habitat. The gorillas were plainly suspicious of the strange object with a glassy eye that I set in front of me. Getting a good image on film was a chancy business too. With lens apertures regularly set wide open and the film forced anywhere between one and three times the normal exposure rating, I did my best to capture something of the gorillas' way of life – at least the small snatches seen when the light provided sufficient illumination. I filmed the luxuriant vegetation that dominated the scenery, the faces that peered at me through it, the movement of dark bodies across small openings and partly exposed animals feeding – until it was obvious the disjointed scenes were becoming overly repetitive. Now and then a gorilla would climb a tree and I could build a little sequence of action. But so few and far between were these little gems of activity, the sense of achievement after capturing one was intense, and usually quite out proportion to the actual value of the sequence.

In spite of what I had absorbed from George Schaller's books and Dian Fossey, I had not expected gorillas to be quite so slow moving nor so quiet in their daily wanderings. My knowledge of chimpanzees and other primates had helped to generate expectations of a more active creature; perhaps even subconscious childhood memories from the reading of *Tarzan and the Apes* still faintly affected my perception of their lifestyle. However, as their behaviour became more familiar, I adapted to the extended periods of waiting for action: the unhurried departure from the sleeping site to begin two or three hours of concentrated feeding; the sometimes protracted rest period that followed; and the long afternoon feed that slowed as dusk approached and preparation of beds for the night began.

Days merged into weeks that passed all too swiftly. By mid-October I had a better, though very superficial, understanding of gorilla behaviour. In turn the animals were clearly recognising me and less inclined to be so tense and wary. I had become inured to repeated showers of rain and long spells of thick mist; the brilliant days of late September were only a memory and sunlight rarely broke through the grey and weeping carpets of cloud. Immobile, wet, and often uncomfortably cold, I spent hours behind the camera waiting for the combination of a good sighting, sufficient light and interesting action.

During the periods of midday inactivity, while the gorillas dozed quietly on their beds of foliage, regularly my thoughts turned to linger on still fresh memories of the recent expedition to Lake Rudolf. With the rarefied mountain air chilling my hands and feet, mental images of bleak, windswept sediments roasting in the hot climate helped to pass the time and divert my mind from immediate discomforts. It was also satisfying to muse on the very good prospects for further explorations.

My association with the Leakey family had long ago deflected me from an intention to concentrate on photographing wildlife, but after several years of constant exposure to their activities I had few regrets about that. Their expanding search for the fossils of hominids and their descendants had introduced me to a wide range of interesting subjects – including now the long-term studies of both chimpanzees and gorillas that Louis Leakey had initiated. As distant relatives of prehistoric man, the social life of Africa's great apes was coming under close scrutiny, and I knew Louis hoped to find someone soon to study orang-utans in the Far East.

While I worked to photograph some of his many fossil specimens, Louis often talked about his need to know everything possible about living primates, and especially the great apes. Fragmented and mute fossils could only reveal details of the physical shape and possible abilities of a creature, perhaps also some assessment of mental capacity and a reasoned conclusion as to what it ate to survive, but how it had behaved in its social life remained pure conjecture. Louis was certain a deeper understanding of modern primate behaviour would help explain how and why early hominids had evolved to produce a line that so swiftly became the dominant species on earth. Through regular exposure I had become intrigued by his fascinating theories on hominid evolution. Although so far allowed to see little more than tantalising glimpses of gorilla social behaviour, the knowledge about early man acquired from Louis gave an additional reason to appreciate the rare opportunity to observe and film them.

With over half my time in the mountains now gone, I found myself looking more often to the future – and wondering if Richard Leakey would be granted further funds to continue his search for fossils. Even as I daily tried to ignore the wet and sometimes freezing conditions, warming my mind with thoughts of heat and desert, he would be preparing a report to the National Geographic Research Committee. Having staked his reputation, and put at risk his future activities in palaeontology, on a claim that the land east of Lake Rudolf would prove to be a prime area for the recovery of hominid fossils, he would be compiling the report with considerable satisfaction. The expedition had revealed a huge spread of ancient sediments by the lake that contained a wonderful variety of well-preserved Pleistocene fossils, but more importantly, the team had found three pieces of hominid bone – two of which were sections of massive australopithecine jawbones. On the value of these discoveries alone he would surely be able to justify a request for funds to support another, more wide-ranging search. Having been involved with all of Richard's field exploits since 1964, and very much aware of his self-confidence and persuasive abilities, I did not doubt for a moment that he would be successful. One way and another, for five years he had exercised a considerable influence on my career as a photographer. If all went well in Washington, I was certain to play a part in a second expedition to Lake Rudolf.

I had first met Richard in 1959 when he was only fifteen. Had we then been able to look into the future, both of us would have been amazed to know we would one day be working together. At the time I was in partnership with three friends, managing a motor workshop, tuning high-powered engines and mainly absorbed with the workings of mechanical things. My partners and I held the Jaguar Car franchise for East Africa. We favoured sports, racing and rally cars, and to me the study of ancient sediments, fossil bones and stone tools was a subject that could not have been more remote from my interests. But the following years had brought many changes. In 1961 I had married Heather Martin, a veterinary surgeon whose work with wild animals had earlier brought me into contact with Des and Jen Bartlett. Des was cameraman to Armand and Michaela Denis, famous among other achievements for a decade-long run on BBC television with a wildlife programme called *On Safari*. We had met when Heather was called upon to give veterinary advice on the many and often exotic animals in the Armand Denis menagerie. Des had later chosen our workshop to attend to his collection of safari vehicles. Over a period of several years he had also drawn me deeper into photography, generously letting me try out some of his expensive cameras and make use of his large and well- equipped darkroom.

Just as an early attraction to motorbikes and sports cars had in the mid-fifties led me to abandon a career in agriculture, this fresh exposure to photography suddenly opened up an unforeseen opportunity to return to an open-air life. In 1962, just as Kenya was heading inexorably towards independence from colonial rule, Des Bartlett invited me to join him at Armand Denis Productions. With the uncertain future of motor engineering in mind and tiring of an urban existence, I jumped at the offer. With few regrets I brought my seven-year spell in the motor trade to an end and took up a career in photography. Then, only eighteen months later, in May 1964, though very much a novice cameraman, I was taken on by the National Geographic Society to provide photographic coverage of Richard Leakey's first major palaeontological expedition.

Now, four years later, huddled against the cold on a high, dormant volcano, I found particular pleasure in anticipating another season in the arid hinterland of Lake Rudolf. It was an enjoyable exercise to counter the cold with images of the desiccated land and the vast spread of sediments still to be combed for the remains of ancient ancestors. Thoughts on how to create fresh interest and diversify the photographic record regularly occupied my mind. Whiling away time in this pleasant fashion, I could not know that Richard's influence and intervention in a dispute in Washington would cause me to miss his next expedition altogether!

On the southern slopes of Mount Visoke I had long since located the last of the gorilla study groups – Group 5. If a morning contact was broken off early,

I respected Dian's request that the animals should not be subjected to the stress of being followed. Nemeye and I would retreat, and, if time allowed, go in search of another group. Regularly we returned to sleeping sites three or four days old to follow up fading trails. It was hard work, but as a result I covered the full expanse of the research area several times. Growing knowledge of the mountain and its numerous ravines enabled me to draw a fairly accurate map on which to detail the wanderings of the groups, and to pinpoint their various sleeping sites. Nemeye's eyes were sharp and from long practice he rarely failed to keep on course. Following his often instinctive lead, I had quickly honed my own long dormant tracking abilities. It was not hard to follow a gorilla's spoor, but when tracks crossed and recrossed and old mixed with new, it was necessary to be highly observant and attentive to detail.

Group 5 consisted of seventeen members that included three and sometimes four silverbacks. Throughout my stay they hugged the south-east slopes of Visoke, but in spite of their proximity I was drawn still to the families of Geronimo and the impressive 'old man of the woods' – Rafiki. With his small band of four males, Rafiki was apparently shadowing the seventeen members of Group 9. Several times I had heard the two great silverbacks beating their chests in noisy confrontations, but had never been anywhere near close enough to witness what was going on. The distinctive and exciting sound of energetic chest beating carried great distances across the mountain slopes, often mixed with a curious hooting and roaring that made me long to be able to see and film what was happening.

The sharp ridges facing the north-west were now criss-crossed with fresh gorilla trails. It seemed evident that Geronimo was doing his best to lead his family away from the five males, covering a good deal of ground in the process. But old Rafiki was persistent and seldom far behind. Some days, while following and attempting to stay on course through the maze of tracks, I was quite uncertain which group would be encountered first. Many times I wished for the magical ability to soar like a bird and view the whole scene from above the obscuring vegetation.

One misty morning, creeping silently along a fresh track of wet, broken foliage, I turned a bend and looked straight into the eyes of a bulky gorilla, ten feet ahead. Half turned away, the creature was looking back at me over its shoulder. Female? Male? I could not tell. Its mouth gaped open, seemingly ready to accept the peeled stem of a thistle held up in a large fist. The eyes and face registered a look of total surprise, quite comical really – but only for a second. Shock replaced surprise and a coarse, very loud scream erupted from its throat. I turned away immediately, starting to crouch down as the gorilla lunged out of sight with another violent scream and a thunderous crash of breaking plants. As it vanished from view, I gained the distinct impression that the scream was reverberating; above and below several invisible gorillas had taken up the cry. But more seriously, a growing and nerve-racking sound was coming from directly ahead. Already on my knees, I could only listen to the incredibly loud roaring and smashing of bushes heading my way. A large body burst out of the foliage where I had surprised the first gorilla. Somewhat rigid with alarm and the sharp edge of near panic, I forced myself to look away. All noise and motion ceased abruptly and a potent smell strongly reminiscent of a human sweating in fear drifted over me. As the moments of silence extended, I glanced up, cautiously, briefly. It was Rafiki, not the leader of Group 9 I had been expecting. Great shaggy arms stiffly supporting his barrel chest, from my lowly position he looked enormous – and definitely much too close. His wide, angry eyes stared me down and he gave out a strange sound that was more like the suppressed whinny of a horse than anything else. The tension was almost palpable, but already, relief that nothing serious had happened so far was flooding over me. I took another guarded look at the truly awe-inspiring primate. The hair on his prominent sagittal crest stood up, increasing the bulk of his massive head. He was moving his pursed lips, but now the direct stare of his eyes lacked any sort of menace. I lowered my gaze submissively, very much aware that my heart was thumping away like a bass drum. I felt curiously elated as the tension eased. My desire to see a mature male gorilla at close quarters had at last been granted – and with considerable added drama. Stiffly, the huge animal backed away a few feet. I glanced up in time to see him snatch a fistful of leaves and shred them through his large canines. Then he turned and disappeared into the foliage. The excitement of the close encounter had been extreme. The image of this great silverback called Rafiki looming over me, powerful and utterly dominant, remains etched in the memory of the event. I felt genuine and profound respect for the old man of the mountains. I was the intruder in his high mountain domain, and with one swift, noisy demonstration he had well and truly put me in my place. I did not know it then, but I was to meet this old gorilla many more times, and he would never fail to impress.

In spite of all the cattle I'd seen and the sounds of poacher activity heard before Dian departed, I was surprised that my weeks in residence had brought little further evidence of them. The cattle seemed to have melted away, and one or two wide-ranging sweeps with Nemeye had produced no fresh signs of poaching. The few primitive shelters we found gave no indications of recent occupation. There were no more cattle hoof prints; the muddy game trails showed only fresh buffalo tracks and the small prints of duikers and bush-bucks. Nemeye and the woodman offered their opinion that the herders and poachers had quickly become aware of my arrival and actually believed me to be some sort of important official. This made me laugh, but they could have been near the truth. I was in the habit of wearing a beret that sported a small badge, which together with a camouflage jacket gave a distinctly military appearance that could easily have created the wrong impression.

By the beginning of November I had become thoroughly hooked on gorillas, wanting to see and learn more about them, and, in spite of the miserable weather, not a little sad the exhilarating experience was coming to an end. Dian was due back and I was starting to think of all the work awaiting me at home. The remoteness of the research camp and the erratic Rwandan mail system made communication with the outside world a frustrating process. Dian had already cabled to let me know she would return at least a week later than planned. Then another cable arrived, offering me the chance to film the fitting of radio transmitters to some elephants in Tanzania. Unable to find out quickly if any delay on my part would upset the project, I worried about the added time and became anxious to get going. In the end Dian arrived two weeks later than we had arranged, partly because she had been held up several extra days in Nairobi while her luggage flew on elsewhere.

Making full use of the extended term, I tried hard to finish off my supply of film on significant action, while true to form the weather did its best to nullify the effort. Incessant showers and clinging mists kept the heavy foliage drenched with water. Conditions on Mount Visoke were depressing. In spite of growing familiarity with the ways of the gorillas, my contacts were if anything less productive. I was nearly ready to quit – even beginning to think seriously of setting off for home without waiting for Dian. By now actually in Rwanda, she had sent a message apologising for her delay and pleading for me not to leave. She desperately wanted to discuss all that had happened in her absence, but still had to change money, drive to Gisenyi and then Kisoro in Uganda for supplies, and so on. Already into the second week of November, I could only hope the elephant operation would stand the unavoidable delay.

As if to compensate a little, the foul weather eased and the final days with the gorillas produced a stroke of luck. While climbing with Nemeye to find Group 8 for the last time, the sound of powerful chest beating suddenly started up only a ridge away. Clambering carefully to a vantage point, we looked down on a shallow valley. Perhaps a hundred yards away many gorillas were spread out on a nearly treeless slope. As always the abundant vegetation obscured most of them, but knowing I would be too easily seen in any attempt to get closer, I had to be content with our position and the reasonable, though distant, view.

Two silverbacks were in direct confrontation: Rafiki, his silvered shoulders obvious, and another I could not immediately identify. Already the two had broken down great swaths of foliage, making their actions a little easier to see. Every now and then one would start a soft hooting call that slowly speeded up and increased in volume. At the peak of this call the challenger rose up and lumbered forward, violently slapping bulging pectoral muscles with cupped hands and changing the rapid hooting to a loud roar. The move forward was very short, perhaps five to eight paces, and finished with the challenger dropping back on to his hands to complete the run. As I watched, one initiated a charge that brought him right up to his opponent – where the foreshortened view through my powerful telephoto lens made them appear to be only inches apart, but they were certainly within two or three feet of each other. Fully expecting some violent physical contact, I was astonished when nothing happened. As the two heavyweights came face to face they kept their heads sharply averted, twisting them first one way and then the other. If they made eye contact at all it could only have been for a fraction of a second. The undoubted power of their superb muscles and huge jaws remained a latent threat throughout the several confrontations that followed. Neither would give way: it was a sort of stalemate position. The two would back carefully away from one another, strutting stiffly, then work up to another chest-beating display, or perhaps a noisy, foliage-smashing run towards one of the few onlookers close to the action.

Throughout most of this marvellous demonstration I was in agonies of frustration. As I began to film the wonderful scene, I heard my camera motor change pitch and begin to slow – my Nicad battery belt had reached the end of its charge! I could have shouted with rage. What an impossible time to choose to fail. My spare belt was back in camp – also flat. The extended period of work waiting for Dian had taken the batteries to their limits and I was literally furious with disappointment. Poor Nemeye crouched at my side couldn't understand why I was so angry. Hastily stuffing the offending belt under my shirt and round my waist in the desperate hope that some body heat would help generate a fraction more power, I tried hard to conserve the last scraps of energy and filmed only the spurts of real action. The motor slowed seconds into each shot and I knew the end frames of each scene would be heavily overexposed. The battery finally expired and I viewed the closing minutes of the power-play through binoculars. Their clarity allowed me to identify Rafiki's opponent as Uncle Bert – Dian's name for the head of Group 4. The confrontation was nearly over. The two silverbacks sat down some distance from each other, while around them individuals began to stir a little and start eating. Uncle Bert made one more rush into the foliage. He ran right over a cowering female, thumping down hard with a heavy fist on her broad back, and for good measure added a hefty backward kick before vanishing from sight.

With the camera out of action I could do no more than enjoy the rest of the day just watching the gorillas and pondering the significance of the extraordinary display. I had been very surprised to see the two gorillas approach each other so closely; either could have reached out and begun a spectacular fight. But obviously had they grappled with one another their long canines would have come into play – with deadly effect. Did they ever really fight, or had gorillas evolved a fine tension-dissipating demonstration that allowed them to eschew damaging combat? I did not know. As the two families moved apart, feeding and studiously ignoring each other, I wondered how the various individuals had interpreted the event. The two males would surely encounter each other fairly often. But did they indulge in the same sort of behaviour each time, or had I just been privileged to see a rare demonstration? As the gorillas dispersed, the light began to fade under heavy afternoon clouds. Despondent over the battery failure, but very pleased to have witnessed the spectacle of a full-blooded confrontation, I withdrew from the scene.

Dian finally returned to her camp on 10 November. Though visibly exhausted from a day of hard motoring and the climb up the mountain, it was plain she was pleased to be back. While she unpacked, I gave her the news of her gorilla groups and laid out my sketch maps to show the complicated wanderings of the four families. We continued to talk for hours as I related the main events of the past fifty days. She had little to say about her holiday in America, but was very concerned about Alan Root. Having spent some time with him, she was able to tell me he was greatly discouraged by continuing complications from the snake bite; his damaged hand was recovering very slowly and he was currently fighting a losing battle to save his index finger. She didn't say so directly, but I felt she was relieved to find that her camp was clean and intact.

Back in the musty old tent that night, active thoughts about the gorillas kept me awake for a long while. The seven weeks spent amongst them seemed to have evaporated like a dream, but one that surely would be vividly remembered. Describing for Dian all that had happened during the period had refocused my mind on many exhilarating encounters, and some fascinating glimpses of gorilla behaviour. Keeping a record of the movements of four separate families had involved much long-distance tracking over Mount Visoke's steep ravines and ridges, and the heavy exercise had definitely improved my level of physical fitness. But the gorilla adventure was over; for the next two days I would be travelling hard to get home, then moving on again to film animals living in a very different environment.

Suppressing an urge to spend time showing her exactly where the groups were located, I said farewell to Dian and the pleasant little research camp and left the next morning, positive in my own mind it was most unlikely I would visit again. I was sad it was necessary to rush away, but I had pressing matters to attend to and Nemeye would soon lead her to all the right places. Except for a brief pause to drink from a stream where the cultivated fields began, my string of porters galloped down the boggy trail non-stop, then sped on across the wide expanse of cultivation to reach the road in under an hour. This time I had no difficulty whatsoever in keeping up their pace.

Demaret was waiting with my Land Rover, and I called in to say goodbye to Monsieur Descamps. Since he knew I would arrive at the Rwandan border when the post was closed, he promptly persuaded me to stay for lunch. With my schoolboy French over three decades behind me, conversation with the Descamps family proceeded with many smiles and nods but little real understanding; however, a bottle of French wine seemed to ease the difficulties. I reached the Rwandan border well after opening time – but still had to wait for the customs officer to appear from his own lunchtime relaxation. I was asked to open up my Land Rover, a request that always caused some apprehension at the various border posts. My boxes of assorted equipment invariably aroused interest and speculation – and sometimes created difficulties.

On this occasion the first item to be checked was a sack full of bones: gorilla bones. Dian had asked me to deliver the complete skeleton of a silverback to Dr Leakey at Nairobi Museum. The skeleton was all that remained of Whinny, the former leader of Group 4. The sack was opened and the set of rather human-looking bones precipitated a flurry of concern and a torrent of questions in French and Rwandese. With exasperation, the senior customs official finally condescended to use Kiswahili and demanded an explanation. In answer, I opened up the separately packed and magnificent gorilla skull, which promptly drew awed comments from officials and onlookers alike. Never before had they seen such a huge and strange primate skull, indeed none had ever seen a gorilla, though undoubtedly live gorillas roamed the upper reaches of Mount Muhavura looming high in the sky behind the customs post. The skull went from hand to hand, the massive sagittal crest, the great molars and huge canines causing particular comment and excitement. My boxes of equipment were now ignored, my passport received the required stamp and I was permitted to proceed the short distance to the Uganda barrier, a few yards ahead. I wondered what reception the remains of old Whinny would accord from the Ugandans. But there was no need for concern; my papers were in order and the Land Rover excited no interest. Within minutes I was on the way to Kabale and the comforts of the White Horse Inn sixty miles ahead.

Much to my relief, the extra weeks spent in the Virunga mountains did not affect the elephant project; I had worried needlessly and discovered there was more than a week to prepare. The documentary division of MGM Studios wanted film coverage on Howard Baldwin, an electronics specialist and an expert in the making of radio monitoring and tracking devices. Howard had already assisted George Schaller with equipment for his research on the lions of the Serengeti Plain. Now he was to continue some work with elephant researcher Iain Douglas-Hamilton in the Lake Manyara National Park. Two young elephants were to be immobilised with a dart gun and fitted with radio collars.

Unfortunately the project did not go well. Now three years into his study on the elephants of Manyara, Iain knew the area intimately and could identify his subjects with an ease that I envied. We found the right herd with a minimum of fuss, and after two aborted attempts Iain put a dart into the first elephant. In spite of the sting from the projectile it hardly moved, very nearly going down in a perfect position as the drug took effect. But then the matriarch and members of the herd nearby became restive and noisy. Gathering its ebbing strength, the young elephant staggered off to join them, collapsing out of sight. We could just see other elephants trying to raise their fallen companion. Using his vehicle to create a diversion, it took Iain precious minutes to persuade the herd to move away. The collar was fitted in record time and the elephant was back on its feet minutes later. Sadly, the radio ceased transmitting the very next day – the elephant had succeeded in breaking it. Howard decided it would be unwise to fit the second unit until it could be more securely protected.

Although the project had failed, before leaving Manyara I elected to complete the record of the darting with scenes showing the collared elephant going about its normal daily life – a little effort that caused some unexpected excitement. Finding the youngster in the acacia woodlands without the transmitter functioning was no easy matter. I spent hours searching, and when I did locate it the cover was very thick. Manoeuvring slowly to find a good camera angle, I was suddenly given a rude shock. On the periphery of my vision I saw movement through the back window of my Land Rover – a large elephant was approaching at some considerable speed. I floored the throttle, but it was already much too late; I was in the wrong gear anyway and the response was poor. With a loud squeal of anger the grey bulk closed on me and with a resounding crash made solid contact with the back door. My vehicle leaped forward and gained a few yards; bushes, termite mounds and trees forced me to follow a tortuous course and all I could see in the rear-view mirror was a close-up of tusks and a large trunk. The chase continued for a substantial distance but luckily no serious obstacles blocked my path. At last the vision in the mirror vanished in a cloud of dust. Circling slowly to get a good look at my assailant, I discovered it was one of Iain's favourite elephants. Named Boadicea, she was an imposing and respected matriarch he had pointed out to me the previous day; a fine lady who was given to aggressive behaviour and spectacular bluff charges. She shook her head at me contemptuously and swung away to rejoin her family.

I went back to Iain's camp to deal with the damage and give him the story. He was thoroughly amused, but also intrigued that Boadicea had pressed her charge to make physical contact. We could only conclude she had become annoyed at the vehicle grinding through the bushes near her family, and having caught up with it simply decided to press on and complete the rout. I managed to straighten out the bent rear door and close the two neat holes where her tusks had penetrated. Then we went out in Iain's open vehicle to visit the irritable lady. True to form, she gave us a sensational demonstration – charging to within a few yards. The noisy rush towards us brought a vivid recall of the mighty Rafiki bearing down on me. For a tense few seconds I wondered if having dealt with one intruder a short while earlier, Boadicea was actually going to dispense with bluff! But Iain was satisfied with the lively performance, deciding her attack on me had not significantly altered her attitude to vehicles.

I was soon back home and immediately caught up in the effort to speed up and finish work on the new house. Heather and I had been living in tents on our land, but with new year assignments that would probably take me away for long periods, it was essential now that the building be completed to a stage where we could actually live in it. Alan Root was still in deep trouble with his hand. If it failed to respond to specialist treatment there was a strong possibility he would need help with his filming commitments. In particular, final coverage to complete the film about George Schaller's lion study was becoming quite urgent. With our small labour force, Heather and I battled on through December, finishing off the roof, arranging plumbing and electrical work: ordering doors, windows, fittings – the prospect of actually moving in seemed many months away.

The new year came all too soon. I took on an assignment to shoot stills with a *National Geographic* television crew covering the activities of the famous wildlife cameraman, Heinz Sielmann, and thereafter pressure to overcome the backlog of work at home became intense. By now in America, Richard Leakey was putting forward his proposals to the National Geographic Research Committee for the continuation of work at Lake Rudolf. Using a film made from material I had shot on the initial expedition, he was also due to give his first public lecture in Washington. I waited with some impatience, keen to hear how he was getting on, but when a letter came there was no word about funding. He wrote instead to tell me he was aware the research committee was currently in serious discussion with his father about the gorilla project. Without elaborating, he advised me to be prepared for further involvement.

Within a fortnight a cable arrived from Bob Gilka, director of photography at *National Geographic*. It was brief and to the point. Dr Leakey had suggested intensive stills' coverage on Dian Fossey should begin immediately, and asked whether I would be interested in the assignment on a long-term basis. Prepared by Richard's letter, I began seriously to consider a total disruption of all previous plans. Knowing that filming the gorillas was an important assignment Alan particularly wanted to retain and complete, I needed first to check his reaction. Then, if I took it on, I would miss the expected season of research with Richard: work I had practically taken for granted and was looking forward to. The words 'on a long-term basis' in Bob Gilka's cable were surely significant. I knew for certain Dr Leakey had in mind Jane Goodall's research on chimpanzees in Tanzania – where for some years photographic work had fully occupied the energies of her husband, Hugo van Lawick.

January ended in a flurry of cables and letters and it became clear I could take over the gorilla assignment if I wished. As yet I was unaware of considerable earlier consternation in Washington, and that Dian Fossey had little knowledge of what was being planned. Dr Leakey had apparently questioned an initial decision to offer me the gorilla assignment directly, suggesting that, since I was married, it was unlikely I would want to take on the lengthy commission. Instead, he had in mind a young man he thought might be suitable for the work. On the point of accepting his advice, several members of the research committee had turned to Richard for his views on the matter, and it was he who persuaded them to at least ask how I felt before committing themselves to an unknown person. This suggestion promptly involved Richard in a row with his father, who, though objecting strongly to what he saw as interference, reluctantly agreed it was perhaps the most sensible course to take. I discovered later that Louis had a partial obligation to the person he had put forward; the young man had a wealthy father offering financial support for anthropological studies in Africa, and Louis, it had to be admitted, had an urgent need for funds to finance his many research projects.

By mid-February things came to a head. I had written to Dian to ask about her thoughts on the matter, and with some amazement discovered in her reply an apparent ignorance of what was happening, though she did admit to having received letters from Dr Leakey that mentioned photographers. By the end of the month I had flown to Washington to discuss the assignment and to meet everyone concerned at *National Geographic* headquarters. With a return to the gorillas now certain, there followed a frantic endeavour by Heather and myself to complete our house: at least to the point where she could use it in my absence and be more secure. Our plans to finish off the interior went by the board. As soon as all the doors and windows had been fitted, we struck our tents and moved into the bare shell, spreading out our camping equipment and a scanty collection of furniture to make the rooms look less barren.

Up at her remote camp Dian had her problems too. Her work had come to a complete standstill as she struggled to revive and sustain two baby gorillas: youngsters that had been specifically captured by Rwandan national park guards for Cologne Zoo in Germany. From the two letters she sent as I prepared for a long stay in Rwanda, it was clear she was distraught and worried. I was also concerned to learn she had still not been fully consulted over final decisions on photographic coverage. To compound her difficulties, she said visitors kept turning up, and she had shortly to contend with a man being sent by Dr Leakey to act as a possible assistant for a census of the gorilla population. Reading between the lines, I gained the distinct impression she did not want yet another person on hand to add to the stress.

On 2 April I was ready to go. I felt very sad to be missing the push north through the wild country east of Lake Rudolf. Richard had received a fresh grant and with usual thoroughness was already making preparations. If nothing else his field season promised to be adventurous. He would be exploring new territory as far as the border with Ethiopia and, to ease the strain on hard-used vehicles, was planning to use camels to survey the more difficult areas. I consoled myself with the thought that photographing gorillas would be equally exciting. Although the conditions would sometimes be tough and uncomfortable, I knew that tracking, watching and photographing the great apes would bring more than adequate compensation.

Assignment with Gorillas

In spite of ominous storm clouds that reminded me strongly of the first visit, I reached the Visoke camp without getting wet. My string of porters had increased considerably in numbers, but this time it was less of an effort to match their fast rate of climb. Dian was not so reserved with her greetings, but an underlying abruptness in her manner did not make me feel particularly welcome. She was, however, grateful to receive all the many items I had purchased for her in Nairobi, and plainly impatient to show off the captive gorillas.

Her cabin had recently been extended with a new section that was now providing temporary accommodation for the gorillas. Following her through a connecting door, I saw that the room was festooned with quantities of favoured gorilla food plants and some decorative foliage. Pressed together and squatting on the planks of a workbench, the two orphans eyed me apprehensively. When Dian moved to reassure and pet them, it was immediately obvious she had their complete trust. They looked healthy too; clearly she had done a fine job in pulling them back from what she described as near death at the hands of rough and callous captors. The work had given her a marvellous though stressful opportunity to handle a pair of wild gorillas: something she had never even dreamed of being able to do. Although normal research had been abandoned, she had acquired much valuable data just watching the pair and attending to their needs. However, the fact they were due to be handed over for shipment to Germany within a matter of weeks weighed heavily on her mind. While the two gorillas responded to her attentions, she expressed grim determination to try to do whatever was necessary to prevent them from being exported.

With the light fading rapidly under cloud cover, the familiar chill of late evening air began to penetrate. I paid off my porters and hastily searched for a place to set up my small tent. Everywhere I looked the soil was soft and damp, so I settled on a level site across the gurgling stream, thirty yards beyond the cabin. Clearing a patch on the moist ground I quickly erected the tent. Lightweight and sandy coloured, it had been purchased for use in the Lake Rudolf deserts; set in the verdant mountain vegetation it stood out sharply and I regretted not having bought something in green. Stacking my kit and camera equipment in the restricted space, the realisation that this flimsy canvas structure would be my home for many months finally settled in. The assignment was going to be a long haul, and with pleasant memories of the comfortable cabin, I had cause to wish that Dian had been able to construct more than one of them. The man who had come to survey the gorilla population had not stayed. I wondered wryly if the decrepit and mouldy tent that served to accommodate guests had helped put him off. Apparently, after realising how difficult and demanding the task would be, with commendable frankness he had admitted he was not the right person for the job.

The next four weeks were filled with activity almost exclusively connected with the gorilla orphans. Each morning, while they were isolated in a large cage of wire netting attached to the side of the cabin, Dian and her assistants spent hours cleaning out their room, removing all the wilted foliage and faeces, washing down and disinfecting the floor, bringing in fresh food and more vegetation to decorate the walls. If the weather allowed, at least two periods of near free-ranging walks took place each day. On these excursions the gorillas were like a pair of delightful pets: responsive, trusting and increasingly playful. Strongly attached to Dian, their initial apprehension at my presence quickly evaporated. Within a matter of days they began to treat me as another companion. With memories of the elusive wild gorillas still strong, it was a special and rewarding experience to be able to handle two of the creatures and to examine their bodies in detail: their faces, hands, feet, and long coats of hair. I made full use of the situation, shooting many pictures and rolls of cine-film. I was able to help Dian maintain better control over the sometimes boisterous pair; to thwart their occasional dashes for the thickets on Visoke, and to make it possible to take longer walks in the beautiful hagenia woodland.

At first, with an air of calm and disciplined thinking about the orphans, Dian did her best to maintain control over her feelings in front of me. But she could not keep up the facade. I had arrived at the peak of her anger and frustration over not being able to defeat the plan to send them to a zoo. She desperately wanted to try to release the pair in the wild, and had already refused to hand them over to park guards sent up to take them away – even on two occasions to the conservator himself. The weak and ineffective man had quickly gained the upper hand by reminding her the Rwandan government had approved the captures – even threatening to have more infants seized if she failed to cooperate. It was a measure of Dian's strength and his weakness that he had to use such tactics. She suspected that two gorilla families had been decimated during the captures and knew the conservator was not bluffing. Though prepared to defy government officials to the limit of their patience, she knew her charges would have to go in the end. She firmly insisted the animals were not fit to travel, which initially had been perfectly true, but lately the conservator had seen their healthy state for himself. Time was running out. During the weeks leading up to the final date set for departure, only one hope kept her from despair: an increasingly desperate hope that there would be sufficient response to her appeal for help from the international conservation community. She had sent letters to every important person and organisation she could think of, and could only wait to see if they would have any effect.

The days slipped away quickly and Dian began to lose her self-control. Although little was directed towards me, I became an uncomfortable and unwilling witness to the full range of her emotions: from laughter and smiles on the woodland walks, to bouts of angry rage and quiet tears. Though each day was filled with activity and many moments of real pleasure in the company of the animals, the injustice of the situation kept playing on her mind. I felt she was becoming emotionally unstable. Her temper was mercurial, and her three African staff members suffered verbal lashings if they made mistakes or failed to follow directions with alacrity. In spite of the photographic opportunities, there were times when I wished I had delayed my arrival for several weeks.

Between bursts of activity related to the orphans, there was ample time for me to go out and make contact with the wild gorillas. I was impatient to get started, but when I voiced the intention to do so Dian swiftly vetoed the idea. As she would not let her staff anywhere near the gorillas, it was only with my assistance that she was able to take them on the extended excursions into the woods. Since the two were providing an unrepeatable opportunity for observation and pictures, she was adamant I should forget about fieldwork and concentrate entirely on the work at hand. In conceding to her wishes, for the first time I realised there could be a conflict of interests in the weeks ahead. Unfortunately, all too soon a depressing situation was to develop that threatened to sour the whole nature of the assignment.

In a desperate last bid to placate annoyed government officials and to try again to persuade them not to send the gorillas to Germany, at the end of April Dian left the mountains and rushed off to Rwanda's capital, Kigali. She returned exhausted and defeated. I had long since offered to handle the unpleasant task of delivering the pair to the airstrip at Ruhengeri. A wooden crate had been constructed and, to familiarise them with it, had been placed in their room for many days. The playful gorillas were completely unafraid of the ugly box and increasingly used to being confined inside for short periods.

When the fateful day for departure came there was no reprieve. It was 3 May – a bad day from beginning to end. As soon as the youngsters had been enticed into the crate and secured, Dian vanished in tears. She had lavished a great deal of care and love on these two creatures, tended their wounds, brought them to good health and taught them to trust human beings. She had counted on being able to hold on to them and attempt a return to the wild with one of her study groups. Their departure was devastating and would seriously affect her mood for many weeks to come.

The porters were two and a half hours late. Twelve of them took turns carrying the heavy, awkward burden. When we arrived at the roadhead hours later, the Land Rover was nowhere to be seen. I sent off a runner to find out what was wrong and a further hour passed before it came. The journey down the appalling road seemed interminable, and at Ruhengeri things got worse. At the airfield the light plane hired to transport the pair to Kigali was still waiting, but now it was discovered the crate was too big to pass through the loading door. I had taken along some tools in case such a situation arose, and set to work immediately to modify the box. Amazingly, in spite of the sawing and hammering the two long-suffering animals gave only the occasional whimper.

At last the job was done. The gorillas accepted and drank the milk mixture I prepared for them, much to my surprise. Then, impatient from hours of waiting and anxious to complete his task, with a roar of engine noise the pilot taxied away and took off. Nursing a deep sense of sadness, I watched the plane disappear out of sight. The two youngsters were now definitely beyond recall. I reached camp after dark, drained of energy and looking forward only to a warm bed and some relaxing sleep. Listening to my report of the orphans' final, harrowing departure from their mountain home, tears welled freely in Dian's eyes. Almost choking with suppressed emotion she retreated into her cabin to hide her distress.

From dawn to dusk the next day, Dian worked with her men to clean out the gorilla room and erase all signs of their presence. By evening the only evidence of their long stay was the external wire cage attached to the end of the room. The following morning routines governed by normal research began to fall into place, but there was little pleasure to be gained from them. With seasonal rains well established, the wet and dark conditions combined with Dian's depressed state of mind to make the return to the field almost unpleasant. The situation was not at all what I had expected and I did not like it. As one difficult day followed another, I began to feel my presence was something of a burden to Dian. I was keen to work on my own, but thinly masked by a brittle politeness, Dian revealed a continuing intention to control my activities by insisting that we should work together. Not wanting to add to an already difficult atmosphere, I deferred to her wishes. To obtain plenty of pictures relating her to the gorillas, both Bob Gilka and my photo editor in Washington had stressed the importance of working consistently with Dian; human interest was a prime consideration for the magazine. Time was not a factor, so I settled for peaceful relations – and the hope we would soon have some success with this aspect of the work.

At first we searched north and then west, deep into Zaire, locating the gorillas of Group 9 on the further limits of their normal range. Dian had not seen this family for over seven months and all our contacts were short and remarkably poor. We switched to looking for Group 5, finding them far off in the east – equally unresponsive and evasive. With Dian present I was expecting to improve on the mild successes of my caretaker period, but she persevered with a series of contacts conducted mainly at long distance. The generally poor sightings we had of gorillas were of little value to me, nor could I see how they advanced her research in any positive way.

In this atmosphere of polite tension I began to suspect that Dian was testing my resolve and patience. Though on occasion she relaxed and made an effort to be pleasant, she clearly intended to remain the researcher in charge and maintain full control over my role in her project. Resentment over not being properly consulted as to how and by whom her work would be photographed obviously still rankled. I knew she greatly admired and respected Alan Root; he was a well-established wildlife film-maker, also a friend, her preferred mentor and the man she had always wanted for the job. As one unrewarding day followed another, I began to wish it were possible for him to take over again. But his accident had cut him out of the running. Unfortunately Dian was making all too plain her reluctance to accept his replacement.

Holding to mainly static positions, we spent many numbingly unproductive hours in the rain and mist. Cold, wet and generally in poor humour, we tracked, stalked and watched the gorillas. Occasionally one or two curious individuals would expose themselves and I could go to work. Using telephoto lenses, I managed some acceptable shots, but if any of my movements appeared to cause apprehension on the part of the gorillas, Dian would urge me to be more considerate and careful. On some of the more distant contacts I suggested manoeuvring to get closer, but she did not approve. The situation was putting my patience and temper under severe strain. I began to develop my own resentments, but a recall of the circumstances that had placed me in the mountains – and the considerable expense already incurred – were sufficient to make me determined to avoid open conflict.

We seldom spoke during the contacts. Interminable periods spent crouched in dense foliage with nothing to do except wait for a break led me to exercise my mind. I thought often about the expedition to Lake Rudolf, soon to begin, but recollection of heat and wind and dust now merely accentuated the trying situation and did little to distract me from the daily discomforts. I thought about the future, trying to imagine what lay ahead in the months to come. I watched Dian and the way she worked, becoming aware as one hard day followed another that she was not physically well adapted to the gruelling hours of walking and climbing at over ten thousand feet – something that had not in any way been apparent during the first visit. By moving at a deliberate and slow pace, stopping often to scan the terrain, or pausing for long periods to listen for sounds that would betray the whereabouts of gorillas, for a short while she effectively concealed the signs of distress. Nemeye, or a new young assistant called Vatiri, always led the way, carrying her backpack, slashing occasional plants to clear the path and following up the gorilla trails. He would be admonished for going too fast, but it was not long before some long and steep climbs were tackled – then it became obvious Dian was exercising a good deal of will-power to overcome and ignore a persistent lack of strength. Her face and breathing clearly showed heavy strain and her manner sometimes matched it. Adapting to her pace added to the hours of initial searching and tracking and exaggerated the differences between us. The mainly unproductive contacts were not really helping either of us, adding to my conviction that Dian was waiting for me to break out and do something she could disapprove of. Suppressing impatience, I waited for her attitude to change. Unfortunately, belated letters in response to her pleas on behalf of the two orphans kept coming in, serving only as reminders of the failure to keep them from a lifetime in a zoo.

During the meals we ate together, with occasional and rather unsubtle comments Dian had soon made it obvious she was not particularly happy to be sharing meals. As there had never been any suggestion that I would have to be completely independent, aside from helping with the cooking there was little I could do about it. During our discussions about the gorillas I felt obliged to constrain my opinions to avoid argument; otherwise we conversed reasonably freely, but had little in common to keep small talk going. From what she said, it surprised me to learn she was not pleased with some aspects of her relationship with the National Geographic Society, particularly their control over the pictures she was taking. She was unhappy, too, that her funds were still being channelled through Dr Leakey, the main reason being that she suspected he was diverting some of the money for other projects. Also, having little money of her own, she was upset over a recent decision that no grant would be forthcoming to assist her during a future term of study for a doctorate.

In spite of occasional days where the weather and our awkward association improved, as May drew to a close my store of patience ran out. If I was going to continue, it was essential to make myself fully independent of all Dian's facilities. Then perhaps it would easier to exert some pressure to follow my own concept of what I had been assigned to do. The seven weeks spent alone with the gorillas the previous year had been a marvellous experience; I had returned expecting greatly improved opportunities, but so far they were not forthcoming. My original enthusiasm for the assignment had nearly evaporated. In a moment of pure frustration, I dashed off a long letter to the *Geographic*, carefully laying the tentative foundations for a possible withdrawal.

Using the excuse that I had to track down funds sent to Kigali, and then go on to Nairobi to renew a re-entry visa for Kenya, I arranged to leave the camp. No sooner had I done so than a welcome change in the weather matched some improved contacts with the gorillas. Following two gruelling forays into Zaire to keep up with Group 9, and by good fortune finding Group 8 again, Dian unwillingly admitted to near exhaustion. I took advantage of her condition, and for two enjoyable days savoured the pleasure of tracking and working alone with Nemeye. Close to the Bishitsi bluff we found old Rafiki, apparently on the trail of Geronimo again, and both families in a slightly more cooperative mood.

Descriptions of the encounters drew Dian out again, and with some careful manoeuvring and pure luck I managed to engineer a situation that produced the first good pictures with gorillas plainly visible in the same picture with her. While backing away from Group 9, we spotted Rafiki feeding and moving slowly towards the fallen trunk of a massive hagenia tree. Anticipating that he might climb up it, I urged Dian to move forward to the base of another fallen tree. The flat terrain allowed me to back away many yards and employ a telephoto lens to foreshorten the distance between Dian and the spot I hoped a gorilla would appear. Not realising what I was attempting to do, Dian frowned and scowled her disapproval as I moved away. Almost on cue, Rafiki emerged from the undergrowth at the base of the tree. Followed by the youngest of his group, a blackback given the name Peanuts, he climbed with regal poise up the trunk, stopping at the top to rest on his elbows and stare at Dian. The scene not only described the nature of the difficult forest terrain, but also captured the essence of Dian's tenuous relationship with the magnificent creatures. Realising the setting and positioning were perfect, Dian turned to smile at me. She gestured carefully for me to come forward, but I shook my head and kept shooting. After the contact was over, with some annoyance she questioned why I had insisted in backing away so far. My explanation mollified her, but not until my photo editor sent duplicates of the scene did she appreciate how the tele-lens had improved the composition of the picture.

I left the camp in better spirits, but it was still a relief to be walking away from the wet weather and the disturbingly oppressive atmosphere. Back at home, I felt a reluctance to speed up a return, spending nearly three weeks attending to my own affairs, gradually shaking off the nagging desire to cut out of the assignment. I had quickly found out that several of my letters sent from the mountain had gone astray; letters trying to smooth out Dian's personal photography problems had been delayed or lost and many other explanations, requests and decisions affecting the research study were hanging in the air. Several of Dian's letters had been lost too, greatly adding to the confusion. The gorilla project was still a minefield of misunderstandings, making it difficult to regenerate any feeling of enjoyment for the task ahead.

On returning to Rwanda late in June my mind was made up. Photographing gorillas was too interesting and exciting an assignment to pack in: ridiculous even to think of giving it up. Though I felt sure there would be some confrontations, I would stick it out no matter what problems arose. In this frame of mind, I was quite unprepared for what lay in store.

During my long absence the weather pattern for Rwanda had changed abruptly. Skies were clear and practically no rain had fallen. Fine, grey volcanic dust now covered the roads near the mountains and river beds were nearly empty; everywhere grass was turning brown and crops withering under a blazing sun. On the slopes of Mount Visoke the heavy vegetation looked wilted, and up at the research station the little stream had dwindled to a silent trickle. Dian was surprisingly pleasant: quite definitely in better humour. *National Geographic* had written to let her know she would have to start writing up her experiences soon. An article on her work had been scheduled for early publication in 1970 and this had obviously pleased her enormously.

The breakdown in mail communications was slowly being overcome, but there were still a few crises that needed attention. Because of a lack of grazing in lower regions, cattle were now roaming the woodlands in large numbers, and hunters were extremely active. Many uninvited and unwelcome visitors had been climbing up to the camp – some annoyingly truculent – demanding to be shown the gorillas and expecting to use Dian's meagre facilities as a base. Adding further pressure, within a few weeks another man selected by Dr Leakey would be coming to deal with census work. Dian had also sacked two of her African staff for incompetence and the men had responded by threatening to cause trouble. To cap all this, the camp was in imminent danger of running out of water.

Perhaps it was the news about the magazine article that put Dian in better spirits – or maybe the fact I would now be entirely self-contained, yet on hand to help with the welter of difficulties. Although there was an international furore going on about their capture, evidently the emotional distress created by the gorilla orphans had faded. Whatever the cause, the atmosphere was quite different and Dian made small friendly overtures in a transparent bid to improve relations. I was able to help mediate in solving a few problems with her assistants, and, to counteract the threat of trouble from those who had been sacked, employed an extra man to guard the camp. But beyond saving water in cans and buckets, nothing could be done about the rapidly failing supply.

Dian's strictly negative attitude toward my work had changed also. I began immediately by going out independently, spending four days trying to get some value from the most reclusive of the gorilla families – the nervous Group 4. After this promising start, in an amicable and serious effort geared to provide fresh material for the proposed magazine article. I accompanied Dian most days for nearly three weeks. It was a useful period that confirmed she had come to terms with my presence, but at the same time the dry weather created conditions that altered and lengthened the ranging patterns of the gorillas, quickly revealing the true limits of her physical strength.

Although the mornings were bitterly cold, the sunny weather made work on the mountain slopes much more pleasant. For a while the gorillas of Groups 4 and 5 ranged within easy reach, but as the dry spell extended into July the animals began moving on routes that took them regularly above eleven thousand feet – and significant distances from camp.

I was beginning to recognise individual gorillas more easily and starting to learn the names Dian had applied to them; one or two were Kiswahili, while others obviously had sentimental meaning for her. Uncle Bert and Flossie were names of a favoured uncle and aunt, and drawing on her interest in classical music, the silverbacks in Group 5 had been called Beethoven, Bartók and Brahms – in fanciful reference to the different quality of their vocal sounds. Although one or two of her names had vague association with a perceived quality of character, most had no particular significance. Dian began to talk about the gorillas more readily and I came to realise she was intensely sympathetic towards them. She was not afraid to be anthropomorphic in her descriptions, nor to expose her emotional responses to gorilla activities, especially where situations involved an animal in any sort of distress.

My work did not require me to conduct any sort of behavioural analysis, but because of Louis Leakey's oft-expressed belief that intensive studies of the apes would help shed light on the possible lifestyle of hominids, the subject interested me a great deal. Apart from compiling a visual record of all gorilla activities, I intended to see what I could make of their social life.

As the gorillas adjusted to the presence of two observers, I began to accept that there would be no short cuts to taking sensational close-ups. Most of our contacts tended to be conducted at some distance, with binoculars constantly in use. But even so, there were few opportunities to shoot good pictures where the animals were not reacting to the presence of humans. Dian had told me of two extraordinary and exciting incidents with the five males of Group 8: one day they had come near to the same tree she was using, and had even followed her after the contact. Peanuts, the youngest member of the family, had once apparently taken a book from her, and on the same day had caught hold of her boot and tried to pull her from the branch where she sat. These sort of interactions were exactly what I needed, but they consistently failed to materialise. Though my knowledge of gorillas and their responses to humans was still limited, I found Dian's description of the 'physical' approaches by Peanuts a little far-fetched and hard to reconcile with the general behaviour I had so far witnessed. Except for the one rewarding encounter before I had left, for the most part Group 8 remained strongly inhibited, the five members firmly keeping their distance at every meeting.

The drought continued and the mountain vegetation wilted further. It became very difficult to move quietly through the dried and dying leaves, which made good approaches harder to achieve. In search of succulent plants, the gorillas led us many times over the rugged terrain well above eleven thousand feet. Though not always enjoying the exertion required to climb there, I liked the upper reaches of the volcano. As one ascended, the vegetation changed gradually until giant groundsels and the fine-leaved lobelias began to dominate. Great bunches of helichrysum became more frequent, and on some of the ridges close stands of weirdly shaped giant heath trees flourished, their branches draped with flowing streamers of blue-grey lichen, or sometimes knobbled with clumps of bright-green moss.

On the upper portion of Mount Visoke, many of the ravines narrowed to steep-sided gullies made dangerous by loose pumice and slippery, moss-laden banks. After Dian balked at crossing some of them, I discovered she had been hiding a deep fear of heights. But more seriously, the lengthy climbs, which usually took two or three hours, quickly depleted her reserves of strength. Will-power was no longer enough and the ascents became painfully protracted. Although she tried hard not to show any distress, exhaustion etched her face and demanded frequent rests. She apologised for causing delays, blaming chest problems from her heavy smoking habit. Earlier observations that she was physically unsuited for the job she had taken on were now swiftly confirmed. She could only partially overcome the disadvantage by practising a form of mind over matter. I could not help recalling the decidedly unpleasant and difficult weeks that followed the departure of the orphans, positive now that much of her early attitude stemmed from a reluctance to reveal her limitations in front of a stranger. Since my return from Nairobi she had gallantly tried to keep up a demanding schedule of fieldwork, but now she was acquiring a gaunt, weary look that caused more than a little concern.

As an understanding of her situation grew, I began to lose some of the mild disdain I felt for her research methods and to feel some sympathy for her. I was no champion mountain climber myself and had no difficulty appreciating the physical strain she felt. In my youth, nearly fifteen years of recurrent malaria and the intake of extraordinary amounts of quinine had affected both my physique and stamina. I, too, felt a depressing lack of strength when climbing heavily laden at altitude. While in the army many years earlier, scouting and patrolling at high altitudes on Mount Kenya, I had to contend with weeks of climbing effort that had at times brought me uncomfortably close to the condition I now saw in Dian.

Her study brief was to try to find out all there was to know about the mountain gorillas of the Virunga volcanoes: to continue and add to the behavioural research conducted by George Schaller in 1960, and to assess how many of the animals still survived. The project was no easy undertaking. Louis Leakey had no doubt selected her for the task on the basis of a perceived strength of character and uninhibited enthusiasm; and his own personal conviction that women made better and more consistent observers than men. But since he had never visited the actual location, he was quite unaware just how demanding the conditions for her would be. Beyond a brief grounding in behavioural study at the Stanford University Primate Centre, she had set out to tackle the work with no academic training. Her personal, first-hand knowledge of Africa and African animals had been acquired during one whirlwind and somewhat contentious private safari in 1963. However, although her frail constitution was inhibiting and restricting some of her fieldwork, she had absolutely no intention of abandoning what she had set out to do. Taking into account the traumatic difficulties suffered during the early months of her project, experiences I knew full well would have overwhelmed most people, I had to admire her fortitude.

After three months in her company I had come closer to understanding what Dian was up against, physically and mentally. In the friendly atmosphere that now prevailed, conversations flowed more easily. She hesitantly revealed that aside from the physical aspect she had other worries, in particular her capabilities for the academic side of research. She knew Schaller's published work on mountain gorillas was a superb example of a study conducted in depth. His discerning and analytical approach had revealed many features of mountain gorilla behaviour – and his detailed descriptions made fascinating reading. Although Schaller had not been able to go very deeply into their social behaviour, mainly because of the same observation difficulties that plagued

Dian, in two and half years she had so far found very little to add to his perceptive and meticulous work. Whenever we touched on the subject, she freely admitted to feeling overshadowed by his achievements. In spite of having had four gorilla groups under observation from her Rwandan camp for two years, her subjects remained only partially habituated and persistently hard to see clearly. After opening the gates to some of her inner thoughts, Dian realised there was no need to try to conceal her physical weakness nor to try to impress me with a demanding schedule of fieldwork. With confidence growing that I was committed to helping her research, her earlier perception of me as critical intruder was soon forgotten.

To accommodate the separation of feeding and cooking arrangements, on my return I had reorganised my tent. Although it was very cramped, the thin canvas structure had become a cosy though somewhat chilly refuge, with the functions of workroom, kitchen, dining room, bedroom and wash-place all packaged in one small area. Well endowed with blankets and a large sheet-lined sleeping bag that easily countered the bitterly cold nights, a comfortable bed ensured restful sleep; judiciously placed shelving and stacked boxes took care of my possessions, leaving a few cubic feet of space in which to stand and move. A sturdy wooden table acted as a desk and general workbench, and my kerosene pressure lamp supplied ample though noisy light. The lamp doubled as a very effective heater and clothes dryer: a great asset, since one seldom returned from work in a dry state. Wet clothing hung from the ridge pole above the light quickly dried in the stream of hot air, but it was very necessary to keep window vents open to avoid a build-up of fumes. I had a gas heater for added comfort during the colder evenings, but it burned with a harsh sound that disturbed concentration so was seldom used. I did all my cooking under the tent flysheet on a small kerosene stove, soon becoming an expert at juggling stacked saucepans to deal with my largely tinned supplies. To provide entertainment and a link with remote happenings in the outside world, I used a sophisticated Braun T1000 radio. A small collection of books helped to fill in the brief periods available for relaxation.

The radio was in full use on the night of 20 July. The day had been a long one: an early photo session to try to illustrate the hazards of the stinging nettle zone, followed by seven hours in the vicinity of Group 4, while Dian went off with Nemeye to try to locate the restless Rafiki. I was tired, but fully alert to an extraordinary event taking place far beyond the confines of the planet. With an earphone plugged into my ear – along with millions of others around the world, I waited in curiously anxious suspense for the crew of the American 'Eagle' Lunar Module to complete their preparations for a landing on the moon. It seemed hardly possible that such a daring mission could succeed!

Since I have an aversion to hearing radios blaring in the wilderness, I always used an earphone to listen in. However, earphones do tend to cut out external sounds. As I lay in the warm comfort of my bed, concentrating on distorted transmissions from the moon and Mission control in Florida, some equally distorted sounds reached my ears – like someone shouting. Wondering if the space craft would land safely, convinced something would go wrong at the last minute, I had no intention of missing the final moments to touch-down. I ignored the increasing yells – but it was no good. Unable to understand the lack of any response, Dian rushed over my narrow bridge across the stream shouting that she had been robbed! The urgency and anger in her voice was now plainly audible, but Eagle was seconds away from contact with the lunar surface and I could hardly bear to put down the earphone. By the time I opened the tent flap Dian was cursing and swearing and totally unimpressed by talk of men on the moon.

A case had vanished from the cabin, apparently while she was in the kitchen. She had been working late, preparing for her journey to Kigali, and had then gone out to the kitchen to prepare a snack. Looking for the case shortly after, then frantically searching, she could not find it nor readily believe it was actually missing. Beyond searching yet again, calling and confronting the staff with the loss, and looking by torchlight for any sort of evidence as to what might have happened, nothing more could be done. The case had definitely vanished, and with it everything of value that Dian possessed: passport, money, jewellery, travellers' cheques – and her latest funding cheques from *National Geographic*. Also gone was another cheque to finance the new survey man, Michael Burkhart, already in Rwanda and due to be met the following day. Just when financial constraints had eased and it seemed things were beginning to run relatively smoothly, a devastating blow had fallen. Dian was terribly upset, understandably very angry and close to tears.

Well after midnight I returned to my tent, not looking forward at all to the next day. 'Eagle' had landed safely, but I was somewhat mollified to learn the crew were still hours away from venturing out on to the moon's surface. Great excitement still prevailed and I lay fitfully awake most of the night so as not to miss the momentous occasion. Before dawn, thoroughly caught up in the suspenseful moment, I listened as Neil Armstrong put his space boot down on the dusty soil of the moon and spoke his famous line: 'That's one small step for man, one giant leap for mankind.' I wanted nothing better than to listen further to the incredible events taking place so far away, but the sun was due and more down-to-earth matters needed urgent attention.

At dawn a fresh search of the surrounding woodlands showed up some footprints. Before long theft was confirmed; the case lay abandoned and empty behind a tree only two hundred yards from the camp, a few loose papers scattered in the dewy grass. Dian was not worried about the cheques, they could be stopped, and the actual hard cash loss, though serious, was not too great. But the loss of her jewellery and sentimental trinkets upset her badly. With her mental tranquillity and carefully laid plans in ruins, she borrowed all the money I had available and set out to meet the census man. Police would have to be informed, and a visit be made to the American embassy in Kigali to send cables about the cheques and arrange for a new passport. The incident was disturbing, highlighting the vulnerability of the camp to anyone with thievery in mind.

It took Dian nearly two weeks to sort out the problems caused by the theft. In her absence I concentrated entirely on Group 4, mainly because they were conveniently close and using an area that had become very familiar the previous year. The period actually marked the tentative beginnings of what would in time develop into an extraordinary association between humans and gorillas; but that relationship lay far in the future, and for the present I struggled to improve the level of habituation. The collective shyness of the family made most contacts difficult and good picture opportunities were rare, but I persisted because of better chances to record some chest-beating behaviour.

Now infinitely more careful and skilled at manoeuvring in the dense foliage, I had long since learned that the gorillas were endowed with senses not much more acute than those of humans. Unlike the numerous duikers, bushbucks and buffalo, they seldom reacted to wind-borne scents. Their eyesight was obviously very good, and I judged their hearing to be superior to mine at least, though possibly it was just that they were more acutely aware of the sounds reaching their ears. In the concealing undergrowth it was this hearing ability I had to contend with most. Though the initial period of stalking was invariably exciting, to keep fully alert and tuned in to all the sights, sounds and smells had at first required determined concentration. It had taken a while to reach and maintain a high degree of awareness, to analyse everything my senses picked up and avoid letting my brain cut out seemingly irrelevant but often important bits of information.

Many contacts were established before any visual sighting, particularly when a gorilla detected a sound and was certain it did not come from the immediate family. There would be a 'questing' chest beat – a soft thumping that seemed clearly to mean 'I hear you – who is it?' The gentle patting of one's leg or chest to duplicate the sound would supply the required information, letting all within earshot know the persistent human intruder was lurking again. Having developed an acute longing to see more of the animals at close range, I had to be content with distances that forced the regular use of telephoto lenses. Lack of success in taking more than an occasional meaningful picture was already beginning to cause some frustration.

Dian returned at last with her new assistant. Tall, well-built and bearded, he gave every indication of being a suitable person to tackle the mountains, only his comments and tired eyes gave any sign that he had found the climb to camp somewhat heavy going. After days spent dealing with the aggravating problems generated by the theft, Dian was not in a good humour. The police in Ruhengeri had been helpful at least – overzealous if anything. Three of her former camp employees now languished in jail, and several policemen had climbed to camp to confront the four current staff members. They had arrested Sehegeri, the man I had employed as a guard: a big, powerful, somewhat sinister-looking man I had purposely selected because he appeared competent to deal with trouble. In her own mind Dian thought Sehegeri was the culprit and inclined to lay some of the blame at my door for employing him. I was not so certain and reminded her of the foolish thing she had done a few weeks earlier. After counting a thick pile of Rwandese franc notes recently exchanged for dollars, she had naively waved the fat wad in front of the camp assistant, Nezarwanda, gleefully explaining that the money meant she could keep the gorilla work going for a long time. Even if he was not the thief, it was more than likely Nezarwanda had been unable to resist mentioning the money to the rest of the staff. Any one of them could have done the deed – but then all at their quarters would have known who had been absent from their tent at the critical time. It seemed most likely to me that one of the men she had sacked earlier had taken his revenge.

Adding to unease created by the theft, the continuing lack of rain was another worry. The camp stream had ceased even to trickle and only a few shrinking pools of discoloured water remained. Foliage everywhere was badly wilted and turning yellow. It was possible to spend the whole day on the mountain without getting any clothing wet, but the hot days made lengthy spells of climbing a tiring and sweaty effort. The gorillas continued to favour the higher altitudes, travelling unusually long distances to search for succulent plants.

While Dian attended to chores in camp, I took Michael Burkhart out for his first introduction to gorillas. It was unfortunately a day that began with an extended period of tracking. After four hours of scrambling about the upper reaches of Visoke, visibly tiring and probably suffering from the altitude more than he let on, my companion had to give up. Guiding him back to the top meadow for an easy walk back to base, I went on to locate Group 4, ironically finding them only a hundred yards from the path he had taken to get home. Sorry that he had not held on just a little longer, I felt some misgivings about the wisdom of sending an inexperienced person out to do a difficult job. There was no question the task ahead was a daunting one. Michael Burkhart was the second person Louis had selected to count the gorillas, and to be anywhere near accurate, his work would involve locating all the groups and individuals living in areas administered by three different nations: Uganda, Rwanda and Zaire. He appeared to be physically strong and healthy enough, but he would also have to remain well motivated, self-reliant and unaffected by isolation and the hardships of roughing it for months in difficult conditions. Dian was determined to get him set up on his own with the minimum of delay. Still upset by the theft and not at all happy at having to feed, train and establish a new assistant, she was in an uncompromising mood. Given a bare seven days of instruction that did little to counteract visibly waning enthusiasm for his project, he was shown how to read and follow gorilla tracks, and how easy it was to count nightbeds to determine the number and rough composition of a family. He would have to do his best when it came to identifying the animals to avoid duplication. When listing sex and age, much of his data would surely be guesswork. Even with the habituated study groups, Dian and I were unable to determine the sex of some of the subadult gorillas; at the time both of us were unaware we had already made faulty assumptions.

Although he would have the help of competent Rwandan assistants, Burkhart still had a language barrier to overcome, and lacking experience and field craft, he was going to find it both exciting and difficult to contend with the reactions of completely wild groups. We decided he would make a start on the northern face of Visoke, just over the border between Zaire and Rwanda, where a crater called Ngezi with a small lake at its foot showed on Dian's map. Since reports from local people said the lake had not dried up in the drought, a camp would be put down somewhere nearby. Having never visited the place, we had to accept the general belief amongst our assistants that Zaire park rangers never came anywhere near the area.

The setting up of a new camp gave an ideal opportunity to vary my picture coverage, so I went along to record the event and give a hand. Situated at roughly ten thousand feet, Ngezi proved to be a beautiful location. To the east of the tiny lake, a scatter of low, bamboo-covered craters stretched towards the eroded bulk of Mount Sabinio. To the west, Mikeno reared high and dominated the horizon. Thick haze restricted views of the low country to the north, but the visible land appeared to be sparsely populated. To keep the camp well hidden, with some difficulty tents were set on a high, narrow ridge well above the small stretch of water.

We spent three days surveying the immediate surroundings, finding evidence that gorillas certainly frequented the area. But all the signs were stale: a few sleeping sites and scattered individual nests, all overgrown and clearly weeks or more old. Compared to the heavily utilised slopes on the other side of Visoke, the Ngezi section appeared for the present to be out of favour and uninhabited. Michael Burkhart would have to travel much further afield to find his first subjects. The only excitement came when we stumbled upon a few bones on a game trail. They proved to be from a gorilla skeleton and many more were dug up at the spot. Sadly, the all-important skull was missing.

Expecting to find many gorillas, I for one had been keen to experience their reactions on first contact. Our failure to find any was a setback, and poor Burkhart seemed to have lost even more of his initial enthusiasm. He was not at all happy when the time came for Dian and me to leave. He would have to range considerable distances from his base, and even though none of the local people knew where it lay, it was obvious he felt apprehensive about his position on the wrong side of the border. Dian had no sympathy, however; he had been selected by Dr Leakey to tackle the long delayed count of gorillas and the time had come for him to get on with it.

Nearly mid-August, and still the drought persisted. Cumulus clouds grew daily in the sky, but steadfastly refused to part with any moisture to relieve the yellowing and parched vegetation below. The last of the drying pools in the bed of the camp stream had scum on the surface and were turning an unpleasant orange colour. Kanyarugano, a new man now in charge of camp chores, found one small, clear pool downstream some distance away. Every day he carried out cans to fill with water for drinking and cooking. Washing clothing had become a problem and bathing water was reduced to a minimum.

A week after the Ngezi camp was established, high above the now dried-up meadow, three members of Group 4 gave me my first truly close and 'peaceful' gorilla encounter. While I lay prone in an awkward position, seeing little and waiting patiently for the right moment to head for a suitable tree, the silverback moved and passed close above. His family began to follow the lead, some pausing to feed on a few miserable thistle plants. Moments later, a subadult and two youngsters named Simba and Papoose stopped at a gap above me and gazed down. With what might have been collective confidence they turned together and pressed timidly forward. Stopping only five or six feet away, they stood shoulder to shoulder and looked me over with evasive eyes – tiny Simba squeezed in the middle. Astonished by this approach, taking infinite care I lifted a camera. The light was awful, making it hard to focus on the dark, shadowed faces. Regretting that moments like this had to be viewed through layers of glass, trying desperately to keep the camera steady for the slow shutter speed, I exposed several frames. Each clack of the shutter made the gorillas flinch. I caught sight of the silverback above, twenty feet away and watching with a concentrated stare. The three held their position for several seconds, then retreated noisily, causing the silverback to give a suppressed bark of concern. The brief event stimulated a vision of what might become possible in the future – inducing a small measure of confidence that such close shots would soon become easier to obtain.

Though still constantly frustrated by the shyness of the gorillas, by now I had settled more comfortably to the work. From the moment of return at the end of June I had taken care not to infringe on any aspect of Dian's time in camp. Beyond joining her to describe and discuss daily events and plans, and perhaps enjoy the warmth of the cabin fire for a while, in the pleasant atmosphere that now prevailed I was wholly content with my separate existence. What little free time remained after a day's work was spent writing up field notes and camera reports, dealing with a growing flow of correspondence and preparing for the next day. There was plenty to do to keep me occupied. I was used to being on my own; isolation had never produced the loneliness I had seen affect others with varying degrees of severity. Dian seemed to cast be in the same mould, and separating our feeding arrangements had eliminated a major element of strain. However, I was in for a surprise that caused a brief renewal of tension, but which was soon to lead to totally unexpected changes in our relationship.

Early one night as I drifted on the verge of sleep, the sound of footsteps brought me fully awake: someone had crossed to the entrance to my tent and was working at the zip. I sat up and called out loudly in Kiswahili: '*Nani?*' (Who is it?)

'It's me,' came Dian's voice.

'What's the problem?' I asked, but she merely opened the flap, stumbled in the darkness and sat down heavily on my bed. I repeated my query, but she reached out and held on to me. While we sat for long moments in an awkward embrace, I waited for some explanation. 'What's wrong?' was all I could think of to say.

Finally the response came: 'There is nothing wrong, I just need someone to hold on to.'

I listened while she thanked me for being so understanding and tolerant of her physical difficulties with the fieldwork, going on to say that she really appreciated the help I had given her with Burkhart and the new camp. Then she kissed me and without thought I resisted. Dian reacted quickly with a mercurial turn of temper. 'Why did you do that?' she shouted. While I entreated her to hold on a moment and not to take offence, she pushed away and left abruptly. Listening to her departing footsteps, wondering if I had misread her intentions, I slipped out into the cold, groped for my shoes and hastily slung on a jacket. Stepping out of the tent, I heard the door of the cabin slam. The sound shattered the chilly silence of the camp and effectively damped my intention to go over and apologise. The difficult days of April and May had not endeared me to Dian, but since her change of attitude I had come to respect and like her much better. Our association had remained formal, but pleasant and almost entirely neutral. Now, suddenly, a new element had surfaced that promised complications.

The next morning Dian was curt and aloof. Intending to say I was sorry for hurting her feelings, I was immediately put off by her manner and remained obstinately silent. We studiously avoided any mention of what had occurred and friendly relations remained distinctly chilled for several days. I worked on alone with the gorillas for a while, regretting the return to a superficially polite atmosphere. But it did not last long. I came upon Rafiki one morning and found his group in a more responsive mood than usual. Little persuasion was needed to induce Dian to try for a close encounter for the cameras. Though the gorillas failed to give us what was needed, Dian's return to a congenial disposition let me know she had chosen to ignore the incident. But the casual, independent nature of our working alliance had taken a jolt that was not so easily set aside.

Including the months I had spent on Visoke in 1968, my notes now re-corded a total of just over two hundred and sixty hours in visual contact with gorillas. *National Geographic* had insisted stills should take preference over motion-picture coverage, but with half a year of work completed, as yet there were no really outstanding results. Though able to move much closer to the evasive creatures, my best shots were mainly of individuals taken at a distance with telephoto lenses. I used Ektachrome high-speed film most of the time, but even so was forced to use wide apertures and slow shutter speeds: most often 1/30th of a second, but frequently at 1/15th and 1/8th. I invariably carried a small tripod, but it was seldom possible to make it steady enough for the long lenses. To be certain of a sharp image it was essential to have the camera jammed against the trunk of a tree or a solid branch, but these supports were not always available and I had to accept that soft images from camera movement would spoil many frames.

August ended with a welcome storm that lashed across the volcanoes and broke the long drought. A rush of flood water off Mount Karisimbi quickly scoured out the stagnant pools of the camp stream. Within a short while it was flowing strongly with a supply of silt-laden but fresh water. The parched soil soaked up the heavy rain and wilted vegetation began to recover with astonishing rapidity. Weary of climbing to the upper reaches of Visoke nearly every day, I hoped a fresh growth of their favoured plants would soon entice the gorillas to return to lower levels.

September came in with clouded skies and fitful showers of rain. The golden tinges of water-starved and dying leaves gave way to the green of fresh growth; foliage laden with moisture became the norm once more, making it easier to move quietly. But I missed the sunshine and began to look forward to a planned break at home. Though remarkably fit by my standards, the constant, heavy exercise was taking its toll. My weight had reduced drastically and clothing hung loose on my frame. No matter how much I ate I seemed to be burning up the energy and drawing still on slim reserves.

On the northern portion of Visoke Michael Burkhart was apparently having little luck in finding many gorillas. Notes from him for Dian arrived sporadically, but the reports were strange and oddly worded. It was impossible to decide if he was merely trying to be flippant and amusing; whatever the intention it was hard to assess what he was actually achieving.

At this point a letter came from Heather that immediately overshadowed gorilla matters; she wrote that I would be pleased to know the second East Rudolf Expedition was over and Richard had told her about a spectacular find. My immediate reaction was one of both delight and dismay. Obviously I had missed a very special event. Richard had at last found a hominid skull and the information gave me considerable incentive to hasten away and see what all the excitement was about.

On reaching Nairobi I quickly followed up the news. In his office at Nairobi's National Museum, Richard showed me a remarkable fossil skull, describing with understandable pleasure the pure chance that had led him to the site where it lay. Resembling the famous *Zinjanthropus* skull found by his mother at Olduvai Gorge almost exactly a decade earlier, the fossil was a beautifully preserved specimen of an australopithecine hominid. Holding the ancient skull in my hands, I could sense the glow of achievement that gripped Richard. I recalled the time I had expected him to find a skull to match the jawbone discovered at Peninj – and now he had almost stumbled over one nearly five hundred miles further north. This incredibly old piece of mineralised bone represented for him an assured place in the records of palaeoanthropology. It also justified the faith placed in him by the research committee of the National Geographic Society; five years of endeavour in a field dominated by his parents had finally produced a reward that exceeded all expectations.

The skull had no name beyond the scientific label coined by Professor Raymond Dart: *Australopithecus* (southern ape). Richard had no desire to have any of his team's important finds tagged with nicknames. The fossil was marked with museum reference letters and number: KNM-ER 406, and henceforth would simply be known as 406. Examining it with all the reverence due to a distant prehistoric relative, I had to suppress disappointment at missing the chance to cap my record of Richard's fossil-hunting career.

As no significant bones of an australopithecine skeleton had yet been found, visualising what sort of living creature had carried the head was an impossibility. Over the ages the teeth had been eroded away, but the root cavities indicated they had been very large. Its prominent sagittal crest and widespread cheekbone arches were intact and truly impressive; I reckoned the bulky muscles that must have covered the cranium in life would have closely rivalled those of a gorilla. Watching gorillas eating for hours on end, I had wondered about the powerful muscles that worked their jaws; their diet consisted almost entirely of soft vegetable matter, though some of it was coarse and fibrous and needed to be well crushed to aid digestion But still, it seemed to me they had an excess of power in their jaws. If the missing teeth had been anything like the huge grinding molars of Mary Leakey's *Zinjanthropus*, the 406 hominid had certainly been well equipped to cope with a diet of raw and coarse plant material – but what sort of a body and digestive system would the creature have possessed? To extract sufficient nutrition from their vegetable diet, gorillas had large and specialised guts, which gave them their distinctive corpulent look. Anatomists had determined that the australopithecines walked fully upright, but what sort of figure a bipedal herbivore would have cut was difficult to imagine. The vision of a corpulent vegetarian did not quite fit my image of a hominid striding purposefully through the open woodlands and savannahs of prehistoric Africa. But perhaps the 406 skull had belonged to a creature whose carbohydrate diet consisted of fibrous roots, seed pods and hard nuts, and who might also have been a partial omnivore – in which case surely a leaner and more athletic body would have supported it.

Now I learned that Richard's success in the field had been outstanding in more ways than one. In addition to the nearly complete skull, fragments of a second one had been found, and to the huge excitement of the archaeologists, Kay Behrensmeyer, a young American geologist newly attached to the team, had located two sites where primitive stone tools were eroding out of ancient volcanic tuff. For five years I had accompanied Richard on a variety of expeditions and field trips, filming and photographing all that happened, and compiling a photographic record that lay in boxes in the *National Geographic* archives – unused because there were no startling new discoveries to warrant an article. On 27 July when 406 was found, I had spent a rewarding day close to two gorilla groups, and was well pleased with the pictures the contact had provided, but I would have been more than pleased to have been present when Richard found his hominid. At last his efforts had hit the world headlines, making it virtually certain the *National Geographic* magazine would publish an article.

Burying regrets over a lost opportunity, I ended my break by spending several days photographing the skulls for Richard. With good reason, he confidently predicted a third and expanded expedition would be mounted in 1970. Two seasons of wide-ranging exploration had defined the extent of the main fossil-bearing deposits, confirming an incredible richness of fossils throughout the area. Preliminary dating work by scientists from Cambridge University, had already set the age of the tool site at about 2.6 million years, so it was clear the region held exciting potential. The initial ground search had been completed and an immense amount of work lay ahead: literally hundreds of square miles would have to be subjected to more precise and thorough searches. Archaeologists would be kept busy excavating tool sites, and geologists put to the test to unravel the huge puzzle posed by the broken, complicated stratigraphy of the sediments.

While I photographed his fossils, Richard talked about his plans for the coming year and hoped that I would be free to join in again. The thought of new discoveries yet to be made was a powerful incentive to try to make sure I was, but it was impossible even to guess how much longer gorillas would claim first priority. Six months remained of the year I had undertaken to cover the gorilla project, but there were already indications the period could be extended. The two of us were committed to exhilarating, long-term projects and I hoped it would be possible to find some way to enjoy them both.

Heavily laden with fresh supplies and purchases for the camp, I set off on the long journey back to Rwanda. During the hours at the wheel I tried hard to look into the future, but it was a futile exercise. A new expedition to Lake Rudolf would not start until June of the following year – plenty of time, I thought, to give me a good chance of joining it – but so much remained to be achieved with the gorillas. Mulling over the subject and arranging plans neatly in my head, little did I know what complications lay in store.

Dian greeted my return with an enthusiastic welcome; an uncharacteristic display that was not entirely due to pleasure at seeing me. She was in the throes of yet another crisis and wanted help. During my absence her new assistant had given ample reasons for her to conclude that he was quite unsuitable for the census work. But Burkhart had been personally engaged by Dr Leakey, so she had spent days agonising over the situation. She had already written letters of explanation to Louis, and by cable he had given her permission to terminate the man's appointment if she wished. In spite of this, uncertainty over the best course to take remained. She had purposely delayed making any move until I returned.

Before leaving for Kenya I knew that the astonishingly vague reports from Burkhart were causing Dian concern. Since then she had received several others and had become convinced he was irresponsible; she had also been informed by porters and her staff that he was smoking bhang or hashish, and putting very little effort into fieldwork. Together we examined the strange and irrational reports covering six weeks of work. There could be only one conclusion: the young man had become something of a liability and should be pulled out before further funds were wasted. Still troubled by the situation, Dian made up her mind and sent a runner to the Ngezi camp with a letter.

The reaction was swift. Michael Burkhart appeared the next day to confront Dian. She faced his first angry demands to know what right she had to turn him out before calling for me. Quickly drawn into the acrimonious arguments that followed, I had to make it clear I was party to the decision, and that he was being fired purely as a consequence of his own behaviour and lack of responsibility. A survey to count the gorillas had long since become urgent, there was a great deal of territory to cover and he had already wasted valuable time and strictly limited funds. Anger and bluster soon evaporated; accepting the dismissal Burkhart left in a resentful but subdued mood. To add to his discomfort, because local elections were taking place, all offices and shops had shut down and there would be no immediate action. He would have to wait at Ngezi four more days. After he had gone Dian expressed her relief and gratitude for the backing I had given her, admitting that had Burkhart been less belligerent and pleaded for another try, she would have found it difficult to stand firm. Not wanting to finish the matter alone, she asked me to help close down his camp and take him to Gisenyi for a flight out.

Climbing the scenic trail to Ngezi, I found myself wishing Burkhart had been a success. I was as eager as Dian to know how many gorillas lived in the area, and briefly contemplated making use of the camp to explore it myself; it would be relatively easy to work west and locate Group 9, interesting also to track down the group known to utilise the slopes to the east. But I was not a free agent and the idea soon faded. Burkhart had by now accepted his fate. He seemed relieved, almost pleased to be leaving. No longer resentful, he conversed quite amicably on the journey to Gisenyi. But his trials were not quite over; the light plane that was to take him to Kigali failed to turn up. Ultimately he had to go by bus – a rugged ride lasting six to seven hours in overcrowded conditions over appalling roads.

Dian was by now thoroughly depressed by the whole affair. In spite of the nonsensical reports Burkhart had written, she remained uncertain she had done the right thing, and worried how a count of the gorillas would now be accomplished. Deciding to remain in Gisenyi, we booked in at the old Palm Beach Hotel, familiar to me from a disturbed twelve-hour stay during a

National Geographic assignment four years earlier. At that time the hotel had been dirty and badly run-down; a very rowdy group of local officials had occupied the bar below the bedrooms, carousing until the early hours of the morning and ruining any chance of some much needed sleep. Now the hotel was considerably cleaner and being managed by a friend of Dian's. I was introduced, and for the first time met Rosamond Carr, a charming and soft-spoken American lady who seemed quite out of place in her current occupation. Later Dian explained that Ros had suffered some financial troubles with her small farm on the lower slopes of Mount Karisimbi. She had only taken the job to help tide her over the difficulties. In a matter-of-fact way, she explained that it was from Ros Carr's place that she had set out to restart her project after escaping from Zaire. So far, what little I knew about Dian's early days in Zaire and Rwanda had come from Dr Leakey and Alan Root. With the mention of her escape I felt it was time to ask about her Kabara experiences. But she was reluctant to talk of them and shied away from my questions with a few terse replies.

The unplanned break in Gisenyi gave a first time opportunity to photograph Dian away from the mountains, so a pleasant morning was spent in the colourful African markets purchasing fresh fruit and vegetables, and many unnecessary items that helped overcome strong objections to the cameras. Later, as Dian wanted to see another very special friend, we drove south along the narrow, winding road that hugged the edge of Lake Kivu.

Turning into a cramped driveway, we stopped at a rustic little house on a small promontory curving out into the lake – a delightful setting by any standards. A diminutive woman came out to meet us and I was introduced to Madame Alyette de Munck. Dwarfed by Dian and myself, Alyette greeted us in sharply accented English and warm smiles of pleasure. She was clearly very pleased to see Dian, while I was given a long look of frank appraisal. With her brown hair cut short like a man and showing the first wisps of grey, her lined but beaming face gave no hint of the distress and tragedy she had suffered in recent times. I knew little of the relative events of the past few years, but enough to give me an unusual perspective on this undoubtedly courageous and tough little lady. She and her family had suffered serious problems after the Belgian Congo became independent and slipped rapidly into civil war; in a short space of time she had lost her husband, then, in horrifying circumstances, at the very time Dian had been organising a restart for her research in 1967, her son and nephew had been brutally murdered at the Congolese border post near Kisoro. I knew that in spite of the tragedy, she had been of great assistance to Dian, helping her to search for a new place to set up a base, and later providing her expertise and personal funds to construct the cabin. In time I would come to know Alyette well: kind and generous, with a restless energy that never seemed to flag, she was one of the few people welcome to visit the Visoke camp.

The relaxed day away from the mountains did wonders for Dian. With artful make-up, a change of hairstyle and clothing, she had again transformed her appearance. The break allowed her to release the pent-up tensions of past weeks and to ease some of her depression over such an early failure of the gorilla count. I had worked with her for close on seven months now, but this was the first time I had seen her well away from the mountain environment and dressed as for a visit to some smart restaurant. With the difficult weeks in April and May a matter of history, our independent camp arrangements had set a pattern of existence that was relaxed and undemanding, and we had gradually become amicable friends. Although we had only a shared interest in the gorillas as common ground, conversation flowed much more freely. I had not forgotten the incident in my tent, and subsequently Dian had made it plain that she felt happy with my company. At the dinners we had together at the hotel, almost the only guests in the large dining room, the persistent topic of gorillas and related work faded. We sipped on imported French wine and exchanged small items of information about one another's past. I learned she had a wealthy stepfather, and gathered most of her childhood had been difficult and somewhat unhappy. But she was reluctant to talk much about her early life and managed to extract far more details of my past than I of hers. She did reveal that it was an early accident with a horse that was the root cause of her breathing difficulties: she had fallen badly and broken a rib that damaged one of her lungs. She admitted freely that her heavy smoking habit compounded the problem, adding, without being specific, that she had recently become more worried about her lungs. Already she had made a serious effort to cut down on smoking, but still remained concerned and felt she should have her chest examined.

Inevitably, talk returned to centre on the gorillas. Though my assignment had several months to run, Dian pressed me to declare if I was prepared to stay longer if necessary. It was obvious a great deal remained to be accomplished with the gorillas, and work on material for a lecture film had barely begun. But the attractions of Lake Rudolf still lay in my mind and I felt unable to commit myself so far ahead. If the National Geographic Society were prepared to fund her on a long-term basis, as they were doing with Jane Goodall's study of the chimpanzees, Dian had no other commitments in her life and intended to continue her research. She felt sure that in the fullness of time she would extend what was known about gorillas well beyond the scope of Schaller's work, but retained an uncomfortable uneasiness on that score. For over two and a half years she had amassed piles of field notes, but as yet nothing really significant had come out of her observations. And when it came to a population count, although the will was there, she had neither the time nor the strength to conduct a survey on her own.

When Dian revived her worries about the census problem, it led to something we had discussed earlier – a plan to make a patrol across the border to visit Kabara, the main purpose of which would be to relocate and count the gorillas she had started to study in 1967. Kabara lay roughly five miles in a direct line from our Rwandan base, but Dian had never dared to penetrate that deep into Congolese territory on her own. She felt an obligation to do something constructive about a census and Kabara seemed the best place to make a start. I wanted to see the famous meadow myself, so we agreed the time was right for a reconnaissance. But first, Dian would take a short holiday in Nairobi to see about her chest and discuss census and other project matters with Dr Leakey.

Around the mountains the weather was fast returning to a more normal state. Rain began to fall with greater regularity and the fertile earth absorbed it greedily. The vegetation continued to sprout quick-growing shoots that promised to erase all signs of the severe drought. The crisis over Michael Burkhart had effectively disrupted field work and I had not seen much of the gorillas. While waiting for the elections to finish and camp staff to return from voting, I had made a few excursions – quickly discovering that poachers and cattle were present in considerable numbers.

Over a wide sweep of the high saddle between Visoke and Karisimbi, the woodlands were full of scattered cattle herds and riddled with an alarming number of trap lines. This called for some urgent action, so together with Vatiri and Nemeye Alphonse, a new assistant who had taken the place of my old friend of the same name, I spent hours collecting and driving the cattle down towards the park boundary and destroying the snares. I wished for some official power to do more than just chase the animals out of the park. The conservator came up to the camp very occasionally, always accompanied by several raggedly dressed guards, a few sporting battered old rifles and ammunition of dubious reliability. The man acknowledged and accepted our own anti-poaching and cattle round-up efforts almost as a subordinate. Knowing that 'mademoiselle' was prepared to pay a small bounty for any people his men caught operating illegally within the park, he usually made the effort to pay a visit when he was out of pocket. Having exchanged the normal polite formalities and listened to our reports and complaints about the cattle and poachers, he would order his men to start a patrol, then stay at the camp, talking and taking tea and biscuits. The men would go off to comb the forests nearby, almost invariably managing to arrest one or two young herdboys, and perhaps lift a few snares. But they never seemed to be able to apprehend any of the wily poachers. We all knew that in spite of promises from the conservator to deal sternly with the captives, they would soon be set free and would return to the park again.

With preconceived and firm ideas about the sanctity of man-made game parks and reserves, Dian looked upon intruders in the Parc des Volcans almost as enemies, reserving particular hatred for the hunters whose primitive but effective methods caused much suffering to their prey. I detested the activities of the hunters too, and felt considerable animosity towards the cattlemen and their beasts, but even so found it difficult to regard either with the same unswerving enmity that gripped Dian. Having lived all my life in Africa, like many of my friends I suffered conflicting emotions about the European style of rules and regulations that had been imposed upon the indigenous inhabitants of Africa. As a boy I had been an avid reader of the stories of adventure related by early explorers and professional hunters, some of whom had slaughtered uncountable numbers of animals for sport and profit, and occasionally 'the pot'. Later I had accepted without question the rigid regulations that applied to special reserves, wilderness areas and 'Government land', also the sometimes curious laws determining the ownership of all wild animals: laws that made every hunter a poacher if he ignored them and instantly restricted access to former common land. Countless Africans for whom hunting was part of a normal, traditional way of life were affected. With good reason most were confused and angered by the decrees that made their ancient craft illegal and unacceptable.

Feeling uncertain about the rationale that had led to the imposition of strict 'game' laws, contemplating the motives of the men hunting and trapping in the Virunga park induced some further soul-searching. Economic necessity drove most of them to endure the risks and hardships of a hunter's life, and as a visitor to their country I was hardly in a position to justify my actions against them. Knowing very well that were I in their position – totally ignorant of worldwide environmental issues and the steady decline of wild animal populations – my outlook would be quite different. However, it was relatively easy to ignore the hunter's point of view and respond to the urge to protect what was clearly the last sanctuary for the great apes of Virunga. The threat posed to gorillas by the snares and the frequent sight of dead and dying antelopes made it easy to generate a heightened state of animosity. But still, many of the patrols to disrupt the activities of the hunters left me vaguely unsettled.

To provide pictures of anti-poacher work, Dian accompanied me on several of the snare-hunting patrols. Destroying the simple snares gave her great satisfaction, but she hated it when we found a victim caught up in a deadly noose. The obvious signs of a lingering death often reduced her to tears. Most of the animals we found were dead: mainly the beautiful little red duikers. But occasionally we came across one still alive, exhausted from hours of struggle at the end of a line attached to lengths of bamboo or springy saplings. Many times I was led to an abandoned line of traps by the whiff of putrid flesh, finding a decomposing carcass caught up in a noose. The trappers valued their wire nooses, but used many others woven from perishable materials; when a poacher moved to a new site these were simply left to rot where they had been set – able to perform their lethal function until time and slow decay destroyed their strength. Piles of snares, together with weapons and tools captured from fleeing poachers and herders, threatened to crowd out the small camp store. However, the campaign had the required effect and the invaders withdrew from the immediate saddle area. It was sobering to remember that the region covered by our anti-poaching activities affected only a few square miles. I shuddered to think what was happening in other sections of the park outside our small sphere of influence.

Although I had taken many hours away from gorilla work to destroy the ever-sprouting snares, it was not often I caught up with the wary men who set them. One particular occasion sticks firmly in mind because my anti-poacher action backfired. While in Washington, before the assignment began, I came across a shop called Spy. Amongst the many fascinating cloak-and-dagger items for sale was a slim aerosol can, the label of which claimed the contents to be similar to the chemical sprays used by police to incapacitate fractious criminals. Along with an unpronounceable name describing the chemical, the sinister black can carried the appropriate name 'Subdue', and promised instant nausea and vomiting at the touch of a button.

Late one evening, as I made my way back to camp through the nettle zone, the unusual sound of voices came to my ears. Soon I saw glimpses of the owners: two men were heading directly towards me on the same trail, one carrying a bundle of bamboo rods on his head that bobbed up and down above the high nettles. Having carried a can of Subdue in my pack for months, more as a weapon for possible self-defence than anything else, at last I saw a chance to test its effectiveness. Stepping back quietly into thick cover to ambush the pair, I burst out moments later in the path of the leading man – deadly can of Subdue at the ready. The leading man froze and was bumped from behind by his companion. Closing in with a loud yell I sprayed both with a jet from the can. A breeze blew a good quantity of the stuff back in my face, stinging my eyes with vicious intensity and forcing them firmly shut. The poachers meanwhile collected their shattered wits and bolted. Eyes streaming and throat dry, wondering if I'd received enough of the chemical to make me ill, I could only wait and listen to the men crashing away through the nettles. Nothing drastic happened; gradually the stinging subsided and I was alone in a quiet forest, eyes watering profusely and a bundle of bamboo at my feet. I could only wonder what effect the action had on the two poachers. They must have been confounded by my strange antics and both had received a full measure of the spray. If the chemical had stung their eyes as much as it did mine, they must have had great difficulty seeing where they were going: at the very least they would have suffered plenty of nettle stings.

On the way down to Gisenyi, taking Dian to catch her flight to Kigali and Nairobi, I collected a batch of mail from the post office at Ruhengeri. Among the letters was one that effectively obliterated all her immediate worries. Al Royce, my picture editor in Washington, had written to send congratulations; one of my photographs of Dian out in the woods with the two gorilla orphans had been selected for the cover of the January 1970 issue of the magazine. The news was a total surprise. With great pleasure I handed Dian a colour copy Al had included. Her first reaction was one of disbelief, followed by a welling of happy tears. Overwhelmed by the knowledge she was to appear on a front cover that would be seen by millions, she flew away from Gisenyi in an almost euphoric state of mind. Watching the small plane take off and disappear, Dian's emotional response stayed in my mind. My gratification at attaining the prime spot on the magazine remained fresh too, but was tempered by thoughts of a different and more troubling nature.

Following close on the departure of Burkhart, my relationship with Dian had suddenly become more intimate than I ever believed possible. The situation bothered me more than I cared to acknowledge and seriously affected my thoughts about the future. From the hard and irascible person who had nearly driven me to quit, a more feminine and amiable personality had slowly emerged. On my return in June, Dian's attitude of polite sufferance had slipped, giving way to frequent smiles and genuine laughter. Both of us had come to terms with the fact that we were to be isolated in one another's company for a long while, and making the best of it seemed the only satisfactory approach. The assistance I had been able to give her with a series of crises had been gratefully accepted, but it was perhaps my uncritical acknowledgement of her physical limitations and working methods that really tipped the balance. I had come to like Dian and to respect her unshakeable desire to make a success of her difficult task. And now I was unintentionally caught up in a sensitive and unforeseen affair that split my emotions into separate compartments. I was happily married and loved my wife, but nevertheless had to admit I was flattered by Dian's now undisguised interest in me. But was I being mercenary and accepting the situation to ensure continued tranquillity – or was I simply drawn to the new and distinctly more attractive personality that had surfaced? I could not decide and was thankful for the moment to be working on my own for a while.

With the saddle area cleared of snares, I began tailing Group 4 again, and only a day later found blood and afterbirth in one of the night nests. Exhilarated and anticipating the sight of a new baby, I followed the gorillas with extra care and caution. With my ability to identify each individual quickly and accurately still uncertain, after hours of quiet manoeuvring and observation I had seen no sign of a new infant on any of the females; I could not even be positive I had spotted all of them.

Over the following days disappointment grew. Uncle Bert led his family off Visoke and headed west on to the lower slopes of Mount Karisimbi, almost halfway to the Kabara meadow. I felt sure we would soon meet up with some of the Kabara gorillas, but no sounds or visible evidence gave any indication they were using the region. I managed positive identification of the five adult females, but there was no new baby. Since the placenta I had found gave proof of a birth, I could only conclude the baby had died and had been abandoned where I had failed to see it. For the first time though, the nervous young silverback presented a decent opportunity for a good picture. Normally very careful to remain hidden, he amazed me one afternoon by moving out of thick foliage only thirty feet away. He sat next to a female named Flossie, apparently unconcerned by the lack of cover. Flossie was holding her young infant and here was a chance for a first shot of a mother and baby next to a big male.

Squatting in full view, Uncle Bert's eyes betrayed only mild irritation at my presence. During the first shots he merely watched and pursed his lips, but when I moved slightly to obtain a better view of the mother and baby, the spell broke; he pushed past Flossie to enter thick cover, venting some of his annoyance by thumping her hard across the back with a heavy arm. In situations like these, all too few in number, I was beginning to suffer from a mild form of buck fever. The closer I got to the great apes, the more difficult it became to contain inner excitement and suppress my anxiety to get better photographs. I had to exercise considerable self-control to stop my hands from jiggling unsupported cameras.

The Group 4 family was rapidly becoming my favourite; I had learned all the names Dian had so far applied, and was finding it easier to recognise individuals from different angles. Every gorilla had distinctive combinations of nostril shape and nasal wrinkles, making frontal recognition fairly easy. But side and back views could be a real problem. One or two of the animals were still unnamed. An elusive old female I kept referring to as X had gradually become Mrs X; she had a baby that had been confused with Flossie's infant, so for a while both were called Simba. Although still nervous, the group was responding to repeated visits. One of the subadults was beginning to make reasonably close approaches towards Dian and myself, and for that reason was given the name Bravado. Thought to be a blackback male, much later 'he' was discovered to be a female, causing some confusion in the study records.

By now I had decided the Group 4 gorillas would be my prime subjects. Although Group 5 occupied a more easily accessible area to the east and south of the camp, and formed a larger family with two, sometimes three, silverbacks, frequent encounters with poachers and herders kept them wary and less cooperative. The five males of Group 8 were still sought out regularly, always with the hope they might repeat the very close approaches Dian had recorded before I arrived. Sadly the Group 9 gorillas had almost faded from the scene; for some unknown reason they had shifted their range further to the north and beyond practical reach from camp.

November started with storms that brought back memories of my caretaking period the previous year. In the faint hope they would ease, the survey of the Kabara area was put off until later in the month. Feeling rested after her holiday in Kenya, but reluctant to tell me much about it, Dian spent many days with me in further attempts to shoot pictures of her close to the gorillas. The sorely needed, close-proximity shots still eluded us, but the prospects were improving.

Then one morning the work routine was interrupted when Dian was bitten by a dog, an incident that would later have far-reaching effects. Preparing for the day in the pale light of dawn, I was startled by several high-pitched screams and curses. Abandoning a half-cooked breakfast, I rushed over to the cabin in time to see a mangy-looking dog release Dian's leg and back off. It slunk away at my approach and vanished behind the cabin. Indignant and slightly shocked by the attack, Dian explained she had just emerged to brush her teeth when the dog appeared. Wagging its tail in a friendly manner, it had walked past her and in through the door; then, without any provocation, it had turned round, leaped forward and latched on to her left shin with great ferocity. Fortunately, the dog had tried to bite through thick socks, stout jeans and long underwear so its teeth had not broken through to the skin, though the red bruises showed how hard it had tried. We decided the animal was very likely rabid and made absolutely certain it had not breached the strong material of the jeans. It was a nasty experience for Dian, and with other complications was to lead to a painful course of anti-rabies injections the following month. My breakfast was a charred mess when I returned, but later in the morning a good contact with Group 5 helped Dian to overcome the shock of the incident. The day was made memorable by brilliant weather and some unusual, crystal-clear views of the volcanoes to the east. Sadly the fair weather did not last and our delayed visit to Kabara was made in dreary, wet conditions.

Accompanied by our gorilla assistants, Vatiri and Munya, and a gang of sixteen porters, under a low ceiling of heavy cloud Dian and I followed familiar ground for about an hour. Soon all the known trails were left behind and we struck out west, having to do without sight of Mount Mikeno as a guide. The inevitable rain began to fall, soaking us all, but it failed to dampen anyone's spirits. The porters chattered in their usual fashion for a while, until I warned of the possible chance of meeting a Zaire ranger patrol, then they quickly lapsed into uneasy silence.

Following vague and clogged game paths, we crossed a series of shallow valleys, seeing two sets of old gorilla signs that gave some mild encouragement. After three hours of slow progress, through the trees and gloomy underside of cloud we saw steeply rising ground that could only be the eastern flank of Mikeno. Guesswork navigation had led us to exactly the right spot. We broke out of the forest near a swampy stretch of water, beyond which lay the open grass of the large and famous meadow. Dian walked forward, puzzled – something was missing – then we saw the collapsed remains of a rusty corrugated iron roof. The wooden cabin that had stood here since the early 1930s was now a pathetic wreck.

An ideal and beautiful location for a base camp, the Kabara meadow had seen many famous visitors: kings and princes and other notables, not the least of whom had been the American naturalist, Carl Akeley. Though he had shot several of them for a display at the American Museum of Natural History, Akeley had been the first to mount an expedition to study the Virunga gorillas. However, with his work barely begun, Akeley had died and been buried here on 17 November forty-three years before. We had missed the anniversary of his death by two days.

After examining the wreck of the cabin, Dian led me to the western edge of the meadow where Akeley's remains lay. The headstone that had marked the grave was missing and only a low-walled, open square containing a few white-painted lava rocks remained. We searched the surrounding bushes for the headstone but failed to find it. While Dian removed encroaching plants and tidied up the grave, she admitted to feeling conflicting emotions about Kabara. She was pleased to see the place again, but depressed by recollection of the events that had forced her to leave. I had tried several times to get her to tell me all that had happened during those dark days, but apart from inferring that she had been very badly treated while detained at the town of Rumangarbo, she invariably shied away from the subject, saying that she preferred not to revive unpleasant and traumatic memories.

Our Rwandan porters were now visibly troubled at being so deep into Zaire and anxious to head for safer ground. We held them back to help prop up the cabin roof to make a shelter for Vatiri and Munya, then, with dire warnings that failure to return on time would cost them the chance to be hired as porters again, let them hurry away. Later, I wandered around the edges of the meadow hoping to see beyond the forest fringes, but evening mist merged with the overcast sky and shut out the views. I wondered what the first Europeans to visit had seen. There would certainly have been far fewer humans at the base of the mountain, and over half a century of growth would surely have changed the look of the forest. Following those who had come to hunt and shoot the gorillas, Carl Akeley had arrived a decade before I was born. He had hunted gorillas as well, but his fascination with the country, and curiosity about the little-known giant apes, led him to persuade the Belgian colonial powers to establish a national park to protect the area. My growing knowledge of the region, and particularly its high-altitude vegetation cover, had made me wonder how much longer the hagenia trees would dominate the scenery. There were remarkably few saplings to replace the ancient trees, many of which were already losing their giant limbs. Though they flowered profusely, there was virtually no regeneration. If the gorillas' Virunga sanctuary could survive the rising tide of humans, I felt sure future times would see changes in the look of the beautiful woodlands.

For four days we worked hard to survey as much of the territory as possible, discovering that cattle and poachers had used part of the region extensively during previous months. Only two small gorilla groups were contacted, both terrified by our appearance and retreating swiftly to break contact. By counting night nests we determined the first consisted of eight members, but saw only one individual who faced us briefly before the family fled. In the forest south of Mikeno we found no evidence of gorillas at all, but did bump into a group of men heading for Kabara up the old access trail. Our presence probably thwarted the men from filching material from the old cabin. Though they did not stay long, their appearance disturbed us; with two days to go before our porters returned, we worried that a ranger patrol might hear news of us and climb to check on us.

We located the second group of gorillas on Mikeno, high above a great canyon called Kanyamagufa. They kept their distance, chest beating, screaming and plainly very disturbed. We could count no more than six before they retreated out of sight up the mountain. On an attempt to backtrack and find their night nests, the hazardous slopes of the canyon gave Dian a very hard time. Trying to hold to easier ground we lost the trails, and finally, in mist and pouring rain, abandoned the search.

Breaking camp early, we were relieved of further anxiety when a line of porters emerged from the trees by the waterhole. Bad weather had cut much of the enjoyment of the Kabara visit, but I was still pleased to have seen the area. Several weeks would be needed to conduct a proper census, but at least we knew some gorillas were there still. We had covered a lot of ground and expected to find many more of the animals, or at very least more evidence of their tracks and sleeping sites. Four days' work and only fourteen gorillas accounted for: was this an indication that numbers had declined drastically since mid-1967? Dian was pessimistic and inclined to think so. As she had been unable to identify any of the animals, the possibility that we had actually seen the same group twice could not be ruled out.

As December approached I arranged to return home for Christmas. With eight months gone, the slow progress in obtaining any remarkable material weighed on my mind. So far only the contact with old Rafiki exposed on a fallen tree had resulted in fine shots, and I was becoming sceptical that the encounters Dian claimed to have experienced early on were as close as she had described, but she insisted that the two of us together inhibited the animals, particularly when I tried manoeuvring for better angles.

Al Royce, and also Joanne Hess in the lecture division, sent a steady stream of information and encouragement on the stills and cine. Both knew that the gorilla study could bear no comparison with Jane Goodall's chimpanzee research, but that did not influence my desire to match to some degree the extensive coverage of chimps that Hugo van Lawick had achieved over the years. Having actually visited Jane's camp in Tanzania, Joanne in particular was aware that the chimpanzees had responded beautifully to the establishment of a large number of special feeding stations. They were easily enticed to come and accept bananas at these points and at the campsite: a state of affairs that allowed consistent and close observation – and also many fine opportunities for pictures. Dian too had visited Jane's camp, but only briefly. Though impressed by Jane's work, she was very conscious of the critics who claimed that by provisioning her subjects Jane had partially compromised her study of natural behaviour.

During his short stay in 1968, Alan Root had persuaded Dian she should not attempt to get in amongst the animals: her job was to remain a detached and unobtrusive observer, to be as neutral as possible in her contacts with them. The gorillas after all were having to accept an association with humans forced on them unwillingly; one should accommodate to this fact and in turn accept contacts conducted mainly under their terms. Since they were not animals that could be drawn in by offers of foreign foods, enticing gorillas to come to her had not been a viable proposition anyway. I had so far respected Dian's wish that I follow her general field techniques and avoid inhibiting natural behaviour by forcing close approaches. Although increasingly tempted to press forward and follow when the animals moved away, I resisted the impulse, trying instead with extreme care and stealth to ease in as near as possible during the initial approach. By being slow and patient, it was often possible to reach good positions without being detected. I had made some fine observations that way, but could not operate cameras and remain concealed; as soon as I was discovered the gorillas slid shyly behind the foliage. I began to have doubts about obtaining sufficiently varied and exciting film footage, though on the basis of what she had seen already, Joanne was cautiously optimistic. Al Royce on the other hand was happy with the illustrations for the January article; in fact he was already looking ahead to a second, and stressing the need for new situations that would place Dian closer to her subjects.

Before leaving for Nairobi I spent a pleasant afternoon on a long-ranging climb up Mount Karisimbi, following the course of the stream that flowed through the camp. For two days previously Dian and I had made further patrols to get rid of intruding cattle. The work had given fresh opportunities for photographs of her in action, driving the beasts away from Visoke, destroying the cattlemen's temporary shelters and collecting various belongings they abandoned in their haste to run away. Now I wanted to survey the higher slopes on Karisimbi and see if cattle were present there too. I needed also to think seriously about the coming year and my future with the gorilla study.

With a light pack, I followed the camp stream, entering a beautiful patch of hagenia forest at the edge of the high meadow. The banks soon became heavily overgrown, forcing diversions to search out easier game trails. Although there was a plentiful supply of their favoured food plants, none of the gorilla study groups utilised this particular area. Poachers and cattlemen on the other hand used it constantly, and quite likely it was their activities that accounted for the absence of gorillas.

As the angle of the slope steepened, plenty of buffalo prints showed on the muddy pathways but evidence of cattle rapidly diminished. The forest was unusually quiet, not even the twitter of birds or warning whistle of a duiker marked my progress. I climbed steadily, examining the trails, listening for sounds of anything that might be near, all the while sampling the varied scents of wet soil, damp foliage and rotting vegetation. With senses fully occupied absorbing details of this unknown ground, for a while more serious thoughts took second place. When all sign of cattle had long since vanished I continued to climb, enjoying the physical exercise and looking for an open place with a good view.

Breaking out at last on to a small grassy meadow, I looked back at the diminished outline of Visoke. At a glance I could see the entire range I traversed so frequently in search of gorillas. Narrow shafts of sunlight played through the clouds, briefly outlining sharp ridges on the mountain and dappling the woodlands of the saddle with patches of light. I rested for a while, aware that a light-grey curtain of rain forming in the east meant the return to camp would probably be wet. Low-pitched thunder grumbled ominously from clouds concealing the upper cone of Karisimbi, easily persuading me it would be wise to give up the intention to climb higher.

Enjoying the spectacular view and watching the slowly approaching rain, I relaxed on a bed of tussock grass and allowed my thoughts to turn to the immediate future. On reaching Nairobi in three days' time I would become involved again with Leakey matters. Joanne Hess wanted me to give priority to the filming of Richard's hominid finds; shots that were urgently needed for inclusion in his latest lecture film. Louis Leakey wanted new pictures for a comparison of some Olduvai fossils, and had asked for me to handle the work.

A new year was only three weeks away, and early in 1970 Dian would be leaving to start a two-month period of work at Cambridge University in England. When she returned my assignment contract would long since have expired. I had written to Bob Gilka in Washington, saying I was willing to carry on until Dian came back – and beyond that if necessary – but had no idea what the response would be. There was little doubt that Richard would be mounting a third expedition to follow up the successes of 1969, and I retained a desire to be part of that adventure. It was possible I might be able to arrange for assignments that alternated between the fossil fields and these fascinating mountains, a prospect that was pleasing to contemplate.

My associations with anthropologists and archaeologists had involved me in many discussions about the possible lifestyle of pre-human creatures. It was an interesting and demanding mental exercise to try to determine how and why hominids had evolved and moved so swiftly away from an ape style of living. Subsequently, the wonderful chance to follow and watch gorillas had not provided much help in that respect. Though in many ways spectacular and awe-inspiring, gorillas were too specialised, they seemed to lack any exceptional mental agility and had so far, to me at least, displayed a mainly tranquil social behaviour that seemed unlikely to throw much light on reasons for the changes in the hominid line. It had to be admitted that the mainly distant contacts were not allowing a good view of their full range of behaviour; subtle facets of it were still well concealed behind the thick vegetation. The very luxuriance of the foliage – full of edible food supplies – ensured that little mental or physical effort was needed to keep the gorillas' large appetites satisfied. But there were surely other aspects of their life that exercised their relatively large brains. They lived in cohesive family units, where members were seldom beyond aural range of one another, and perhaps it was here that significant features of their social life might be revealing. There was so much yet to learn, and I for one particularly wanted to know how they avoided interbreeding.

When it came to attempting an understanding of hominid behaviour, Jane Goodall's lengthy study of the chimpanzees was a much better model. Her subjects lived in an area that combined forest and open savannah, and they utilised both environments. Their social life was complicated and mentally demanding, they were apparently quite frequent meat-eaters, sometimes actively hunting their prey, and had also been observed using modified natural objects as primitive tools.

Though impressive in size and strength, mountain gorillas were reclusive herbivores with very limited ranges; they lived precariously in a rapidly shrinking habitat constantly invaded by humans, and as a result were already coming close to extinction. In fact, with the current lax control over human activities in the mountains, there was serious cause for a belief that very few would live to see the twenty-first century. Even Dian's research and my photographic work could be considered intrusive. What she and I were doing would one day surely lead to increased public interest and a desire on the part of many to come and see the animals – but would there be many gorillas left? The hasty survey of the Kabara area had not been encouraging; and what of the other volcanoes – how many groups were there? A census must be conducted soon... My thoughts switched between gorilla matters and fossil exploration as I tried to decide where my priorities lay. There was still so much to find out about the gorillas, but then a few hundred miles to the east, Richard Leakey's latest activities had created a longing to share in the excitement of new discoveries.

The several millions of years that covered the rise of early hominids through to *Homo sapiens* were a fascinating period. During many sessions photographing specimens from his collection of skulls, Louis Leakey had often talked about them, describing specific features for me and the way he interpreted the position of various skulls in the fossil record. The skull from Olduvai he had named *Zinjanthropus* was a representative of the australopithecines: short, thickset creatures that had coexisted on the African woodland savannahs with another hominid called *Homo habilis*, or handy man. *Homo habilis* was Louis's name for an apparently small and gracile creature who was assumed to be more skilled in taking advantage of the resources of an open savannah habitat; a creature whose teeth suggested an omnivorous diet and who was most likely the maker of the many stone tools found at Olduvai. For reasons yet to be assessed, the australopithecines had not survived, whereas *Homo habilis* had gone from strength to strength – the postulated ancestor of the creatures that evolved with remarkable speed to become the complex beings known as *Homo sapiens*. As yet, very few hominid specimens had come to light, providing slim evidence for his theories, but Louis would become very animated in discussions about them. It was easy to be persuaded that what he had to say was entirely correct. To him, morphological differences in the growing array of fossil skulls, jawbones and skeletal fragments spoke volumes, as did the prehistoric living sites and primitive stone tools associated with some of them. Certain factors in hominid social behaviour must surely have accelerated their evolution, but unfortunately the fossil record could reveal virtually nothing about lifestyles. Louis was consequently very keen to draw on the information coming from the individual studies of primate behaviour, in particular those he had initiated to cover the African apes.

Having watched gorillas for several hundred hours, I found it absorbing to speculate on the reasons why the australopithecines had become extinct. They apparently walked upright and possessed larger brains than their primate cousins of the forest. They had teeth that indicated they were well adapted for surviving on coarse vegetable matter, and they had lived over a huge spread of land from South Africa all the way up the Rift Valley to Ethiopia: a vast territory that provided a very wide range of habitats. Why then had they not been able to continue to thrive? What was it that caused their demise, while their less venturesome and presumably less intelligent relatives in the form of gorillas and chimpanzees flourished? Could they not have retreated to the forests if conditions affecting their more open, woodland habitat became too harsh for survival? Did they in fact come to a dead end quite quickly, or did they fade out slowly in a modified form yet to be discovered? Since evidence of their existence amounted to only a few incomplete skulls and jaws, some teeth and scraps of arm and limb bone, it was impossible to determine the circumstances that led to their disappearance. To help trace the intriguing path of hominid evolution with any accuracy, many more specimens would have to be recovered. In the semi-deserts surrounding Lake Rudolf, Richard and his team had brought to notice a huge and fertile field for fossils and seemed likely to make many significant discoveries; it was frustrating to be engaged on a particularly choice assignment that seemed likely to prevent me from recording them.

Behind me Karisimbi was beginning to take a beating. I could hear wind and rain thrashing the vegetation on the upper reaches of the mountain, while in direct contrast all the forest below seemed calm. The curtain of rain from the east had advanced steadily, taking on deeper hues of grey as the density of rain increased. To the north, a huge cumulus cloud bulged in the sky, and below it mist was spreading above the Bishitsi bluff. For a few more minutes the rivulet by my side slipped gently, almost quietly, over a smooth bed of rock. But soon, fuelled from above, the flow changed dramatically to become a noisy torrent. It was time to get moving, but the extraordinary visual spectacle that was developing held me captive, easily displacing thoughts of man and beast and future activities.

The growing volume of water splashing and tumbling beside me was another distraction, a reminder that this small stream was part of the longest river system in the world. Commencing perhaps two thousand feet higher, the water from the storm was setting out on an impressive journey. It could one day possibly reach the city of Alexandria at the delta on the Mediterranean Sea, over four thousand miles away.

In my youth, I had learned that the Nile had much to do with the history of East Africa and, with a touch of romantic reasoning, had always believed it was the location of the river that was responsible for my presence in Africa. Starting early in childhood, enjoying the drawings and pictures, but struggling to understand the elegant and complicated grammar, I had delved into books about the adventures of explorers who searched long and hard to locate the main source of the Nile. Only much later did I come to understand why it was so important for early imperial powers to know exactly where the head-waters lay. Little did I know that many years later I would come to live a few feet from one of the river's most distant tributaries, and to participate in a project aimed at a better understanding of mankind. Had the source of the White Nile been found to lie further west, history would surely have taken a different course; my father would never have settled in Africa and I would not have landed up beside this turbulent extremity of the mighty river. However, intrepid explorers eventually discovered the main source lay nearer to the east than the west, and the knowledge had set in motion a project that eventually influenced the lives of a great many people – including my father.

When dawn broke across the edge of Africa on the first day of the twentieth century, the British had already embraced a vast area of land in the wide, vaguely defined boundaries of an East African protectorate. With considerable difficulty and aided by thousands of Indian 'coolies', hardy engineers had also laid three hundred and fifty miles of railway line. The iron tracks stretched from the ancient port of Mombasa to the edge of the Great Rift, and within two years would reach far-off Lake Victoria, the vast reservoir at the head of the White Nile. Securing access to the sensitive Nile catchment area was not the only reason for building this thread of steel in the wilderness: the threat of expanding German influence in Tanganyika, a treaty with Uganda's Kabaka, Mwanga, British commercial interests, and a strong desire to suppress the widespread slave trade gave added justification to the extraordinary and seemingly wild enterprise.

My father, Ronald John Campbell, was born in 1890, at about the time the British Empire was at its peak. He became a army officer, a major in the Royal Artillery Regiment. Shortly after the First World War ended he learned that the British government had just scrapped the sprawling East African protectorate. Boundaries had been redefined and the territory had been declared a colony of the Crown under the new name of Kenya. Partly to justify the huge expense of constructing the railway, and with special concessions being offered to men retiring from the armed forces, an active campaign was under way to attract settlers to the new colony. Some fellow officers from my father's regiment had already emigrated, among them his good friend Albert Martin, whose sister he happened to be courting. Soon taking the bait also, my father sailed to Kenya in 1924, where he began a new life by learning something about the difficult art of farming in Africa. No records survive to reveal what happened for the next year or so, but by 1926 he had purchased some land, and persuaded Olive Martin to come to Kenya and marry him.

Although my parents lived in Africa, I was born in England, at Harrow, on 29 October 1930. Not an auspicious time by all accounts; the devastating effect of the Wall Street money market collapse the year before still gripped the world, and like thousands of others my parents were struggling to avoid financial ruin. Since the cost of a sea voyage would have been no small expense, I have no idea why my mother returned to her homeland for my birth, but there must have been good reasons. Perhaps after three years in Africa she wanted to see her relations and friends again, and to bear her second child in less hazardous conditions.

After a month or two in midwinter Britain I was carried off to Africa; a journey my mother later told me was definitely the worst she ever undertook. For some reason she was obliged to join her ship at Marseilles, and had first to make her way by train and ferry across England, over the Channel and through France. She was never a good sailor, and on this occasion apparently nor was I, thereby contributing in no small way to her discomfort. The next stage was another train ride, a journey of five hundred and fifty miles on the Kenya–Uganda Railway: the now famous line across the spine of East Africa – and still thought by many to be an insane venture in the wilderness. Ignorant of the past history of the railway and no doubt stressed by the continuing rigours of travel, I was carried north-west from the coastal town of Mombasa to Nairobi. In Nairobi, in all probability, my mother visited her brother 'Bert' Martin before going on to cross the equator in forested highlands at nine thousand feet. From the cool heights of the highest railway station in the British Empire, our train would have descended slowly to the town of Eldoret, then branched north to head for Kitale – our destination and the most northerly station in the colony of Kenya.

At the time of my arrival, Kitale was well established. The small town stood at little over six thousand feet above sea level, midway between a massive extinct volcano called Mount Elgon and a forested mountain range known as the Cherangani Hills. Dominating the view to the west, Mount Elgon was said to have the largest base of any volcano in the British Empire, and beyond its summit of fourteen thousand feet, lay the protectorate of Uganda. Topping out at eleven thousand feet, the Cherangani Hills were less significant, but their eastern slopes fell away in a spectacular drop to the floor of the Great Rift Valley. Quite unaware that in time many features and events associated with the Great Rift would strongly influence my life, I spent my childhood in the environs surrounding Kitale. I began absorbing the wonders of Africa from the confines of a thriving white farming community, with only books to make me better aware of the rest of the huge continent and its varied indigenous peoples. Often, looking back, I felt regret that I was born only just in time to sample the twilight of a pioneer era, and in particular that my father's circumstances did not allow for adventurous travels. When I was only two, the combination of drought, locust plagues and the continuing effects of the depression had forced him to sell our farm and seek employment in the town.

Kitale was situated in the middle of the Trans-Nzoia district, a fertile region of nearly fifteen hundred square miles lying to the north of the Nzoia River. The area must surely have been a wildlife paradise before it was opened up to farming, but I was many years too late to see the spectacle. Though a variety of antelopes and many smaller animals were still plentiful, elephants, rhinos and other big game had been pushed back into the forests of Elgon and the Cherangani Hills. Leopards still roamed the gallery forests of the river valleys, but lions were scarce and seldom seen. In spite of the altitude and the mainly temperate climate, Kitale was sometimes referred to as the capital of death valley, a sinister title acquired from half-joking acknowledgement of the huge population of malarial mosquitoes that bred so successfully in the swamps nearby. All too many people in the district had been struck down with the disease carried by the insects, sometimes with fatal results. Unfortunately, it was not long before I too became one of the victims. Throughout my childhood and into my teens, frequent and serious bouts of malaria affected not only my physical abilities, but also to some extent conditioned my attitude to life. I was to become something of a loner and obliged to wage a long fight against the negative effects generated by years of repeated illness. Because my mother was a petite five foot and my father no more than five foot seven, she was ever convinced that my growth to over six foot had been induced by the long periods I spent in bed.

When the swollen stream at my side suddenly increased in volume, it broke the enjoyment of the view and idle reminiscences. Visoke was still visible, but its outline was quickly vanishing behind a wall of rain. A deep blanket of pure white mist rolled ponderously over the forest by the distant Bishitsi bluff. Thunder growled almost continuously in the dark, turbulent clouds that now stretched to envelop Mikeno. Still enthralled by the magnificent scene, I wished my camera could capture the vast panorama that so distinctly showed three converging weather systems. It was definitely past time to go.

As I began the long descent to camp, a strong wind laced with hailstones swooped down from Karisimbi. Plunging into the undergrowth, I was chased all the way back to the top meadow by a ferocious storm, a few brilliant discharges of lightning cracking down to help speed me on the way. For once, buoyed up by some pleasant thoughts and my imminent departure for home, I almost enjoyed being caught in nature's violence. In the dark of the storm all traces of my tracks on the way up were soon lost, but the lie of the steep slope helped keep me roughly on course. Soaked but exhilarated, by chance more than design, I broke out on to the meadow and followed the now greatly enlarged tributary of the Nile back to my tent.

When I began the journey home it was with the sense that everything seemed to be going well; whether I followed the fossil hunters, the gorillas – or both – the year ahead was bound to be very interesting. I felt curiously light-headed, but for a while ignored the sensation. It was my practice to leave camp after midday and drive only as far as Kabale in Uganda, where some relaxation and a good night's sleep at The White Horse Inn was always welcome. As I drove up the winding road to the Kanaba Gap, this time my ears began to ring unpleasantly. When I reached the hotel an hour later I knew something was seriously wrong. By midnight I was suffering from a very sore throat and a rapidly rising temperature. I awoke from a very bad night, feeling acutely unwell. In a muzzy haze and head splitting, I set off, determined not to risk being caught in Uganda should the infection get worse. Motoring on through the day and into the night, I forced myself to keep going and reached home in an unsteady daze at two in the morning. There, ministered by my lady vet, I collapsed into bed for a period that lasted many unpleasant days. It transpired I had contracted a particularly virulent form of flu, and I vaguely remembered that one of the men at camp had been similarly struck down only a week earlier.

An overhead aerial view of Mount Visoke. The Karisoke research camp lies at the base of the mountain in the small L-shaped glade at the centre-bottom of the picture.

The southern face of Mount Visoke, with the first Karisoke cabin just visible in the trees by the grassy glade in the right foreground.

Lips compressed and head turned away, a gorilla female beats her chest to express her worry at the presence of a human intruder.

In the early days of the study the gorillas were very wary and used the thick foliage most effectively to stay out of sight. Here, a silverback male peers suspiciously at his observer.

Coco and Pucker, the two juvenile gorillas captured in 1969 by Rwandese park guards for Cologne Zoo in Germany. The pair survived only nine years in captivity and died in 1978 within a month of each other.

Dian restored the traumatised youngsters to good health, and it was a special and rewarding experience to be able to handle them and examine in detail their faces, hands, feet and long coat of hair.

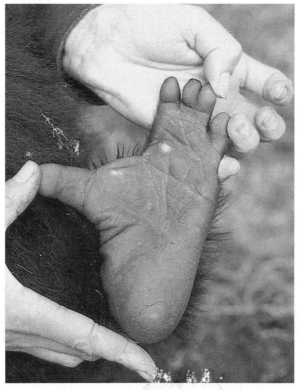

Coco's foot, showing webbing of toes.

We spotted the silverback Rafiki feeding and moving towards a fallen tree trunk. Anticipating he might climb onto it, I urged Dian to move forward. Followed by the young blackback Peanuts, Rafiki climbed the trunk, and by moving back and using a telephoto lens I was able to foreshorten the distance between Dian and the big silverback. For the first time I had managed to shoot a decent picture of Dian in visual contact with one of her elusive subjects.

Lightweight and sandy-coloured, my tent had been purchased for use in the Lake Rudolf deserts; set in the verdant mountain vegetation it stood out sharply and I regretted not having bought one in green.

Hoping for a day's work, men anxious to be hired as porters cluster around Dian's old Land Rover.

At the head of a line of porters, Dian sets out to establish a camp at Lake Ngezi for her first assistant, Michael Burkhart.

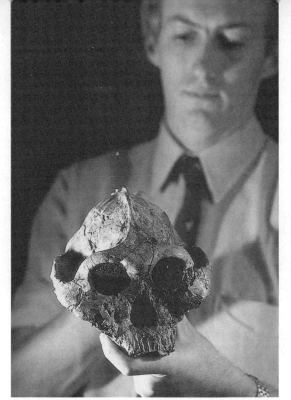

In his office at Nairobi's National Museum, Richard showed me a remarkable fossil skull, describing with understandable pleasure the pure chance that led him to the site where it lay.

Captured from fleeing poachers and cattle herders, pangas, axes, bows and arrows, muhoros, cooking pots and nooses from snares were taken and held back at camp.

For the first time the nervous young silverback presented a decent opportunity for a good picture. Normally very careful to remain hidden, he amazed me by moving out of thick foliage only thirty feet away. He sat next to a female named Flossie, apparently unconcerned by the lack of cover. Flossie was holding her young infant and here was a chance for the first shot of a mother and baby next to a big male.

Having destroyed a young hypericum tree to make a day nest, Mrs X of Group 4 sits in it and warns others of my presence with a chest-beating display. Her infant, Simba, is below her.

Unaware of her own destiny, Dian tidies up Carl Akeley's grave at the edge of the Kabara meadow where he had died forty-three years earlier.

For only the second time since the beginning of the assignment, I was able to photograph a long play session between the subadults. On this occasion the gorillas allowed me to climb a spindly hypericum tree overlooking their playground – a close, exposed position that only weeks earlier would have caused them to disperse and hide.

Looking like the Grand Canyon in minature, a view of the Peninj sediments, where a survey headed by Richard Leaky in 1963 led to the discovery of a beautifully preserved australopithecine jaw.

Dian and her gorilla trackers, Vatiri and Nemeye, look over the dismembered remains of a silverback gorilla found by Alyette DeMunck on Mount Sabinio.

Down to All Fours

On returning to Rwanda at the end of December, still shaking off lingering effects of flu, I found Dian in a low, almost dejected state of mind. She too had fallen to the same infection, but had suffered a much worse time; a soaring temperature and renewed worries about her chest had compelled her to seek help at the hospital in Ruhengeri. There, the doctor who treated her insisted the incident with the dog could not be ignored. Since Louis Leakey had thoughtfully sent her anti-rabies medication on first hearing about it, she had been persuaded to undergo the painful, fourteen-day course of injections. She had convalesced with Ros Carr and had been forced to postpone her flight to England for a week – a delay which, as it turned out, was to bring a wonderful stroke of luck.

Dispirited by her illness and increasingly apprehensive as to how she was going to adapt to academic life, Dian was not looking forward to the months to be spent in England. Dr Leakey had always insisted she must acquire qualifications that would carry weight in scientific circles, and had eventually obtained funds for her to do so, but with departure imminent, concern over how she was going to handle the complexities of behavioural analysis had increased.

With the camp staff enjoying three days' leave to celebrate an extended New Year holiday, the new decade opened quietly on an unusually low level of energy. Both of us were not only under par, but also affected by a nagging sense of stagnation in our work: a condition aggravated by cloud-filled skies that presaged a wet start to gorilla watching. It was also depressingly noticeable that the Watutsi cattlemen had again taken advantage of our absence. To regain some strength and dispel her uneasy feelings, Dian chose to abandon further preparatory work for Cambridge and spend the remaining days out in the open with me. The presence of cattle demanded immediate attention, so we carried out a short, unhurried patrol to advertise our return and to destroy a new herder's shelter found near the Zaire border; then the following morning, walked out to make the first contact with gorillas in over a month.

The weather was dismal. A low, unbroken ceiling of cloud covered the sky and sapped all colour from the scenery. We walked along the boggy path to the top of the saddle with a fine drizzle drifting in our faces, but it felt good to be active and on the trail of gorillas again. Heading north, we travelled at a leisurely pace, taking time to examine the paths and scan the foggy slopes – listening all the while for any tell-tale sounds that would short circuit the search for recent tracks. Within the hour patience paid off; the snap of a branch and subtle sounds of gorillas feeding allowed us to home in on Rafiki and his companions.

The five males were conveniently placed at the centre of their range, low on the mountain, so little effort was needed to reach their level. Although anticipating a more active response than usual, we were unprepared for the outbreak of harsh screams and smashing of foliage that greeted our appearance. The tumultuous reception effectively stimulated our jaded systems, and there followed a tantalisingly close approach by at least three of the males. But we could only listen as the gorillas advanced, then retired in the thick cover. Since the group remained low and moved only short distances, we persisted with contacts for the next three days. But they were failures; the animals were so consistently shy and uninterested in their observers I did not take a single picture. Then, unexpectedly, Alyette de Munck came up from Gisenyi. Though Dian was unprepared for her friend and not as welcoming as usual, she soon rose to the occasion. To entertain Alyette, she abandoned an intention to start packing and arranged to go out early for a final call on Group 8.

Under a pall of grey clouds, we left camp early and headed for 'the meeting place': a shallow valley on the west face of Visoke where I had filmed the silverback confrontation in 1968. The name had been applied because three groups seemed to meet in the valley more frequently than any other position on the mountain. Without having to do any tracking, we heard, then spotted, Rafiki moving in the thickets several hundred feet above us. We climbed cautiously to a huge, lone hagenia tree and crouched at its base. At first it seemed we were in for a disappointing repeat of the previous, unrewarding contacts. But as we waited, debating what to do next, Peanuts appeared and made a small move down towards us. Anticipating a rare chance for pictures, I asked Dian to go forward a few yards and occupy the foreground. I managed to climb up to the first fork of the tree, and within minutes the elements of the picture I had tried to obtain for so long came together.

Dian lay low and began imitating gorilla feeding actions, encouraging the blackback to descend cautiously a little further. Now only twenty feet separated them, but Peanuts took full advantage of the vegetation to remain hidden. Suddenly he stood to thump his chest, perhaps to relieve tension and impress us, then edged forward to peer down at Dian. For once I had a fine, elevated view over the foliage, but was very unhappy with the dark conditions that were forcing the use of slow shutter speeds. Only the solid support of the tree trunk saved the situation. With the camera jammed firmly against wet, mossy bark I managed to record the extraordinary encounter that followed.

The blackback pushed forward, and to my great delight made his way carefully down the slope in full view. Wide-eyed, lips pursed, but showing only a trace of nervousness, he approached Dian – closing the gap to a bare ten feet before sitting to scratch himself. Smiling broadly with pleasure, Dian imitated his actions for a few moments, then lay back and carefully stretched out a hand towards him. The gorilla appeared to contemplate this gesture for a while, regained his feet, then delicately reached out to make a quick dab at the passive hand. I followed his movement in the viewfinder, releasing the shutter as his big fingers neared Dian's – a fraction too late to capture the fleeting moment of contact. Peanuts sat down again, looking, in human terms, almost embarrassed by what he had done. Dian's face mirrored her emotions: the gentle touch from this wild animal marked an extraordinary and unique moment in her long association with the gorillas. In July of the previous year I had managed a shot of Peanuts making a direct approach to within eight feet of her, a brief few seconds of proximity that had left her deeply moved. Although she had long ago reported an earlier encounter with Peanuts, where she said he had taken a book from her and grabbed at her boot as if to pull her from her perch in a tree, I had come to suspect she had elaborated on a close encounter and had drawn the story from her imagination. Whatever the truth of the matter, this was the very first flesh to flesh contact – with evidence of the peaceful interaction captured on film. Coming only twenty-four hours before her departure, the thrilling event gave her an exhilarating boost, exactly what was needed to help face the difficult weeks ahead. When Peanuts retreated to rejoin his companions, Dian was almost radiant with delight. Below me, wide-eyed astonishment and pleasure showing on her face, Alyette could hardly believe what she had just witnessed. Wiping away shreds of bark and moss from my camera, I enjoyed a feeling of immense satisfaction. After nine months, at last I had photographed Dian in dramatic association with one of her elusive subjects.

With her misgivings about Cambridge submerged by the memory of Peanuts' gentle touch, I took Dian to the Gisenyi airfield the following day. Travelling with all her research records, a typewriter and heavy cases full of winter clothes, she was already worrying she would have to pay a fortune for excess weight. To reduce the load she was wearing several layers of clothing under a fashionable, long winter coat and her bulky appearance was cause for much laughter. How times had changed, I thought, half a year had passed since the abrasive days at the start of the assignment and now we were working together as close friends. The long hours out on the mountain slopes gave little time for relaxation and we had settled to a strangely formal affair. Keeping to the separate facilities that had earlier eased the strain of forced company and shared meals, we maintained an undemanding pattern of independence that suited both of us. Dian had hesitantly become more affectionate and clearly wished that I was more forthcoming. But I retained deep, uncomfortable feelings about Heather and my marriage. Dian was very conscious of the reserve I felt. I had arranged that Heather would come and join me for two weeks while she was away, but I already knew it was unlikely I would find the courage to admit what had happened. The situation nagged at my thoughts, and again I welcomed the circumstances that would allow me to be entirely on my own for a while.

With success in showing Dian next to a gorilla nicely achieved, and determined to reap the benefit of uninterrupted work, throughout the next two months I concentrated heavily on the Group 4 family. Though the bad weather persisted, imposing dim conditions that seriously hindered photography, day by day the gorillas' tolerance of my presence improved – not in definite increments, but very unevenly. Some contacts were peaceful with all the right circumstances falling into place. On others, one or more factors would be against me and nothing positive came of the day. Respecting Dian's wish that the gorillas be subjected to a minimum of disturbance, I had fully developed the capacity for great care and patience in their company. The distances between us were diminishing significantly, but this brought fresh problems. Even though I could regularly approach to within twenty or thirty feet without causing alarm, the foliage remained an obstruction that hindered clear views; the gorillas no longer reacted strongly, but still used the abundant cover most effectively. Time and again it was necessary to back off and seek out elevated positions to get better visibility.

I had adapted to the mountain conditions, but still disliked the wet and cold. Every day began with warmed-up clothing and dry boots at least, but within the first hour of tracking, moisture from the wet foliage soon penetrated. I was amazed how easy it had become to ignore sodden clothing and wet feet – even the bitter cold that so often overwhelmed my poor circulation and numbed my extremities. As Dian had no weather instruments, in June of the previous year I had set up rain and temperature gauges and kept records of the readings and the daily weather. I found that daytime shade temperatures generally reached the mid-fifties but rarely went above 65°F. At night, the high altitude played its part and temperatures regularly sank below freezing, but usually for short periods, so heavy frosts did not occur too often.

During the first months of the assignment I had experienced worrying difficulties with condensation on my equipment. After a freezing night, on several occasions heat generated by a stiff climb penetrated my pack and caused moisture to condense on the chilled cameras; the worst effect being condensation on the inside elements of my expensive cine zoom lens. The opaque film of moisture took a very long time to disperse. After that had happened several times I tried various ways to prevent it. Eventually, by keeping the cameras in their foam-lined boxes overnight, and shifting them to my warm sleeping bag as soon as I got up, the problem was solved; by the time I had eaten breakfast the equipment was sufficiently de-chilled to stay clear of condensation.

Getting out from a warm bed in an ice-cold tent was stimulating but not exactly a pleasure. I countered the daily shock with a routine that eased the transition considerably. From long practice, my mental alarm woke me at five thirty and I reached out to light a small gas lamp, above which was suspended clothing for the day. Then I lay back in pleasant comfort to listen to the radio through my earphone. By the time the six o'clock news from the BBC was over, my clothes were nicely warm, allowing me to slip them on without so much as a shiver.

I did not envy the gorillas sleeping out in the open on their rough foliage beds, exposed to the elements with no more protection than the long hair on their bodies. Clearly they had excellent circulation systems and were inured to the low temperatures. One day I was able to observe a good demonstration of this natural resilience. I had tracked Group 4 into the nettles at the base of Visoke, catching up just as eating ceased and beds were being prepared for the late morning rest. Finding a suitable resting place of my own, I settled to await some post-siesta activity. Shortly, a rainstorm blew up, but with a waterproof wind jacket and durable plastic pants to defeat heavy rain, also a hooded woollen jersey to go under my bush jacket when the cold became too intense, I was well prepared for these weather changes. On this occasion the rain turned to hail that crashed down for nearly thirty minutes, shredding the larger leaves, piling up inches deep in any open space and making the atmosphere feel like the interior of a cold storage room. The gorillas were all but invisible from my position, but when the storm faded and the air grew still, I became aware of several quite distinct columns of vapour rising above the nettles. While I sat, thoroughly chilled and uncomfortable, the gorillas were apparently as warm as toast, their hot bodies steaming and drying off quickly in the frigid air.

Obviously the gorillas had good blood circulation and their coats of long hair were effective in helping to counter the cold, but I longed to know how their nervous systems compared to mine, if they felt things in anything like the same way as humans did. Their ability to push through dense stinging nettles was a constant source of amazement; they gave no indication of any discomfort. In spite of layers of protective clothing, the same plants often caused me much misery. Nettle leaves were one of the gorillas' staple foods and the chemical in the stinging hairs had no detectable effect on their mouths or skins. Did they have lowered sensitivity in their lips and mouths? Regularly I watched gorillas harvest nettle leaves; they stripped them off with an upward sweep of thumb and forefinger, then ate the bundled leaves with relish. The brittle hairs on the stems were up to an eighth of an inch long – well loaded with corrosive acid that caused strong reactions on my skin. To strip leaves as they did would be excruciatingly painful, and as for putting them into my mouth – that would surely be pure torture. On this day, the gorillas were squatting or lying in daybeds made almost entirely of nettle plants. Watching the little steam columns rising after the hail, I envied their capacity to cope so easily with their sometimes harsh mountain habitat.

Shortly after the hailstorm, the first opportunity to witness gorillas confronting another large mammal occurred. While following up trails in the nettle fields, I heard an outbreak of screams and then a strong chest beat. Short-cutting the tracking and hurrying more directly towards the noise, I arrived in time to see an elephant – head raised and ears forward – standing still on one of the main game paths. Suddenly, Uncle Bert appeared and stood to beat his chest. At this the elephant backed up a few feet, then came forward as if to charge, but stopped short and shook its head. Uncle Bert beat his chest again and dropped out of sight into the bushes. Now the elephant came forward again: a short charge that took it out of view. While I tried desperately to reach a better vantage point, twice more Uncle Bert thumped his chest. I pushed on, finding a good position in time to see the elephant back up with a noisy trumpet and retreat down the path to join some companions. It appeared Uncle Bert had won the little contest and his presumed victory surprised me. When I was able to go forward and examine the game path, tracks showed that several of the gorillas had been using it. I guessed the initial outbreak had occurred as gorilla and elephant came face to face. Uncle Bert had responded with a challenge for the right of way. He had not hooted or roared, only beat his chest, and that had proved sufficient to halt and then turn his opponent. I diverted to follow the elephants a short way, optimistic they might return and produce some action for the camera, but they picked up my scent from the eddying breezes. I had to be content with a few scenes of trunks lifted high above the undergrowth like snorkels, testing the air as the small herd swung away to the north.

Previously I had only seen gorillas close to buffalo, and there had been very little reaction from either the gorillas or the buffalo. Elephants were rarely spotted in the research area. Very occasionally tracks showed that individuals and, less frequently, groups of three or four elephants crossed over the saddle between Visoke and Karisimbi. I had bumped into elephants only five times, all loners, and had found them to be very nervous. Buffalo, however, were numerous. They wandered in little groups of up to half a dozen, generally favouring the saddle area and the gentler mountain slopes. Endowed with excellent senses of smell and hearing, they also were shy, nervous creatures who managed to keep out of sight with remarkable ease. Mindful of earlier experiences in the forests on Mount Kenya, I treated them with great respect. Their dark-grey hides merged with the vegetation, and their tendency to remain silent and immobile in the face of danger made it necessary to be vigilant. I trusted it would not be my misfortune to bump into an obscured individual with aggressive tendencies.

I had been able to watch buffalo and gorillas coming together several times, and all the meetings were peaceful. Grazing and moving slowly, the buffalo passed the more static gorillas and appeared to take little notice. I had yet to achieve a clear view of a meeting on a trail, and wondered who gave way when that happened; the relationship between the two large mammals seemed to be very much one of peaceful coexistence. The little forest duikers and the larger bushbucks also moved and fed with impunity quite close to the gorillas. It seemed to me that only the infants and juveniles reacted to the antelopes with any sort of curiosity.

After Heather failed to appear in Ruhengeri on the appointed day, I learned through an exchange of cables that she had experienced difficulties in chartering a light aircraft. In the end she had to revert to an airline and I met her in

Kigali five days later. Always attracted to woodlands and forests, she immediately found the trees and vegetation on Visoke fascinating. Although we sent frequent letters and small cassette voice tapes to one another, my descriptions of the mountain scenery and lush foliage could not match the visual experience: the grotesque beauty of the moss-laden hagenia trees was difficult to describe. As with almost everyone who visited the camp, she soon realised how much extra effort was required to climb about at high altitude. But as a first-time visitor, she found the high mountain vistas captivating and the gorillas awesome. We visited Group 4 several times, also making contacts with Group 8 and Group 5. Though I had tried to explain how frustrating the combination of shy gorillas and thick foliage could be, not until she had seen only tantalising glimpses of individuals did she appreciate what it meant to obtain a good picture.

When the time came for Heather to return home, I had neither salved my conscience nor solved my dilemma about Dian. We drove down to Gisenyi to look at Lake Kivu and to meet and stay with Alyette. Before driving on to Kigali the next day, we went with Alyette to see her second house close to Ros Carr on the slopes of Mount Karisimbi. It had been a pleasant and peaceful period that reinforced my determination not to allow any relationship with Dian to affect the security of our marriage. Having to spend so much time on the assignment had already put strain enough on it. Dian had recently become so openly affectionate I knew difficulties lay ahead. I had painted myself into a corner, and if I opted to continue with another long-term spell I would somehow have to deal with the consequences.

Shortly after Heather returned home, I enjoyed an unexpected, first-time meeting with some truly wild gorillas. Very disappointed by the failure to find any in the vicinity of Burkhart's camp, and having so far taken little time to explore territory any great distance from the main study area, I retained an unfulfilled desire to meet a new family. Leaving camp one morning to spend a day with Group 5, I heard several faint but clear gorilla screams from high on Visoke. Being reasonably certain none of the study groups had been anywhere near the position the previous day, the sounds aroused my curiosity; Group 5 had been in the hills to the south, so if the family was now way up the mountain, something very unusual must have occurred to cause such a long move. I felt compelled to investigate and headed for the nearest ridge path.

On reaching the giant senecio zone at about eleven thousand feet, I began to wonder if the effort was going to be wasted. No further sounds had come to my ears, and I had to cast about for over half an hour before picking up any fresh signs. The tracks were a day old, which immediately eliminated Group 5. I came upon the night's sleeping site, finding only five beds, but surely not made by Rafiki and his four companions. In one of the beds the usual flattened deposits of faeces showed the occupant had slept with a large infant, while in another the dung was fairly small, that of a subadult or juvenile. The three other beds contained the droppings of adults, at least one of which was a particularly large male. Somewhere near me were six gorillas and I imagined all sorts of configurations to account for the unusual number. Now very curious, I followed the tracks from the beds. Thickets of brambles made the going difficult, forcing me to bypass several patches where my quarry had pushed through all too easily. I paused repeatedly to listen but could detect no revealing noises. Progress through the thorny shrubbery was slow and far from silent, so I was not surprised to be challenged by a sudden, full-volume roar. I could see nothing and cursed the difficult terrain that was going to make it hard to get closer. Then two separate and different alarm roars followed the first. Now I really was intrigued: they sounded like adult males. Three big males? Perhaps Rafiki was ahead after all, but then who was the strange female with the infant, and the juvenile? Had the old man at last drawn a female and offspring into his little clan and fled with her across the upper reaches of the mountain? I had to find out. With mounting excitement I thumped my chest with the muted 'I am here signal', following this with munching sounds to give the impression I'd found something good to eat.

Silence reigned. In the still air, only the faint sound of wood being chopped floated up from the camp far below. After 'feeding' for a while, I crept cautiously forward, trying hard with my eyes to penetrate the thickets for a sighting. I experimented with a loud rendition of the throaty 'contentment' growl – still silence! Minutes passed, then sounds of an animal making its way down through the bushes let me know I would soon see who it was. The scrape and crunch of parting foliage came closer, the head of a silverback surfaced above leaves not fifteen feet away; our eyes met and the face registered shock – followed instantly by a nerve-chilling roar. I was looking at a total stranger, a wild gorilla I had never seen before. My imitations had deceived him all too well and now it was my turn to feel anxious. This gorilla was definitely too close and his roar was taken up immediately by two others – they screamed rather than roared – leaving me in no doubt they also were highly agitated. Knowing only too well that full-throated screams coming from a dominant position could presage a serious charge, I remained poised in that uncertain situation where confidence in the belief a gorilla charge is usually a bluff quickly evaporates. I looked away from the angry face and crouched slowly down, hoping his companions could not see me. The thought of three angry gorillas charging together brought on a rush of inner panic. Almost cringing in expectation of disaster, I tried more appeasing rumbles – which in the circumstances were so out of context the gorillas were probably nonplussed by them. Expecting further challenges, quietly I tore and munched more leaves to make feeding noises. A pregnant silence reigned for a full minute and nobody moved. With a small measure of confidence restored, I lifted a camera to the ready and took a look ahead. The face was still there, eyes staring directly and angrily at me, lips strongly compressed. The flush of adrenalin in my body made for unsteady hands, but I managed a shot of the distinctive facial expression – seeing another head appear briefly as I framed a second picture. The faces vanished, then quiet, tell-tale sounds indicated the little group had decided to retreat. The gorillas crossed over a deep ravine, where glimpses of them climbing the opposite bank revealed three large males with unmistakable silver saddles across their backs. Halting on the far ridge, the trio sat to watch me without any apparent further alarm. Through binoculars I examined their nose shapes and marks, confirming all were strangers. The female appeared briefly, a large infant riding her back, then finally the juvenile. I was intrigued by the composition of the family. Obviously these gorillas lived mainly on the far side of the mountain. They reminded me how little I knew about the north-eastern parts of Visoke. If this was Group 6 it was far smaller than expected. As this was the first recorded visit of a new group to the slopes directly above the camp, I wondered if the animals were on a short reconnaissance, or in fact visited often, and by remaining high and quiet had never been detected before. Where I stood now, a bare five hundred feet from the summit, happened to be an area very rarely utilised by Groups 4 or 5. I felt sure the family would have given themselves away long ago had they been regular visitors.

Very familiar with the movements of four groups, I knew how limited were their main territories. In a matter of hours I could traverse the length and breadth of any one family's full range – an area little more than two or three square miles. George Schaller had concentrated much of his research on ranging and territory, but Dian had as yet formed very few opinions on the topic. In my brief experience, the gorillas tended to stay fairly consistently within certain boundaries. Group territories overlapped, but the males seldom led their families any distance across the vague limits. Although the gorillas were able to see for miles across the mountain heights, it seemed the ample supplies of staple foods close at hand gave little or no motivation to explore unknown ground. In this respect, the gorillas were not going to help reveal much of significance to apply to hominid evolutionary processes. I visualised hominids to be wide-ranging creatures who had travelled in family or kin-related bands, foraging and hunting in varied, mainly open country, where food resources were widespread and often in short supply. Expending considerable energy searching for and eating foods with generally low moisture content, they would have been reliant on streams and scattered waterholes. Also, living in country that contained dangerous predators, they would have had to find secure night sleeping sites. Baboon troops closely matched this vision of hominid activity, but mountain gorillas were far removed from such a stressful lifestyle. Nevertheless, they had survived, while their australopithecine cousins had faded to final extinction.

Initially, the gorillas held me enthralled because my image of them was coloured by what I had heard and read long before any personal acquaintance. But I had soon seen for myself that, except in certain circumstances, they were not the threatening, aggressive creatures depicted in the tales told by hunters and explorers. They could be violent at times – usually for a good reason – but overall were remarkably placid, moving without haste and seemingly satisfied with a simple routine of feeding and sleeping. Obviously there was much more to their lives, but until they lost some of their fear and allowed better observation, the finer details would remain a secret. My superficial knowledge of their social activities increased the desire to get to know them better. I yearned to be able to move in close enough to see and film all that was going on within a family. Frustration over their persistent shyness remained high, and with a year of work nearly over, there was cause to wonder if it would ever be possible to achieve such a trusting association.

In mid-March Dian returned to Rwanda and I went down to Gisenyi to meet her. The day started badly with my Land Rover failing to turn up at the base of the mountain, I went on down the road, hoping to meet it, but had to walk for another hour and a half to the Descamps' house at Kinigi. Demaret had been unable to start the vehicle and had run the battery flat with repeated tries. It took me a while to fix the problem, by which time I was hours behind schedule. When I reached Gisenyi, Dian had long since made her own way into the town from the airfield. When I drew up at the hotel she was sitting out on the open forecourt that faced Lake Kivu. Dark glasses shielded her eyes and she greeted me with a coolness that reminded me uncomfortably of earlier times. My failure to meet her at the airfield had been a great disappointment. She had passed the time buying a few groceries and odd things for camp before returning to the hotel to brood over the situation. Explanations gradually broke the ice and her real pleasure at being back in Rwanda soon surfaced. In a chic dress she looked pale but well, and a little extra weight had rounded the angular planes of her face.

She had not enjoyed her term at Cambridge, but it had served to give her a much better understanding of the stricter scientific rules she would have to follow. She was required to return later in the year for a period of at least five months, and was not attracted by the thought of another long spell of English winter weather. Hard physical effort in the dull and cold conditions of Visoke's high wilderness was much easier to deal with.

Stopping in Ruhengeri for mail, I collected a stimulating letter from Bob Gilka. He confirmed *National Geographic* wanted me to continue with the gorillas for a further six months, adding that the illustrations department was extremely pleased with recent results; the touch contact with Peanuts had generated enthusiastic expectation of better things to come. Everyone in Washington felt confident we were well on the way to a second article. There were even indications I could extend the assignment if I felt it necessary. The news pleased Dian enormously, but when we talked about it later I discovered she was formulating long-range plans that would actually halt my work.

While at Cambridge, through the efforts of her professor, Robert Hinde, Dian had met Alan Goodall, a zoologist looking to further his career with research on primates. Following an interview with him, Dian had written to say she had met someone who was not only very keen to study gorillas, but also a suitable person to assist with the running of the project. She had organised that he would come to Rwanda in late July – but had not mentioned she was considering an arrangement that would allow him to have the field to himself.

Due to start a second stint at Cambridge in October, Dian would be away until mid-March the following year. However, before settling in England she intended to spend five or six weeks in America, so would actually be away for seven months. Tentatively, she now presented her plans for Goodall, and suggested I consider halting my work during her absence and commit myself to another full year when she returned. I was not taken with the idea. Gorilla habituation levels were improving steadily and I reckoned a seven-month gap would be counter-productive. But of equal concern was the fact that such a plan would upset arrangements already shaping up for a break at home and a return to the attractions of Lake Rudolf.

The ancient lake had recently been renamed Lake Turkana, and Richard's fossil discoveries were still very much in the news. With an article about to be published by the *National Geographic* magazine, he was approaching the 1970 season with high expectations. When he wrote to ask if I would be available, the prospect of working in the desert sun for a while was too hard to resist; to facilitate the change I had already arranged to be in Kenya at the right time. I remained certain it would be more productive for me to work alone with the gorillas in her absence, but Dian was insistent that the new researcher should have a completely free hand. She proposed that I should continue in the mountains for at least another month, then return to Kenya and perhaps stay to take in the start of the Lake Turkana expedition. After that, a further one or two months in Rwanda would see me through to the arrival of Alan Goodall and her departure. Goodall would then take over until we returned the following March. Now more openly frank that her plan was designed to ensure I would be with her for another long period in 1971, Dian felt positive the arrangement would prove acceptable to *National Geographic*.

I continued to object, but then a letter from Bob Gilka responding to my request to rejoin the Lake Turkana expedition altered the situation; he offered me the option to work for a short time with Richard – if I thought it worth-while – but added I should bear in mind the gorilla assignment took precedence. With this reminder I knew it would be wise to forgo the allure of a full fossil-hunting season, but then Gilka was not yet aware of Dian's suggestion that I match her long absence and the issue remained unresolved.

The rainy season had come early to the mountains, increasing already dense cloud cover and bringing heavier, more frequent showers. The miserable weather and lack of much success with the cameras helped to accentuate my craving to switch assignments for a while. Dian settled to work on her research data, but within ten days had tired of the paperwork. I had been spending time with Group 5 without any great success, and was easily persuaded to go with her to search for Rafiki's little band. The pictures of her touch contact with Peanuts had created quite a stir in Washington, so she was eager to see how he would respond to her reappearance. Absorbed by the improving relations with Group 4, I had not even tried to keep track of the bachelor family, but any situation that held promise was sufficient inducement for me.

Blessed with a rare, bright morning, we went on a slow inspection of Rafiki's main haunts. The lack of fresh trails led us to search further north than intended, turning the pleasant ramble into an unintended five-hour hike that taxed Dian's strength. Disappointment at failing to locate any gorillas was moderated by the pleasantly warm and sunny conditions, and at least the return sweep across the saddle confirmed poachers had not reset any traps in their favoured locations.

Resting now and then, Dian dipping into the tea and biscuits invariably carried in her pack, small talk kept giving way to the more serious topic of the future of the gorilla project. I was still not convinced that a seven-month break was a good idea. I had to admit my yen to rejoin Richard was a disruption that was not really justified, and was prepared to concede the prospects for a long spell with the gorillas in 1971 were very good. Inwardly, my mind kept juggling with the knowledge that I was more deeply involved with Dian and her research effort than I had ever thought possible. Willingly becoming an almost full-time co-worker, I had grown fond of her and concerned for the future success of her work. We now made many joint decisions and I was inextricably caught up in most aspects of the project. Reluctantly, I began to give way; after all, the chances of another hominid skull as spectacular as Richard's 406 being found were very slim. I promised to cut short my stay in Kenya and return to Visoke late in June. I had no idea how I would fill the half-year gap, but provided the *Geographic* accepted the arrangement, I would leave the field to the new man at the end of August.

Having failed to contact Group 8, it was my turn to persuade Dian that Group 4 would respond well, and, sure enough, when we located the family, young Bravado showed a greater degree of curiosity than usual. Once again it was brought home that the two of us inhibited the gorillas a good deal more than one. Bravado alone seemed less affected and I was able to shoot some meaningful pictures. It was extremely difficult in the dull conditions to get good depth of focus. A few feet could make all the difference to visibility, making it necessary to be close to Dian to see any gorilla that came near her. Though I worked with the slowest possible speed settings, frequently using 1/8th of a second when a firm support was available, still the apertures were too large and one or other of my subjects remained outside the zone of sharp focus. Even my pictures of the Peanuts contact had suffered a little from this problem. To solve it I would either have to use faster film or get my subjects closer together. Already utilising grainy high-speed film, I had only the latter option and could not see it working except by pure chance.

Before I returned to Kenya, Dian suggested we try once more to repeat her memorable encounter with Peanuts. I readily agreed, but unfortunately, this time our effort produced precisely the reverse of that first gentle meeting: the worst reaction I had seen from the small group and a few terrifying moments for Dian. I had found Rafiki on Visoke's north-west slope, which meant another long excursion deep into Zaire. Not that this concerned us much as poachers were the only people who visited the area with any regularity. Although Rwandan cattle occasionally penetrated the saddle towards Mikeno, their owners were deeply afraid of meeting a ranger patrol. Unlike the undisciplined Rwandan guards, the rangers from Zaire did not hesitate to confiscate and even shoot the intruding cattle. Fortunately for us their patrols very seldom came anywhere near to Visoke. Had we been obliged to respect the international boundary and keep out of Zaire, two out of the four study groups would be permanently out of bounds, and a third nearly fifty per cent of the time.

Our first meeting with Group 8 was ruined by heavy rain that produced only a distant and poor sighting of Pug and Geezer, but, remembering the unproductive days proceeding the Peanuts event, we returned the next morning. During the long march to reach the group, following soggy and convoluted trails across several gullies, human voices broke through the peace of the wilderness. Because they were loud and clear we thought immediately of a patrol, but from our concealed position the owners remained invisible. We pressed on, locating our quarry nearby on the opposite side of a deep ravine. Realising our relative positions could again give me the rare chance to show Dian making a contact, I suggested she cross over and climb up to the group.

The gorillas were feeding and merely glanced up occasionally as Dian clambered slowly down, then up. Struggling through heavy undergrowth, she managed to get close to Peanuts. Except for the shielding vegetation, the situation looked very promising. Peanuts stopped eating and lay back almost invitingly on some foliage. Encouraged by this, Dian eased carefully towards him. But the blackback could not take the direct approach and backed away. At this moment, with no preliminaries of any kind, Rafiki let out a furious scream and charged down towards her, followed instantly by Geezer, Pug and Samson: even Peanuts turned and added his voice to the commotion. Rafiki crashed through the heavy foliage, halting close above Dian, who sat back and held on to some nearby branches for support. When she made a few nervous pulls at some leaves to simulate feeding, her too-quick movements drew another scream from Rafiki. His powerful voice was magnified in the confines of the ravine and the frightful sound was again taken up by the others. It was all too apparent the gorillas were so highly charged they might conceivably stimulate one another to press an attack.

I had been covering Dian's move toward Peanuts when the charge occurred, but stopped filming lest the sound of the camera or any movement on my part add to the danger. Obscuring foliage almost hid the gorillas and I had no desire to record the event should the worst happen. Whenever Dian made the slightest move the screams were repeated and one or two of the group would lunge forward or whack angrily at the bushes with their hands. Very slowly the tense moments of real danger eased – and finally collapsed. As if to assert their dominance, Rafiki, Geezer and Peanuts paraded almost arrogantly through the foliage before moving away.

Dian was severely shaken: why the sudden surge of aggression from animals that knew her so well? She blamed me for making her climb up from below the group, but I felt there was more to it. The loud sounds of human voices shortly before we arrived had very likely set Rafiki on edge. Then her drawn-out ascent from below and movement towards Peanuts had probably added annoyance to his uneasiness, until finally he sought release with a noisy display of violence. Unfortunately his action generated reactions from the rest of his family, creating a situation that had escalated to a brittle and un-predictable, mob-like situation.

I was not sorry to leave the volcanoes the next day. A high expenditure of energy since the beginning of the year had again reduced my weight. I definitely felt the need for a change of climate. Prior to the incident with Group 8, I had spent many hours keeping in touch with Uncle Bert's family, mainly near the summit of Visoke. Daily squalls of rain were keeping con-ditions difficult and took away nearly all pleasure in the work. The group had been feeding on and amongst the giant groundsels, where low cloud con-stantly swept the slopes and cut visibility to a few yards. It was particularly frustrating not to be able to take advantage of the distinctive alpine vegetation and the marvellous high-altitude scenery. Uncle Bert led his family back and forth over steep and dangerous gullies, where slippery rocks, muddy soil and crumbling lava debris often defeated me, sometimes forcing wide diversions and careful searches to regain faint, rain-washed tracks.

Back at my home in Karen, on the outskirts of Nairobi, I quickly became immersed in a variety of jobs that had been set aside for a year. This was to be the longest break since starting the gorilla assignment and I appreciated the complete change of environment. Gradually I put on weight and regained a tan that had faded away under layers of clothing and clouded skies. As I worked with Heather to add finishing touches to our new house and establish a garden, the days sped by. Mindful of my promise to return to Rwanda before the end of June, I knew there would be little time to obtain any significant pictures at Lake Turkana. But Richard was confident that early excavation work could produce results. When June came, he persuaded me to fly to the lake; if any important discoveries were made later, he suggested the best solution would be for me to fly over from Rwanda for a few days. I might miss the initial event, but would at least be able to share the excitement of a new find. Flying up to Turkana, my pilot a shade anxious about the landing to be made on a very short airstrip, by a few hours only I missed a cable from the *Geographic* asking me to abandon the trip: Edwin, son of Dr Melville Bell

Grosvenor, was coming in to handle the photographic coverage.

Rains throughout northern Kenya had been good for a change, and un-usually heavy over the parched lands east of Lake Turkana. Flying along the eastern shore, I was impressed by the changes the rain had brought. Every-where, long dormant seeds had sprouted and the scattered thorn trees and bushes were in full leaf. The normally arid countryside had blossomed and turned amazingly green. We were heading for Koobi Fora, two-thirds of the way up the lake, where a curiously shaped spit of sand jutted into the water. A permanent base had been set up on it the previous year, and from the air it was a distinctive feature that could not be missed. The airfield, a strip of bare sandy soil, merged with the surrounding earth and was difficult to see. A skilful landing was achieved, but quick and heavy braking was needed to avoid running off the short runway. As the door was opened, a blast of heated desert wind instantly dissipated the cool air of the cabin. I looked with interest over the base camp situated only a few hundred yards away. The ridge of sandy ground was devoid of trees but the site was hard to beat. Near a crescent beach of pale yellow sand, Richard had erected two round metal huts and paved the area around them with great slabs of sandstone. With a large thatched roof placed overhead, the result was a remarkably spacious and cool structure. Nearby, a line of simple thatched and grass-walled rooms or *bandas* provided basic accommodation for expedition members. The cool water of the lake lapped at the beach less than a hundred yards from the buildings – the main attraction for hot and dusty scientists returning from work in the intense heat.

A year and a half had passed since I had last been in this remote region. I had looked forward to seeing it again, and already regretted having arranged to return to the volcanoes for what could be a stay of short duration. Breakdowns with the expedition's heavily used truck and still mired approach roads were causing delays that meant excavation work could not start on time. Within days it became plain little of real import would happen in the time available to me. There were to be two field camps this year: one for the archaeologists opening up the stone tool sites, and another further north for Richard's fossil gang, who would begin digging where the skulls had been recovered. Geologists would continue with the monumental task of mapping and correlating the scattered layers of sediments in the broken landscape. When time permitted, prime fossil-bearing sections would be searched more thoroughly for new hominid and animal remains. The area to be covered was so extensive it would surely take years to complete a thorough investigation.

I could not possibly wait until work started in earnest and flew out after only ten days. In the full heat of midday, our plane lumbered off with barely enough lift to clear the soft sand and erosion gullies lurking at the end of the runway. We climbed into a light-brown haze that muted the green of fresh growth and softened the harsh contours of the land below. I wondered what discoveries would be made over the next three months. The cable telling me Edwin Grosvenor was taking on the photography had caught up, so I knew that I would not be returning to cover any fresh finds. From geologists to ecologists, Richard had gathered together a large team of young and enthusiastic scientists; if nothing else the young Grosvenor would have plenty of activity to record.

At the end of June I began the long haul back to Rwanda, a journey I no longer enjoyed. The route had become very familiar, and though I still took pleasure in the changing scenic views, negotiating the border posts was an unpleasant task. Petty delaying tactics by the officials had become increasingly commonplace; my heavily laden Land Rover as always a prime target for investigation. In response to growing political unrest and opposition to the government and rule of President Milton Obote, along the roads in Uganda it was certain many police and army roadblocks would be in place, as well as the occasional one manned by armed and truculent civilians. The army and police tended to use professional-looking barriers, but the civilians employed anything from logs to a single strand of rope. Getting through the blocks required a good measure of tact and diplomacy. Fortunately, most Africans are naturally loquacious and respond to the traditional demands of verbal etiquette. While my passport and numerous other papers were examined, I found it helpful to divert attention by asking innocuous questions about the weather, or the condition of the roads. Many times it had been possible to deflate a tense and unpleasant atmosphere with polite questions. Another very successful ploy was to ensure that my documents were laced with a few photographs of gorillas; invariably they caused a high level of interest leading to questions and answers that quickly distracted even the most aggressive officials.

Thoroughly soaked by rain on the climb to the Visoke camp, I felt the fatiguing effects of altitude more strongly than usual. Trudging up the steep incline through the downpour, dodging mud holes and rivulets of water on the path, I felt unusually low in spirits too. My visit to the baking fossil beds of Lake Turkana had left me very unsettled. I remained uncertain how the future was going to work out, or even if I was following the right course. The wet conditions depressed me, and the sight of my old tent, now showing visible signs of decay, did nothing to improve my state of mind. I was tired of its cramped limitations and suddenly relieved that there were only eight weeks to go before the new researcher took over.

Dian was pleased to see me back. Having dealt with much of the time-consuming paperwork required by her university studies, she was looking forward to spending more days with the gorillas. In my absence she had experienced a full share of excitements: in a letter to me in April she had described a wonderful contact with Group 4, where she said young Bravado had come up and actually pushed her on the shoulders – the sort of interaction that would delight and satisfy my picture editor. I was sorry to have missed it, but if Bravado would continue to display the same confidence in front of my cameras it seemed I would soon have my shots. Poachers had been active too, killing a buffalo right near camp, and in a near-repeat performance of the November incident, a sick and mangy dog had entered her cabin. This time her natural inclination to be kind to animals was resisted. With the aid of her staff the dog had been removed and quickly put out of misery. She had also taken delivery of a brand new Volkswagen minibus and was at last relieved of the strain of having to put up with the ancient, uncomfortable and thoroughly unreliable old Land Rover that had been her transport for over three years. Perhaps the best news was that she had accepted Alyette de Munck's offer to restart census work on the northern side of Visoke. Alyette was exceptionally tough and fully acquainted with the mountain conditions. Her efforts were sure to be of considerable value. As the true size of the gorilla population could not even be guessed at, Dian was only too pleased to let Alyette try her hand. The entire area encompassed by the national parks of Rwanda and Zaire, and the gorilla sanctuary of Uganda, had been left wide open to intrusion by humans for nearly a decade, so Alyette would also be taking note of any illegal activities. Only the gorillas within the Visoke study area received any effective protection; unauthorised protection at that – but which was fully acknowledged by the conservator. Throughout the rest of the region, poachers, cattlemen, honey gatherers and woodcutters roamed with impunity. Alyette was as fascinated by the gorillas as Dian and myself, and could be counted on to put some real effort into the job.

Squeezing boxes of supplies and gear into my tent once more, I promised myself the next spell in the mountains would be conducted from the luxury of a much bigger tent. I had never expected the assignment to last this long. When the weather over the next few days deteriorated, I had good reason to wish better accommodation was already a reality. On 1 July, light rain began to fall steadily – and kept coming down without a break for fourteen hours. After that, in complete contrast to the drought of the year before, rain fell daily for a week – supplemented by one violent and protracted hailstorm that left deep piles of ice everywhere. With daylight conditions approaching the equivalent of near permanent dusk, I began the routine of gorilla tracking and watching with subdued enthusiasm.

At last the wet weather ceased, abruptly giving way to cool, sunny conditions that dried the dripping foliage and firmed up the soaking soil. With a half-year break looming only six weeks ahead, I felt some pressure to shake off the feeling of stagnation and tried harder to get the best from each contact. When the Group 4 gorillas conveniently worked their way to the eastern limits of their range, to a position above the camp that required no more than twenty minutes of climbing to reach, Dian took advantage of their proximity and joined me to pay them a visit. It was a purely chance decision that led to the first cine scenes of a gorilla coming close to her: also the key contact that led me to insist on making a break from the non-intrusive style of gorilla work we had held to for so long.

Pushing up an overgrown ridge path, we intersected Group 4's tracks, then stalked them in thick vegetation near a deep gully. While I settled in a position with a clear view along a broad gorilla trail, Dian moved ahead a few yards and we waited patiently for developments. Sounds of feeding predominated: the distinctive splat and tear as thistle stems were snapped off and prepared for eating; the scraping of leaves as *galium* vines resisted being dragged from the foliage; and the parting of roots as plants of wild celery were torn from the soil. Now and then soft, contented vocal rumbles and the occasional breaking of wind punctuated the feeding noises. Dian sat and watched ahead, taking a chocolate bar from her pack as the time passed. Minutes later, her face registering excitement, she mouthed the word 'Bravado'. She sat motionless as the gorilla moved into view and hesitantly approached, stopping feet away to watch with a lowered head and timid eyes. Dian's gloves lay on the foliage near her legs and Bravado edged carefully forward to bend down and sniff them, retreating seconds later to resume her careful scrutiny. Hoping to entice the gorilla back, Dian gently offered her chocolate bar, but Bravado was not tempted by the gesture and backed away. The action was short, but I had captured on cine the first, voluntary, near-physical contact between a human and a wild gorilla. Although nothing of any great note had happened, I felt a deep sense of satisfaction; I was using a brand new camera, a replacement for one that had given endless trouble over the past year, and it sounded reassuringly smooth and sweet. After so many months, the few feet of film just exposed represented a clear-cut success. If Bravado continued to display this sort of courage, surely more interesting encounters were bound to take place.

That evening, talking about the event with Dian, I decided the time had come to think seriously about what could be done to improve the chancy, generally obscured nature of the contacts. For nearly fifteen months I had respected Dian's sensitivity about the welfare of the gorillas by conforming closely to her non-intrusive methods. The long period had seen only moderate successes, and though the members of Group 4 were tolerating our combined presence better than ever before, I desperately needed more than just one or two of the animals to trust us. I suggested it was time to give up trying to be peripheral and unobtrusive and to make serious attempts to close the gap between camera and gorilla. Already moving with greater freedom near individuals, I felt an improved relationship could be developed if I began actively following the animals whenever they moved. Dian responded by reiterating her determination to ensure that nobody could accuse her or anyone else of stressing the gorillas. Her work required her to be insignificant – to merge with the greenery – specifically to see behaviour unmodified by a disturbing human presence. Neither of us knew what reactions a more determined approach would bring, and she didn't want me to do anything that would aggravate the groups. I wanted to record uninhibited behaviour too, but if more than superficial coverage was to be obtained it was essential to have good visibility at a reasonable distance. Quite simply, to do better I would have to overcome the vegetation barriers and get the animals to accept more exposed camera positions. We knew my assignment was being extended in expectation of improved results, so something positive had to be done. It was by no means certain a break of six to seven months would be approved, and therefore a strong possibility I would be working solidly in the mountains until at least September or November.

For a long time I had felt we were at a sort of plateau, that significant advances towards better contacts had almost stalled. Nearly four years of hide-and-seek methods had developed a set pattern of behavioural response from the gorillas. They expected their observers to creep furtively about and then settle into more or less static positions. Though there had been a gradual lessening of wary tension, they had adapted to the long-term use of the technique, but still reacted to short-range meetings with almost unwavering nervousness. Convinced that we had reached a stage where different tactics were needed, I persisted, arguing that if at any time the gorillas appeared to be overly worried one could instantly revert to old methods. In the end, though reluctantly, Dian agreed I should perhaps try something new. July 1970 thus marked the start of a period where I began to practise a new strategy.

Busy organising the construction of a new cabin for Alan Goodall, preparing also for her return to Cambridge, Dian could find little time for fieldwork. I was only too pleased to have the gorillas to myself. To get much nearer to the creatures would require an increased measure of respect for their normal habits and social rules; I would somehow have to break down what remained of their fear and suspicion – and that meant testing the limits of their tolerance. Already, just anticipating their reactions was enough to bring on a new feeling of excitement. I intended to experiment with a less visible and submissive style of final approach, and would begin the process by giving up some of my bipedal mobility with a descent to all fours. An upright stance was just too threatening and dominant at short ranges. Gorillas very seldom stood; they did so briefly to grapple with one another in play, or to make a good chest beat – and occasionally to peer above high foliage when something interested or worried them. There were rare exceptions; I had once watched an animal walk almost thirty feet on its back legs, but it was an awkward effort. If the gorillas saw me stand up during a close contact, or caught sight of my face above the foliage looking down, it caused considerable alarm. I had long been creeping about, doubled up and sometimes crawling, but now began to move along their trails on hands and knees, purposefully closing in after first contact, then following and keeping up as the animals moved.

It was a fascinating experience: on a different level I began to appreciate better-trained senses of hearing and smell, and to realise more strongly just how little visual contact the gorillas had with one another. Even at the resting and sleeping sites their beds were often widely separated, with many in completely obscured positions. There tended to be a central core close to the silverback, where perhaps two or three females and their young congregated. Other members could be distributed far and wide: some up to thirty or more yards from the core. Standing and examining the vacated beds each morning, then following up the exit trails, I seldom thought much about this, but down on hands and knees the perspective changed drastically. Now my eyes remained at gorilla level and I had to rely heavily on my ears. The gorillas could no longer detect me so easily though, or know for sure if it was I moving close to them or one of their companions. I experienced many invigorating flushes of excitement – and occasional moments where an increased sense of danger set adrenalin flowing and nerves jumping. As a peripheral observer I usually spent much time carefully searching for a vantage point to overlook the foliage; now I was determined to get the animals to accept me as close as ten or fifteen feet. I wanted to be able to see and film from their level: to be right in amongst a family rather than nearby on the outer fringes. My whole attitude towards the creatures changed at this juncture. They were no longer just subjects to be approached and filmed. I wanted to try to develop good and friendly relations that went well beyond my need to get a camera in amongst them.

Crawling not only reduced visibility and demanded a greater reliance on hearing, it also put additional strain on parts of the body not adapted for quadrupedal locomotion. My kneecaps quickly began to protest and my neck objected to the change in angle. But helped by the strong leather gloves that were part of daily attire, my hands adjusted more rapidly – in fact I soon found it an advantage to copy the knuckle-walking method favoured by the gorillas. They supported their heavy shoulders and chest on the second joints of their long fingers, but whereas their thumbs were too short to play any part, mine were ideally situated to give major additional support. Forcing through channels and tunnels of wet vegetation assured a more thorough wetting than ever before, and my clothing began to suffer extra wear and tear. The cameras rested nicely across my back, but the large tripod was too big and awkward to fit comfortably anywhere. I took to using a small stills tripod instead, but then had to contend with its flimsy instability.

Formerly, the gorillas had almost always been approached after they had left their beds, now I made an effort to reach their sleeping site before they left. Hoping there would be a fairly rapid acceptance of my new tactics, I wanted to get in early and follow as close as they would allow. Since it was not possible to judge how far a group had travelled beyond the previous day's contact site, locating the concealed and sleepy creatures without disturbing them was practically impossible. It came as a pleasant surprise when the first early appearances did not cause a hurried flight. Usually detected before I saw any of the gorillas, the first warning of their presence was either a sudden disturbance in the undergrowth as one moved away, or an annoyed bash at the foliage warning me to stop moving. Occasionally one of the gorillas would thump its chest with the mild 'Who is it?' signal. I would then respond and wait until the family began their morning feed.

As there was no sudden exodus from the comfort of their beds, my arrivals were sometimes early enough to allow glimpses of the gorillas' morning routine. At least an hour or more after first light, individual animals would wake up, yawn and remain relaxed, perhaps shift position and fall into a doze again, or do a little personal grooming. Some would sit, unmoving, eyes open but vacant of expression – almost as if meditating. I could not quite bring into focus the processes of a mind divorced from language, and wished I could know what went on in their heads when they stared out into space. As time passed, individuals would reach out or make a short move to the nearest source of food. Gradually, others followed suit, until several were dispersed in various directions. The actual departure was more or less determined by the whim of the silverback: if he chose to be lazy, his family remained spread out in the vicinity. If he made a positive move, however, the lead was soon followed. Departure from the sleeping site marked the start of serious feeding that usually lasted two hours or more. This was the stage where the majority of my contacts had usually been made, but now I stayed on the fresh paths from the beds, following quietly on all fours.

The first reactions to the crawling technique were very encouraging; many of the gorillas were letting me move quite near with much less anxiety than expected – especially the younger ones. They obviously saw no strong threat in my low posture and deferential attitude. I quickly took advantage, keeping mainly to the silverback's broader trail, often made more distinct when one or two of his females used it as well.

At first Uncle Bert found my presence in his wake disconcerting. He would give short, constrained barks and move to more secure cover whenever he caught sight of me, but his eyes and facial expressions reassured me he was more annoyed than angry. Most importantly, he did not lead his family away. Although not understanding its full meaning, I began to use the guttural 'contentment' growl more frequently. The sound seemed to help reduce tension and convey my peaceful intentions. The thought that I might eventually be able to hold a position within the spread of the family gave tremendous incentive to press on with the experiment.

Reluctantly giving up the growing thrills of crawling after gorillas, I accompanied Dian to meet Alan Goodall in Kigali. First impressions suggested he would be more at home in a lecture room than tramping the mountains of a remote African country, but he soon showed the eagerness that had convinced Dian he would be an asset to the project. To familiarise Alan with what lay ahead, we went on a tour that took in the moderate commercial and shopping facilities of Kigali and Ruhengeri, then before going on to Gisenyi, crossed into Uganda to visit the Traveller's Rest Hotel and Lalji's, a well-stocked general store in Kisoro. Dian's new minibus was a great asset. Blessed with a huge capacity and able to iron out much of the very rough road surfaces, it succeeded in making the long journeys almost comfortable. In Gisenyi, Alan was shown over the lakeside town, introduced to a few of Dian's friends, and finally taken to the house rented for his wife and new child. With memories of the Burkhart fiasco, Dian was going out of her way to make sure the man of her choice would be better prepared for his task.

Sadly, Alan's initial introduction to the gorillas was a letdown. A pre-arranged visit by the Belgian ambassador to Rwanda coincided with his first full day on Visoke. Eager to entertain her important guest and have Alan share with him the exciting experience of a first gorilla contact, Dian insisted we go out together. The result was a very poor and distant sighting of Group 4. The gorillas were made thoroughly nervous by so many observers, and only one or two agitated individuals allowed themselves to be seen.

Suppressing impatience, for the next ten days I helped Dian introduce Alan to the study area and the gorilla groups. As with Michael Burkhart, I could not help feeling that for a person with no experience of working on foot with wild animals, the period of initiation was going to be much too short. Alan was able to see that the fieldwork, though exciting, was a hard, lonely and time-consuming business. Having to deal with the administration of the project in Dian's absence as well guaranteed he was going to be kept heavily occupied. In the absence of any effective official control, anti-poaching and anti-cattle activities in the vicinity of the study groups had to be considered an essential part of the project. Unused to the harsh ways of Africa, Alan was somewhat appalled by this, but at least was able to see something of the problems caused by cattle; we found a great herd of them on the top meadow one morning, and had to abandon the day's gorilla work to conduct a round-up and drive the beasts away from Visoke. One other event conspired to worry not only Alan, but Dian and me, and to throw a little uncertainty over our formerly blithe and trouble-free utilisation of the portion of Visoke that lay in Zaire. Following up the trails of Groups 9 and 8 at the time, we were very surprised to catch sight of a large ranger patrol. We kept well hidden and were not detected, but on the way home were very disturbed to find the patrol had placed some markers on the top meadow where the boundary ran. Later, we heard the sound of rifle fire, but could only wonder what merited the shots. The appearance of the patrol brought on a touch of anxiety about possible difficulties over future incursions into Zaire – and did nothing to help Alan's peace of mind. But as the days passed and no other patrols appeared, we relaxed and hoped there would be no more.

A few days before Dian left for America, another encounter with Peanuts boosted her morale. This time the blackback was more dominant and aggressive in his approach – the scenes I was able to shoot did not have the friendly and gentle appeal of the wonderful touch contact six months earlier. Nevertheless, the fact that he had come right up to her again thrilled Dian; once more a gorilla had helped to counter some of the uneasiness she felt about the long term of study in England.

If thoughts of Cambridge were not attractive, Dian was looking forward to her trip to America with unrestrained eagerness – and especially a visit to *National Geographic*. She would be talking to those involved with her work, viewing all the rolls of film and the now large collection of stills. No longer under the control of Louis Leakey, she would be submitting her own proposal to the research committee for the renewal of her grant. She would be discussing my position too, so I would soon know if her plan for me to leave the field to Alan was approved. I would have to accept whatever decision was made, and on this score there was already trouble in the making.

Before leaving camp, Dian had been severely shaken to learn from Alan that he had developed doubts about his ability to cope with the work ahead. The sudden transition to what he now realised would be a physically demanding and lonely existence had sapped his confidence – to the extent that he finally stated he wanted to abandon the whole arrangement. Watching Dian's handling of Alan over the previous weeks, I had become aware of a change in her manner towards him, an increasing brusqueness and sharpness of voice that recalled the abrasive attitude that had soured our early association. Having done all she could to make sure that her personally selected research associate would be comfortable and properly equipped, she was dispensing with charm and asserting her role as overall controller and supervisor. Her businesslike and uncompromising attitude regarding his research on gorillas had also been made plain. Following long bouts of fieldwork, feeling isolated in his new cabin, Alan had apparently brooded over Dian's different attitude – and especially the lack of any friendly social evenings. Letting all the more difficult and worrying aspects of the job play on his mind, at almost the last minute he mustered the courage to say he could not manage on his own and wanted to leave; it seemed the plan specifically made so that he would be able to do just that had backfired. Dian had been astonished, but had risen to the occasion and somehow convinced Alan that he would be making a terrible mistake if he were to quit.

On the journey to Gisenyi to catch Dian's plane, we discussed the problem. I felt partly to blame for not having been more social myself. If Alan was unsure of his ability to handle his appointment, I was perfectly happy and prepared to stay on – at least until he had come to terms with his task and settled in. Still amazed that the man she had chosen had come close to failing her, Dian could not readily accept the situation, or understand where she had gone wrong. Upset and angry, she decided that all her efforts to ensure Alan's introduction would be smooth and simple had made things too easy. The construction of a new cabin and preparation of a beachfront house in Gisenyi had been expensive and time consuming, and remembering the loneliness and hardships she had had put up with over the years hardened her attitude. She insisted Alan would have to adapt and get on with his work; he had seemed reassured after her talk with him and she felt he would be much happier when his wife and child arrived.

As Alan's presence had effectively stalled the thrills of moving in on the gorillas, I returned to camp determined to make up for lost time. Giving up one more day to accompany him, I reverted to working alone and began again to put my crawling experiment to the test. Freshly energised by the process, I started to spend far more time out on the mountain. If *National Geographic* approved Dian's plan, there were under two weeks left to refine the new approach and build up a little trust. I felt more positive than ever that it was the wrong moment to break off. Within days, however, a telegram from Bob Gilka confirmed that I should take a break at the end of August and consider resuming the work in April 1971. I could do no more than accept the decision and make full use of the remaining days. At least it was certain another long period with the gorillas lay in the future.

Rewarded with several fine contacts that compensated in some measure, I continued to follow the Group 4 family. Uncle Bert gradually accepted that I intended to keep close and began muting his alarm barks to a throaty humph that communicated far less anxiety to the rest of his band. For only the second time since the beginning of the assignment, I was able to photograph a long play session between subadults. This time the gorillas allowed me to climb a spindly hypericum tree overlooking their playground – a close, exposed position that only weeks earlier would have caused them to disperse and hide.

Five gorillas were involved, wrestling and rolling about with obvious enjoyment and steadily flattening the vegetation. Much of the time they just squatted or lay about on their backs, each, it seemed, waiting for one of the others to make a move. Accompanied by soft chest beats and whacks at the foliage, one would eventually initiate a short, playful charge and the grappling games began again.

I could hardly believe my luck. Except for casual glances I was almost ignored. Throughout the whole siesta period, for nearly two hours the performance continued intermittently. From my uncomfortable perch I ran through many frames of film. Thin cloud cover gave the scene a pleasant, shadowless look, but lack of light reduced shutter speeds to the point where it was not possible to freeze the action. Bravado and a female named Maisie dominated the play for a while, then another female came forward and enticed the shy blackback called Digit into some active tussles. Digit was a young male of about seven or eight years who was particularly timid. He happened to be the only blackback in the family, and because he habitually kept to the outer fringes of the group I usually saw very little of him. However, this extended play period brought him out in the open, allowing me to observe him at close range for the first time.

Digit's odd name had been applied in an unusual way late in 1969. By chance I had caught sight of a badly swollen finger on his right hand and reported the injury to Dian by describing an unnamed gorilla in Group 4 who had a damaged third digit. After making several references to 'the blackback with the damaged digit', the word began to stick and it was decided he should be called Digit. For a very long time this shy gorilla never figured prominently in any contact, but following some drastic changes in the composition of his family a year later, Digit was to come to the fore in no uncertain manner.

The day after the play sequence, I kept very close to the group and was made to crawl a considerable distance when the silverback decided to move at least three hundred yards beyond the sleeping site. For a while I thought my presence was the cause, but the big male was in no great hurry and stopped frequently to munch on snacks of thistle and *galium*. The long move accentuated my poor adaptation to locomotion on all fours. My hands were comfortable with knuckle-walking, but my knees became uncomfortably tender and my neck complained at the unnatural angle. I was already used to hearing being the dominant sense, but smell was coming a close second. With my nose closer to the ground, the smells of crushed and chewed foliage were stronger, as were the occasional, pungent strings of dung droppings the gorillas left on their trails.

There were moments when I wondered whether following and keeping so close to the gorillas would in the end pay off; in terms of visibility, most of the time I could see much less than before. Was I pressing them too hard? Was I taking unnecessary risks and in for a shock as one unexpectedly turned on me? All the indicators I could read seemed to preclude a violent encounter, but the possibility I might unknowingly precipitate one hovered in my mind. I had to admit that the pure thrill of tailing these large and powerful apes through the matted undergrowth might be influencing my thinking on the matter. This morning was one where ears were definitely playing a greater part than eyes. Though hearing plenty of movement, I could see little more than occasional dark shapes through the foliage. Then somewhere ahead, Uncle Bert halted in a position he liked and the family settled to some concentrated feeding. It was already late morning and in all probability this would be the site for the midday siesta.

Crawling toward a large hypericum tree, I displaced a gorilla only feet away, but yet still invisible. It was encouraging that unexpected meetings like this no longer produced any vocal alarm, helping convince me I had chosen the right method to attain my objective. Reaching the tree, I hoisted myself quietly above the undergrowth. Several pairs of eyes watched carefully, but jaws continued to chew and nobody moved. A suitable branch curved out high above and I climbed up to it, pausing on the way to pull at strings of *galium* and imitate the actions of feeding. It took many minutes to get to the branch, my pack, as always, awkward and restricting, but the elevation gave a fine and nearly unobstructed view. I could see now it was young Bravado I had displaced.

For over a year these gorillas had seen me take to the trees, but never as close as this. Motionless and sharp-eyed, Uncle Bert watched but otherwise did not react. Apart from distant sightings across ravines, this was the first time I could recall seeing virtually the whole family exposed in such plain view; only Digit remained invisible. While I gingerly adjusted to the precarious perch, the animals lost their acute interest in my antics and concentrated once more on filling their stomachs. For perhaps half an hour the peaceful scene remained little changed: eyes wandered less frequently in my direction; individuals altered positions to reach fresh food plants, slowly relapsing into periods of contented inactivity that normally preceded the construction of day nests.

Suddenly, an ominous crack came from the slender branch that was my main support, but before I could snatch for the nearest firm handhold, the whole bough split away from its joint at the trunk. With my mind already anticipating a painful impact, I plunged to the ground below, crashing heavily on to a jumble of vegetation and tumbling noisily to a standstill some fifteen feet down the slope. Only a brief whinny from Uncle Bert broke the dead silence that followed. Slightly winded, not quite believing nothing hurt, I unwound slowly from tangled plants. High above, the broken branch dangled loosely. I had fallen about eighteen feet, but the combination of springy vegetation and steeply sloping ground had broken the fall. Apart from dents and scrapes, the cameras and binoculars around my neck seemed to have survived the long descent also. I sat quietly for a while, testing my arms and legs, then wiping and cleaning earth from the cameras and listening for sounds from the gorillas. Only the gentle rustling of wind-blown foliage could be heard. I guessed the family had scattered in reaction to the disturbance. My pack lay at the point of impact and I crawled up to examine it. A third camera and some lenses it contained were safe, well protected by foam padding and the small hand towels I used for wrapping.

I rested, cleaning and checking the cameras, and not for the first time thought about the fact that any incapacitating damage sustained in a fall, or an encounter with elephants, buffalo, or even gorillas, might have serious consequences. For some time I had been working entirely alone. Although our African assistants knew which gorilla group I intended to visit and the approximate location, it would be twelve hours before anything could be done if I failed to return by dusk. There were many occasions when I diverted from intended contacts and would be difficult to find. However, I always carried a tin with several large fire crackers: they produced a sound vaguely similar to a gunshot and I had set off many to scare poachers and herdsmen. This was my first serious fall, and on checking the tin felt reassured I could attract attention if the worst happened.

The rustle of foliage snapped wandering thoughts back to more immediate matters. Glancing through a gap in the vegetation, I was dumbfounded to see two gorillas looking at me. Bravado and Papoose were standing side by side, heads bobbing and weaving slightly as they tried to see what I was doing. As I crouched lower and turned to watch, infant Simba pushed between them. Then the trio began to edge forward, hesitantly, peering intently – not at me now, but at the jumbled plants between us. Then I saw the object of their curiosity: like a dismembered hand emerging from the leaves, one of my gloves lay where it had fallen from the tree.

Quiet noises told me others were moving nearer. Macho climbed a tree lower on the slope and squatted to watch; Tiger appeared in the rear of the trio; and behind him, to my great surprise, the large head of Uncle Bert materialised. His appearance caused a touch of worry; would he react to the sight of his youngsters almost on top of me? But he remained a bare ten feet away, looking on with wary eyes but little sign of nervousness. Bravado and Papoose were up to the glove and Simba pushed between them again. I could have reached out and shaken hands had they been so inclined. My cautious movements and clicks of the camera distracted Papoose. She withdrew, playfully dragging Simba with her. This gave Tiger his chance. Keeping his head averted, he brushed past Bravado to strut forward like a silverback in miniature, pausing to check the effect out of the corners of his eyes. Sentinel-like, Uncle Bert followed this performance with wide eyes. I lowered myself to an even more submissive attitude, giving Tiger the confidence to advance to within three feet. His dominant stance held for a few more seconds, then courage abruptly failed and he backed off with less dignified movements. Whatever tensions were present in Uncle Bert suddenly peaked and he disappeared from view with a noisy, intimidating crash.

One by one others followed his lead. Bravado backed away and there was movement from where the females must have quietly sat out the whole of the contact. Savouring the wonderful feelings brought on by this latest show of trust, I prepared to follow – then held back and let them go. I had been granted more than a fair share of luck for one day. With a roll of film that recorded the approach of the youngsters, and some tender bruises to remind me of a fluke soft landing, there was cause to be thankful for a memorable experience and a lucky escape from injury. I wondered what kind of thoughts had entered the gorillas' minds as they watched my startling descent. The cracking of the branch must have set them all on edge, but by holding their ground it seemed they had considered the fall as a normal event, rather than a frightening move; they had certainly shown some curiosity to see what had been the result of it. I amused myself with the thought that in the circumstances their reaction had bordered on solicitude for my fate.

In the few days remaining before Alan took over, I knew for sure a turning point in gorilla habituation had been reached. The new approach was being accepted much better than anticipated, and several of the youngsters had already conquered some of their timidity to become almost bold. But doubts remained that the silverback and adult females would overcome their acute distrust of humans. To prove the point, the day after the fall I was given a good indication of how far I had yet to go. On finding that the group had already left their sleeping site, for once I did not stop to make the usual bed count. This unforgivable break from normal routine caused me to miss signs of a birth, so it came as a great surprise when I caught a glimpse of a tiny pink face on the chest of one of the younger females!

Accentuating the fact that the adults would have to be treated with care and great respect, my attempts to crawl to a position where I could see better and identify the mother met with little success. Accompanied by little Simba, Bravado responded to my manoeuvrings in the undergrowth with another slow, inquisitive approach, once more coming almost to within touching distance. It was reassuring to know I was breeding a good deal of confidence amongst the youngsters – if not yet with the adults. To obtain pictures of the new baby I had to revert to telephoto lenses from a distant vantage point, finding it was the female named Petula who was the new mother.

While the excitements brought on by closer contacts had easily overcome earlier frustrations over lack of headway, anticipation of even better ones made me very reluctant to leave for home. I felt sure the seven-month gap was far too long and would lead to a decline in progress already made. Alan Goodall was as yet a stranger to the gorillas, and he would not anyway be trying to get in amongst them. The period ahead was not going to be easy for him. Unfamiliar with the mountain terrain, struggling also to overcome the language barrier and adapt to African conditions, he was not happy to see me depart.

Though expecting gorilla matters to be put aside, letters from *National Geographic* and Dian soon brought them to the fore again. My most recent results were apparently creating much enthusiasm in Washington; Al Royce wrote with the welcome news that there was now sufficient material for a second article, adding that Dian had been asked to begin work on a new manuscript. The television division was expressing interest too, making it probable that motion-picture coverage would now take precedence over stills. All this was good news and helped dispel reservations about the half-year break.

I began to catch up on disrupted and neglected personal affairs at home, but then Bob Gilka wrote to ask if I would like to cover the work of Dr Bristol Foster and photograph giraffes for a change. Bristol was a Canadian from British Colombia I had met in Nairobi a few years earlier, so it was a pleasure to accept. He had carried out a three-year study of giraffes in the Nairobi National Park, and was now returning to follow up this earlier work and assess any changes during his absence.

Letters from Dian revealed undisguised pleasure at the wonderful reception she was getting in America. For the first time she was basking in the limelight of a genuine appreciation for what she was achieving. But then came a disturbing letter saying she was opposing my expressed intention to visit Washington: something I had been urging so that I could view all the photo material and discuss the problems of movie coverage and sound recording. Reading between the lines, I detected some apprehension on her part that I was playing too strong a role in her project and might deflect some of the kudos. Having contributed most of the visible evidence on her work and subjects, I was not averse to receiving recognition for it, but out of personal interest and commitment I was doing far more than merely taking pictures of the gorillas. It had not occurred to me that she might come to consider me as something of a rival.

By a large margin I was spending more time with the gorillas than Dian. I had now logged close on six hundred and fifty hours in visual contact and had amassed a fair store of knowledge about them. As a matter of course I gave Dian detailed accounts of all my contacts, from nest counts, daily movements and general events – to full descriptions of any interesting or unusual behaviour; all information she gratefully received and incorporated in her research records. The disturbing letter made me suspect different motives for her insistence that I cease gorilla work in her absence. But by now I had adjusted to the situation. The fact that I was virtually committed to another long period on the project helped to dissolve some of my negative reactions. I replied by restating the reasons for taking a trip to America, and tried to put her mind at rest. The new cine-camera I had taken to the mountains in 1969 had been a disaster, with technical faults affecting a good deal of footage. A replacement had changed all that, but I felt the need to view the material and judge overall value for myself. For me it was essential to get to grips with the movie-making, and being unable to see any of the rushes was a serious disadvantage. In the end my letter was rather strongly worded, but it had the desired effect. In her reply Dian said she had accepted my position and raised no further objections. Nevertheless, I knew the exchange marked a minor shift in the way she regarded my activities with the gorillas.

Following the tall giants of the savannahs by vehicle was far removed from the rigours of high-altitude work on hands and knees, so the assignment with Bristol Foster made a very pleasant change. But 1970 was closing fast and once more I was drawn into the Leakey net. Richard was planning a fund-raising lecture tour in the United States and needed a film; one that would aptly describe his six-year involvement in the search for significant hominid fossils. The project was fairly ambitious. It would involve cutting and editing appropriate sequences from lecture films *National Geographic* had produced from my footage, also the filming of major new finds and some extra material to help round out the story. In spite of time constraints that would put me under considerable pressure, I took on the job with pleasure. Just when I most needed fresh exposure to film-making and editing, Richard's requirements provided it.

Several sessions of filming skulls and jaws enabled me to handle all the latest specimens and catch up with the most recent results of the Lake Turkana research. Then the editing of the lecture films kept me heavily occupied, at the same time bringing back pleasant memories of many adventures shared with the fossil hunters. Although a close involvement had not begun until 1964, with hindsight I knew the first glimmerings of interest had actually started in 1959 – the year in which I first met Des Bartlett and Richard Leakey.

In July 1959, Des happened to arrive at Olduvai Gorge in Tanganyika (now Tanzania) at a time of great excitement. Mary Leakey had just found some significant pieces of a fossil hominid skull: the first to come to light in the gorge since it had been discovered by a German entomologist nearly half a century earlier. For Louis and Mary, who had been visiting and working at Olduvai for close on thirty years, the thrill kindled by the discovery was enormous; they were particularly delighted that a good friend and professional cameraman had come at exactly the right moment to record details of the find. The careful excavation that followed exposed many more pieces, and eventually most of the skull was recovered. Des had filmed and photographed the final assembly also, a superb and breathtaking specimen of *Australopithecus* that Louis had named *Zinjanthropus* – known simply as 'Dear Boy' to the Leakey family – and 'Zinj' – or 'Nutcracker Man' to the rest of the world.

Unaware I was destined to become involved in the photography of Leakey fossils, I had seen Des's pictures of the skull in his photo files and in the *National Geographic* magazine. Many articles and newspaper reports on the find had captured the imagination of the world at large, and mine too. In May 1964, when I was assigned to cover Richard's expedition to Peninj, in Tanzania, I had visions of photographing a new hominid specimen of perhaps equal value. Though he knew very well the odds against digging up a skull to match the jawbone discovered at Peninj were great, Richard had been supremely optimistic, and knowing next to nothing about the recovery of fossils, I had found his enthusiasm catching.

Peninj was the name of a river that flowed down the Rift Valley escarpment into the west side of Lake Natron. Close to the river lay an area of ancient sediments, some of which had been exposed by erosion to produce a small gorge much like a portion of Grand Canyon in miniature. While attempting a short cut to Nairobi with Des Bartlett after the discovery of 'Zinj', Mary Leakey had been the first to notice the site. Flying to Olduvai as a freshly licensed pilot four years later, Richard had surveyed the sediments from the air. Set in the wild scenery of the Great Rift, the interesting mini-gorge aroused his fossil-hunting instincts and he resolved to conduct a personal ground exploration.

One quick reconnaissance had confirmed that the sediments were indeed fossil bearing, so he had returned with a small group for a second and more thorough search: one that was amply rewarded by the discovery of a beautifully preserved australopithecine jaw. Because it was the first to be found in eastern Africa, the jaw created intense interest. Louis Leakey easily persuaded *National Geographic* to provide funds for a proper excavation at the site and a wider exploration of the area.

Returning to Peninj for the third time, Richard headed a much larger team. With a thoroughness that would be the hallmark of all his future field explorations, he had laid careful plans. I took on the assignment to cover the expedition with cautiously reserved thoughts about digging for old bones, but had soon revised my opinion of the occupation. The expedition lasted four months and taught me a great deal. I quickly discovered that although searching for and excavating fossils was a serious business, sometimes slow and tedious, many aspects of the work were very interesting, and exploring in the sparsely inhabited country for new fossil and archaeological sites was particularly enjoyable.

Glynn Isaac, an archaeologist working under Dr Leakey, was the senior scientist on the Peninj team. While photographing him at work and listening to explanations of what he was doing, my eyes were opened to the geological wonders that surrounded us on all sides. I was soon looking beyond the scenic spectacle to examine the landscape with deeper interest. Glynn's training allowed him to analyse many distinctive features of the monster rift. As he described what he actually saw, I began to appreciate some of the complexities of his profession. It was very necessary to place the fossil-bearing deposits in their geological context, and so help determine a reliable date for the age of the fossil jaw. Glynn was essentially trying to unravel the fine detail of a gigantic puzzle; he would have to describe the composition and type of sediments containing the fossil specimens and try to correlate his findings with the terrain where they lay. It was my first introduction to the geological extravaganza of the rift system, and I began to understand the significant effect it had had on the prehistory of East Africa. I would never again look at scenic views without being aware of the constantly changing nature and make-up of the earth's surface.

In his position as the expedition's executive leader, Richard relished handling the logistics of the operation. The complex work of geological survey and more mundane excavation chores could be left to the scientists and assistants. He moved at will to any task that needed attention or took his interest. He clearly derived most pleasure from the long forays to explore for new fossil sites in the region. I had seen little of him in the years since our first meeting. Dark-eyed like his father, his light-brown hair bleached by constant exposure to the sun, he had grown tall and slim. Now nineteen, his lean and sinewy physique closely matched my own. Restlessly energetic and very self-confident, he strived to age his youthful appearance by smoking a pipe. As a son of Louis and Mary, he could not help but be knowledgeable about fossil hunting and much of what it involved, but had to accept that the academic side of 'his' expedition would, of necessity, be handled by those who were qualified to do so – in this case Glynn Isaac and Margaret Cropper, a young girl studying archaeology under Mary at Olduvai Gorge. This did not appear to bother him unduly, but after we had talked about it on odd occasions I realised the situation affected him more strongly than he let on.

Although already the owner of a small, but successful safari company, by initiating and organising three fossil-hunting field trips in under a year – the second having hit the jackpot in no uncertain manner – Richard had precipitated a crisis in his life and now had to decide what to do about it. Safari work was interesting, occasionally stimulating, but apparently no longer enough to occupy his active mind or exhaust his abundant energy. An urge to build on his achievement – to continue to find fame in a field where his parents had recently been so very successful was proving too strong to ignore. Thirty-four at the time, I had already been through seven different occupations, but knew for certain I had at last landed in one I could really enjoy. I had left the rigid routines and stresses of a commercial enterprise and moved to a job closer to the natural environment. It was my ambition to work amongst Africa's wildlife and make documentary films. With a term of practical apprenticeship under the guidance of Des Bartlett, I could see myself achieving early success through Armand Denis Productions. I did not envy Richard the choice that lay before him; if he wanted to join the academics he would have to give up the adventurous outdoor life and devote himself to several years of hard study.

Sadly, the extensive excavations at the Peninj jaw site brought nothing to light, so the prime reason for mounting the expedition failed to match expectations. If the skull to which the jaw belonged did actually survive through the ages – it probably lies still in the Peninj sediments, awaiting the slow process of erosion to open its natural tomb. Richard had found his first skull ten years to the month after his mother's discovery – and I missed the occasion.

Breakthrough

The year 1971 began pleasantly with two weeks at *National Geographic* head-quarters. The many hard-working days spent there effectively subdued the revival of prehistoric matters and focused my attention on gorillas. By pure chance the timing of my arrival could not have been more fortunate. At precisely the right moment I was on hand to neutralise potentially serious repercussions to disturbing news that had come out of Rwanda. Both Louis and Dian had sent in reports on recent events in the mountains that had caused acute anxiety to the members of the *Geographic*'s research committee – to the extent that they were actually reconsidering their support for gorilla research.

With a minimum of factual evidence at my disposal, I had to do my best to put minds at rest and counter the unfortunate reaction. First of all, in commendable efforts to try to keep the research area free of poachers and cattle, Alan Goodall had followed my own anti-poaching tactics all too seriously – and had run into trouble. Barely two weeks after my departure, he and Nemeye had come across a large camp of a dozen or so poachers. With courageous, though somewhat rash, enthusiasm, he had rushed the group, firing the pistol Dian had left with him. Apparently he had hit one of the poachers and the man turned on him, fumbling to use a bow and arrow; but Alan had closed in and dragged the weapon away before it could be brought to bear. The poacher had then tried to use a spear before breaking away and making a run for it. Later came the shattering news of a gorilla group said to have been annihilated by Rwandan farmers near a village called Cundura. Dian had been devastated by the report she received from Alan, and conflicting accounts of the massacre from Alyette de Munck and others made it impossible for her to judge what might have been the true reason behind the killings. There were vague, unfounded suspicions that they were related to the shooting incident, and on the other hand, suggestions that a baby gorilla had been captured – but no proof either way.

I was interviewed at length by Dr Leonard Carmichael, the distinguished and respected chairman of the National Geographic Research Committee. During our decidedly grave discussions, I managed to turn the tide of mis-givings about the incidents and secure the future of the gorilla project. Covering all aspects of the work, Dr Carmichael asked many penetrating questions. He was understandably alarmed by the thought that participants in a project funded by the National Geographic Society were implicated in law-breaking activities in a foreign country. I was able to clarify the position concerning the underfunded and poorly motivated national park staff; the advantage taken of their lax control by cattle owners, poachers, honey hunters and woodcutters, and the effect their activities had on the gorillas. Dr Carmichael was an astute man and well aware that what happened in Africa could not be judged entirely by Western standards. He readily accepted my explanation that the conservator of the Parc des Volcans approved and condoned all the anti-poaching and anti-cattle work conducted by myself and Dian. More importantly, he knew in his heart that if the committee was truly concerned for the survival of the Virunga gorillas, continued support was absolutely essential. Ultimately, he felt reassured that the integrity of the National Geographic Society would not be compromised and assured me the members of his committee could be persuaded to approve further funds. Later, in the relaxed atmosphere of a meal we took together, he confided that he was fully aware I was playing a far more active role than that of a photographer. I realised then that Louis and Richard, and no doubt Dian as well, had talked to him about the range of my activities.

It took days to view all the film I had shot since 1968. There was an obvious preponderance of gorillas seen from an observer's point of view, with the animals consistently showing awareness of the camera. There was definitely a need for sequences that would give more subjective coverage. Through our extensive correspondence and by examining the rushes critically as they came in, Joanne Hess was well aware of the filming problems, but still had some difficulty understanding why there was so little sequential activity. Although it was easy to see how wary the gorillas were, it was difficult to judge from the screen how placid and slow moving they could be. The rolls of film contained a highly condensed record of gorilla activities gleaned from hundreds of hours of patient waiting and watching. For me they brought graphic recall of the mountain conditions, of crouching for interminable periods in awkward positions, one eye glued to the viewfinder, waiting for the chance to shoot snatches of significant action, or simply trying to add useful scenes to a sequence suspended by lack of motion. As it was entirely normal for a contented, relaxed gorilla to sit almost motionless for up to fifteen minutes, sometimes even longer, if another nearby began to do something interesting it was all too easy to give up on the first and capture something of the second. It was easy to explain the reasons for frustrating gaps in action, but in the confines of a warm and cluttered viewing room, I found it hard to describe the 'feel' of the mountain environment and the rare pleasures associated with the filming.

Soft, hazy light had produced by far the best results, but the unavoidable use of wide lens apertures ensured a depressing lack of depth in the field of focus. Since a major proportion of the footage had been taken with telephoto lenses set fully open, the degraded images were all too obvious. Exposing for detail on the black gorillas overexposed the surrounding foliage and washed out the greens, making many of the scenes appear as if they had actually been shot in bright light. Scenes shot in direct, bright sunlight were not good; the strong contrast between highlights and deep shadows produced results that were hard and stark, with the gorillas remaining jet black and almost feature-less.

During my stay, Joanne was determined to explore every avenue that might help overcome some of the difficulties. To that end she arranged for repre-sentatives from Kodak to come and look at the material and make recommendations. The bulk of the film used until the middle of 1970 was a Kodak product called Commercial Ektachrome. It had a speed rating of 16 ASA and to obtain a decent image of the gorillas I was obliged to force it two stops to a rating of 64 ASA. Before leaving at the end of August I had experimented with a high-speed film rated at 80 ASA. Although it was more 'grainy', I hoped the faster emulsion would cope with the dull conditions a little better and allow a fraction more latitude.

A screening session was set up in a small theatre at the *Geographic* head-quarters. Since we were to assess the film in the knowledge it would have to stand up to being projected on to the very large screen of Washington's Constitution Hall, it was not just a case of accepting quality that would be presentable for television. Several selected rolls of film were shown to the experts, and when the lights went up they were asked for their comments. For a moment the Kodak men looked blank, then somewhat sheepishly had to admit that they had been so absorbed by the rare sight of gorillas in their natural habitat that they had forgotten to concentrate on the technical aspects. We had to show more of the footage, but were privately very pleased that the content of the film could captivate an audience so easily.

It was obvious that in spite of forced processing the Commercial Ektachrome was producing a more acceptable result than the high-speed stock; the Kodak specialists could do no more than recommend that I con-tinue to use it – the slightly improved depth of focus obtained with the faster stock was definitely not an advantage. Kodak had recently improved the emulsion of their product and I would start using the new film on my return; it was expected to produce superior results, but I was disappointed there was no way out of my exposure difficulties.

It was agreed by all concerned that motion-picture work should now take precedence, and that I would spend a minimum of six more months in the mountains. With the promising reactions to my first efforts to close in on the gorillas in mind, I predicted some really exciting material would be forth-coming in the near future. Looking at all the film and photographs, particularly the shots of Bravado, Simba and Tiger coming so trustingly close, had increased my desire to get back to the habituation process. My application for funds to build a permanent cabin to replace my slowly disintegrating tent was readily approved, and in Washington they could not know how pleased I was about that.

In England, I went to see Dian and found her desperately anxious to return to Rwanda to deal with growing problems; impatient also to start preparing for what promised to be a very busy year. To continue the census work she had taken on Marshall Smith and Jackie Raine, two young American girls both formerly employed at *National Geographic*. Professor Nick Humphrey from Cambridge would be coming to familiarise himself with the project and study the gorillas for six weeks. And for a report to the recently established L.S.B. Leakey Foundation, Allen O'Brien, the founding father of the organisation, would be flying in from California for a brief visit.

There was still a month to run before her term was complete, and Dian was unhappy that Alan had not matched the performance she had expected from him: there were financial problems, and she was critical about many aspects of his research work. She was particularly upset that he had sent her very little in the way of progress reports and field information on the gorillas. Too late, she regretted her virtual insistence that I match her absence from the mountains, ruefully acknowledging it would perhaps have been wiser to have given him more help and a longer period to adjust to the demanding conditions.

In the middle of March I began to prepare for what promised to be the most exciting period of the assignment. Because of interest from the *Geographic* television department, no firm cut-off date had been fixed; for the time being the lecture and magazine divisions would share the cost of my work. A week before my departure for Rwanda, Heather and I had been called upon by Richard to help entertain important guests from *National Geographic*: Drs Melvin Payne, Leonard Carmichael and their wives were passing through Kenya, and had accepted an invitation from Richard to make a brief, unofficial stopover to enjoy a visit to Lake Turkana. During the few pleasant and comfortable days we spent together, touring important fossil and archaeological sites, the gorilla project was a frequent topic of conversation. Both Leonard Carmichael and Melvin Payne impressed upon me that they were expecting my continued cooperation in aiding Dian in whatever way I considered necessary. Aware that I spent much time on matters that were not strictly photographic, they made it clear that this was perfectly acceptable. They felt reassured about the future of the whole undertaking, but remained very concerned with the implications of active conservation measures conducted without proper government sanction.

When I left home, my Land Rover was burdened well beyond its normal capacity, not only with the usual variety of camera gear and supplies, but also a heavy load of slotted angle iron to make a frame for my new living quarters. Poles cut from the surrounding woodland had been used for Dian's buildings, but I was determined not to utilise any more of the dwindling forest trees. The angle iron was relatively cheap and would allow me construct a cabin easily and quickly. Unfortunately, the sheer weight of it on the roof made my vehicle top-heavy and decidedly unpleasant to drive. I had to be careful and took an extra day to complete the journey. The added time actually worked to my advantage, because while I was still motoring through Uganda the Virunga volcanoes were subjected to a violent and prolonged rainstorm. On Visoke the deluge caused tons of soil and gravel to slough off some of the steep slopes like loose skin. Avalanches of water, mud, pumice and mangled vegetation swept through the research camp: a tent was carried away, the African staff quarters were flooded and clothing and food supplies washed out. It was pure luck that some large hagenia trees diverted the raging torrents and allowed the two cabins to escape damage.

Seeing obvious signs of the downpour and glad to have missed being caught in it, I drove slowly over storm-damaged roads towards Mount Visoke. Even from a distance I could see dark gashes on the mountain where tumbling water and debris had gouged the ravines. On the lower, cultivated slopes crops were flattened and some trees had been blown over. During my absence a brand new vehicle track had been driven through to the base of Visoke, thus cutting a considerable distance from the original walk. The road had been constructed with a solid foundation of lava rocks, but the steep gradient and slippery earth capping gave my old Land Rover a hard time. I viewed the new road with very mixed feelings. It would now take little more than an hour to climb to the research station, but I felt sure the easier access would attract many new, casual and disruptive visitors, particularly those who would previously have thought twice about making the effort to walk from the original road.

It took forty-six porters to cope with the load I had brought. Through deep mud and running water, they struggled with difficulty up a new and steep path to join the old trail. On the climb I panted my way up, feeling the altitude and aware I had lost most of my mountain conditioning. On all sides, flattened vegetation and broken branches gave mute evidence of the storm's ferocity. Water ran in places where I had never seen it before, and we arrived thoroughly dirtied by the muddy journey.

The camp stream was still in flood, a heaving torrent of silt-dark water thundering past with an unfamiliar volume of noise. Ugly mudflows disfigured the camp surroundings, and high on the mountain slopes I could see many scars of extensive earth slides. The bridge to my tent had been carried away, also a tree trunk further downstream that had long served as another crossing. I was glad there was no need to use my now thoroughly decayed old tent; Alan Goodall had already gone back to England and Dian had moved to the cabin she had built for him. I settled thankfully into the familiar comfort of her old original.

Dian gave me a graphic account of the frightening experience as the vicious storm had broken the previous day. Apparently an extraordinary display of lightning and violent thunder had preceded fantastic quantities of rain. She had watched helplessly from her cabin as water ran everywhere and the mudflows began. Yet it was amazing how little serious damage had been done. Within a week a flush of freshly sprouting vegetation would begin to cover the ugly swaths of tumbled soil and volcanic gravel. The raging stream fell quickly to a more normal level; but sadly the banks had been swept clean of the many ferns and plants that had formerly given it charm.

Intent on constructing my new cabin before starting serious work with the gorillas, I began the next day. Dian was waiting for her new assistants to return from a quick visit to Tanzania, and in the meantime working with the staff to tidy up the camp. After that she wanted to make a start on her new manuscript: something she had been quite unable to do in the wintry atmosphere at Cambridge. Allen O'Brien and Nick Humphrey were due shortly, and she was particularly anxious to discuss Alan Goodall with the professor. She told me she had exchanged harsh words with Alan before he left and remained despondent over what had happened during his period of tenure. She was also angry he had left behind a chimpanzee juvenile rescued from some men in Gisenyi. The animal was fractious and given to fits of screaming – a sound that grated on the nerves and was out of place in the normally quiet mountain camp.

The rainy season was already well established, as usual bringing alternating mixtures of cloud, mist, rain and occasional spells of sunlight. However, the blue haze that so effectively ruined scenic views was at a minimum. Whenever the clouds parted to let the sun shine through, the mountain peaks stood out distinct and beautiful, and the woodlands looked wonderfully crisp and clean. Underfoot, the dark soil was saturated with moisture, the heavy plant growth it supported sprouting and growing with the usual amazing rapidity.

Labouring over my new cabin, chafing to renew acquaintance with Uncle Bert and his family, my thoughts turned frequently to the last series of meetings, now over half a year old. Recollection of the exhilarating period was a constant enticement to get back to where I had left off. But weeks were to pass before I could concentrate entirely on the gorillas, and then unexpected difficulties repeatedly delayed a return to close and exciting situations.

Time taken to meet and entertain our visitors slowed my construction efforts. The little research establishment had became an unusual hive of activity. Allen O'Brien and Nick Humphrey were collected from Gisenyi and taken for their first sight of gorillas to see Group 4. The animals were near their favourite 'meeting place', but very wary. Although a moderate contact was maintained for two hours, the sight of four observers disturbed and inhibited them. Nick Humphrey would be conducting his own observations for six weeks, but as Allen had one more full day, I took him out alone and tried to produce better results.

Under drifts of fine rain, we tracked Group 4 again. By exercising extreme caution, the pair of us were able to crawl very close before being discovered. I could see Allen was keyed up with excitement at being so near to the gorillas, but he had to remain as frustrated as I had been on my very first contact. I could hear quiet sounds as bodies moved in the vegetation a few yards away. Glimpses of heads and eyes told me that several gorillas were trying to stay concealed as they attempted to see the stranger I had brought. Their mild reaction was pleasing and an indication to me of their improved tolerance, but unfamiliar with the knack of looking deep into foliage to pick out the dark shapes, Allen complained he could see almost nothing. He wanted desperately to move a little closer, so I relented and let him try. But the ploy failed; the gorillas reacted immediately by retreating deeper into the thickets. Mindful of the still tenuous level of trust, I decided against following as I would normally have done.

The day was young, so we began a search further north. The weather improved at noon, a welcome sun breaking through at the very moment we came upon fresh spoor. Within an hour we had found Group 9 in the bottom of a ravine. They were unaware of our presence and we watched them feeding near their day nests. The sun grew brighter, heating the wet foliage and enticing the whole group to recline contentedly in the warmth. The full spread of the family was visible, and sadly there were now only eleven members – down by six since I had first met them in 1968.

By mid-afternoon Nemeye had led Nick Humphrey along our tracks and caught up. Allen remained so keen to achieve a close contact, I allowed him to persuade me to try once more with Group 4. Leaving Nick to enjoy the view of Group 9, we retraced our steps. Uncle Bert had not moved far, but again the group could be heard and not seen. Selecting the biggest of the trampled trails, this time we followed it on hands and knees. As the distinctive sounds of feeding grew louder, I could only imagine what Allen might be thinking and feeling; at least he was thoroughly amused by having to use all fours. We crawled within ten feet of the nearest gorilla before a questing chest beat sounded and the group fell silent. I identified Papoose ahead, straining to catch sight of my companion. While we waited for developments, the sun vanished behind cloud and a steady drizzle began to fall. I had intended to find Uncle Bert, but again my resolve faded; I whispered to Allen, persuading him it would be best to leave a close encounter with a silverback for another occasion. He understood my sentiments and asked if he could try a move forward to Papoose. Knowing the youngster would retreat, I let him pass. Before he had crept more than a few feet, she rose to thump her chest and withdrew hastily up the slope.

After Allen had gone I went back to my building, unwillingly leaving Dian and Nick to follow Group 4. The two census girls were due back and I hurried to finish the job and vacate the cabin for them. With a day to spare I transferred my belongings and was at last ready to renew experiments with Group 4 – at least so I thought. While I put finishing touches to my new abode, Nick went down to collect the girls and Dian prepared for their arrival. It was a day of almost continuous rain, so I felt content to be out of it. But deep in the forests of the saddle area, unobserved, something happened with Group 4 that was to set me back many weeks.

Awakening to a clear sky, pleased with the comfort of the new cabin, I prepared for work. The coming days promised to be busy; Dian intended to have Jackie and Marshall ready to go out on their own as soon as possible, so the pair would need to be given a thorough grounding in tracking and gorilla watching. I had arranged to spend the day alone with Group 4, but seeing the promise of a fine and dry morning, Dian came over to persuade me to join her in a search for Group 8. Neither of us had seen the bachelors for eight months, so there was a very good chance something interesting might happen if we could locate them.

As we walked out, Cindy darting about, pleased as always at being taken for a walk, the sun cleared the trees beyond the glade to the east. It created a morning of the kind that invariably reminded me of the first day I had walked out to see mountain gorillas. Shafts of brilliant light touched the droplets of night rain caught in the pale lichens, setting them glittering like diamonds. Underfoot the soil was almost fluid, the top meadow awash with water. Karisimbi and Visoke reared starkly, their deep erosion gullies sharply defined by coal-black shadows. For nearly two years the slow wanderings of the gorillas had led me repeatedly virtually everywhere on the southern and western sections of Visoke. The land all about was now as familiar as any other I knew: all the slopes, ridges and ravines, and all the many paths and game trails that linked them; even the individual trees, especially those I could climb easily in the endless search for good observation perches. I felt thoroughly at ease and at home, and, depending on the mood, regarded Mount Visoke with a curious mixture of feelings that varied from something akin to affection to straightforward antipathy. Wherever one went on the volcano, moving was never particularly easy – and there were plenty of sections that called for considerable effort. At times I felt altitude-weary; my heavy pack weighed me down and the tripod became annoyingly unwieldy. Often I longed to be free of any encumbrances, to be able to climb with ease and slip more easily through the foliage. But my work demanded I carry a variety of cameras, lenses, spare film and batteries, and the usual complement of rain gear. For the most part I was resigned to the weight and actually felt somewhat incomplete without it.

To balance the arduous conditions and preponderance of unfavourable weather, there were times when it was a great pleasure to be out on the higher slopes, especially when the skies cleared and revealed the stunning mountain views. Invisible currents of air played constantly over and around the volcanoes, keeping the clouds swirling in turbulent and swiftly changing patterns. When the air stood still and the sun shone warmly, the combination of elevation and tranquil wilderness often induced moments of great peace and contentment.

Now secure in the knowledge that we had permission to enter Zaire's Parc des Virungas, a concession organised by Alyette during our absence, Dian and I headed north along our favourite route. We hunted for tracks along the base of Visoke and climbed some of the ridges. Finding nothing of interest, we descended to range far out into the saddle towards the Bishitsi bluff. But our only reward was old and fading spoor. As always, to help Dian conserve her energy we moved at an unhurried pace, taking time to read all the signs and stopping frequently to scan and listen. Before noon the wind increased and dark ranks of cloud began to sweep overhead. Quickly they eclipsed the sun and released a few soft showers of rain, then dropped low to clamp the forest in thick, grey fog. As morning became afternoon, Dian grew tired and decided to return slowly to base along the main game trail. There was still time for me to try to locate Group 4, so we parted company and I cut away westwards towards their last known position in the saddle area.

Alone in the forest for the first time in nearly eight months, I pushed on across the grain of the land. All wind had died and the fog lay over the forest like a damp blanket, accentuating a dull, almost breathless silence. Cutting and pressing through endless tangles of dripping undergrowth, wet and wearing down, faculties still dulled by lack of use for so many months, I felt more than a little out of touch with the wilderness. With concentration fading after the long hours of fruitless searching, I climbed a ridge to intersect the old trail to Kabara – nearly missing through lack of attention the pale undersides of freshly disturbed leaves and traces of broken foliage. Within moments I confirmed that a gorilla had left the signs. Like a discarded load, weariness fell quickly away. With senses reprimed and energy flowing again, I began to follow the spoor.

In the gloomy conditions there was no chance of shooting any film, but if Uncle Bert and his family were near I wanted to meet up and test their reactions in the absence of strangers. The track took me due west, others crossing and mingling with it, and suddenly flecks of rain-washed blood showed on the foliage. I pushed on faster, following the blood trail with some difficulty in the poor light, anxious to find out who was in trouble. As dusk began to drain all colour from the smears of blood, the full-throated roar of a silverback rang through the forest. I had been detected and the anger in the powerful sound diminished my hope that it was Group 4 ahead. Dropping to hands and knees I crawled on, but already it was too dark for anything to come of the contact. With relief I was able to locate and identify Uncle Bert and Old Goat, both clearly agitated by my too swift appearance. I manoeuvred in vain in an attempt to see something of the others, but it was too late. Worried and frustrated, I withdrew quietly to head hurriedly for home before darkness trapped me in the forest. It was unfortunate the major part of the day had been given to the unsuccessful search for Group 8; with ten hours at my disposal I would have discovered who was leaving the blood trail and perhaps what it meant. As it turned out we would never know.

During the days that followed it became apparent something fairly drastic had happened to Group 4. The family remained difficult to approach and observe, travelling fast and in single file to avoid contacts and generally behaving in much the same manner as a nearly wild group. Nest counts showed their number had been reduced by three, and that an infant was sleeping with Uncle Bert at night. Attempts to try to discover the reason and find out who was missing produced no definite answers. Whoever was bleeding when I first intercepted the bloodstains left no further evidence beyond the point where contact had been made. Backtracking had shown only that the animal had bled strongly in its bed of the previous night, and was one of the females; further backtracking revealed nothing that would help account for the bleeding. I was able to confirm that the infant sleeping with Uncle Bert was Mrs X's baby, Simba, and by a process of elimination determined that Mrs X, Maisie and Bravado were missing. Uncle Bert remained nervous and moved frequently, on one occasion leaving Old Goat and her son Tiger so far behind I had to stop following to avoid aggravating the situation.

This unrewarding start to serious filming left me concerned and uneasy. I found it hard to accept that so much ground had been lost; a month gone already and much to do before I could concentrate entirely on the habituation effort. Between Dian and myself, Nick, Jackie and Marshall were given many days of practical instruction in fieldwork. The girls proved to be very willing subjects, but not surprisingly lacked any feel for the wilderness. Dian was eager to get a new gorilla count under way and we debated how best to utilise the newcomers. Lack of funds and equipment precluded separate camps for the present, and under the circumstances it seemed best anyway to let the girls work together while they gained experience; later perhaps, they would have the confidence to go their separate ways and cover more ground.

When the time came for Jackie and Marshall to move out, the mystery of Group 4's change in numbers remained unsolved. I had located Group 8: still up to strength, but they too were unusually nervous. As the gorillas Dian had found south of Visoke at the end of 1967 had never been seen again, we had decided the girls would go to work on the unexplored eastern slopes of Mount Karisimbi. Taking into account the recent massacre of one group, and remembering that the capture of two juveniles for Cologne Zoo had resulted in an unknown number of deaths, it was high time an attempt be made to count the survivors. The girls were eager to start, but also a little apprehensive at being on their own, so Nick Humphrey offered to stay and help them over the first few days.

While I was recharging batteries and catching up on camera reports the next morning, a messenger appeared with a note from Gilbert, the guard who lived at the base of the mountain and looked after our vehicles. Some gorillas were out in the cultivated fields below Visoke; they were worrying local farmers and Gilbert wanted us to come quickly and do something. Group 5 had been ranging close to the boundary recently and apparently had now left the security of the park. This was very bad news and raised the spectre of another Cundura-style disaster. With Group 4 reduced in numbers and difficult to approach, I had begun to accept it might be more fruitful to transfer attention to Group 5; now the animals were miles from our base and out in the open, careless of the dangers outside the park. Dian was very upset by this development and prepared to go down immediately. But as she was still tired from the long hike to set up the census camp, it was easy to persuade her to let me deal with the situation.

Hoping the gorillas had already returned to safe ground, I hurried down the trail. But no such luck; at the roadhead Gilbert directed me to a narrow tongue of uncleared land stretching a quarter of a mile out from the base of Visoke. Thick with weeds and bushes, it lay along a run-off gully to the north of the new road. With considerable relief I realised it was most unlikely Group 5 would have travelled so far from their normal range. One or two women and some children followed me across the fields, eagerly pointing to the central portion of the patch and assuring me the gorillas were in the middle of it.

Voices and the sounds from scattered goats and chickens – all the usual ambient noises associated with human rural activity – floated in the cool air. Wondering what had drawn the gorillas off the mountain in the face of these sounds and hearing nothing, unable to detect any movement, I began to push into the thickets. Then some bushes shook and I moved on, clapping hands and beating at the foliage, trying to guess how the animals would react. A few years earlier this land had been part of the Parc des Volcans and undoubtedly gorillas had roamed here to feed. Gilbert, who had declined to accompany me, said that several gorillas had been seen. I decided they must be members of Group 6, who lived outside the study limits on the volcano's eastern face.

During the years since the area had been excised from the park, the group would have become very familiar with the sounds of humans and their stock. Their main range overlooked cultivated land and the prevailing winds would carry voices to them constantly. I hoped I could get a good look at them, and perhaps see if any of their nose markings would confirm they were the wild gorillas I'd met high above camp a year ago. Beating and clapping to get them going, I saw foliage shift in several places, and came upon a luxuriant growth of *galium* vine they had obviously been enjoying. Now deep in the thickets I could see nothing and heard very little: until one gorilla finally objected to being driven. With a loud scream it smashed through the foliage towards me. I held my ground, feeling the usual rush of adrenalin and the natural instinct to avoid a physical encounter. Out of sight still, the gorilla stopped its charge and turned to beat a noisy retreat. After two years of doing everything possible to avoid causing the animals any stress, it felt distinctly alien to be harassing a gorilla group, but this family had to be persuaded not to leave the sanctuary of the mountain. Close contact with their human neighbours could only lead to some future disaster.

At the vague boundary of the park I caught a glimpse of a silverback. Giving no time to register his nose markings, he turned to face me before disappearing in a steeply rising ravine. Out in the fields, the people who had gathered to watch, no doubt hoping for some entertaining action, began to disperse. Below me, stretching to the east as far as the eye could see, lay an intricate patchwork of cultivated fields. They lapped against the bases of Sabinio, Gahinga and Muhavura, and for a moment I felt a surge of hostility for the intense human activity that it signified. Rwanda, one of the most densely populated countries in Africa, was a prime example of how a high birth rate threatened to overwhelm the capacity of the land to carry the burden.

Over a period of twelve years, close to half of the Parc National des Volcans had been excised and given over to agriculturists. The main purpose had been to ease the problem of rapid population growth, and at the same time generate a pyrethrum industry to help earn desperately needed foreign exchange. The financial backing for this scheme was coming from the European Economic Community, and I knew from development maps that the whole of the saddle between Visoke and the eastern base of Karisimbi had at one time been considered for inclusion in the project. Fortunately, that part of the plan had been scrapped. Had it been followed through, a huge wedge of land up as far as the research camp would have been made available for cultivation and grazing. From my vantage point, I could see a long section of land along the area between Visoke and Sabinio still being cleared; the range of the mountain gorillas was rapidly being reduced to the final and steepest slopes of the volcanoes. In the face of continuing development and ever-increasing pressure from human intrusions, it seemed unlikely the gorillas would be able to survive for much longer.

As I cast about to pick up trails, then backtracked to find where the group had slept the night, gentle rain began to fall. It added fuel to depressed thoughts about the gorillas' short-term future, inducing for a while a feeling of despondency over the months to come. I had been back for five weeks – only two of which had been spent with gorillas – and in circumstances that prevented me from improving habituation levels. My earlier visions of defeating the vegetation barriers were far from being realised. Group 4, though reduced in numbers, remained my best bet, but I could only hope the members were not going to remain nervous and aloof.

Still thinking dark and unusually pessimistic thoughts, I came upon the gorillas' nightbeds and made a careful examination. Four adults had slept close together – one with an infant. Three smaller beds of two young animals and perhaps a juvenile completed the count, and confirmed this group was not the one I had found above camp. I could do no more. Relieved at least that Group 5 had not been involved, in continuing light rain I retired to climb back to the camp.

If my outlook on the photographic work had fallen to an unexpected low, at least the new cabin was a vast improvement on the cramped confinement of the tent I had put up with for so long. I had set in four large Perspex windows that gave plenty of light and good views in all directions. Wide metal shelves provided good work surfaces and storage space, and a cylindrical metal stove I had designed and had fabricated in Nairobi worked unexpectedly well. The heavy metal radiated heat very effectively, keeping a good two-thirds of the cabin warm. Clothing and boots hung above it dried out rapidly, and it had the added advantage of being very economical on wood. Since dead wood in the surrounding forest was being used up at an alarming rate, this was something that would help conserve the slowly dwindling supply.

For a while fieldwork continued as it had for the early part of 1970. Working with Dian I tried to improve on the scenes showing her with gorillas in close proximity. Except by luck alone it seemed, the two of us could not get near enough for good shots of uninhibited encounters. One particular contact highlighted the difficulty and made me determined to accelerate the habituation process. We had taken advantage of a sunny morning to make an early start, successfully contacting Group 4 before rain blew up and spoiled a mildly promising situation. We waited in the cold drizzle, watching half-obscured individuals feeding in the dripping foliage. Suddenly Dian grasped my arm and whispered urgently, directing my attention to a gorilla she swore was carrying a new baby. Desperately I tried to confirm the sighting and we eased forward to try to identify the animal. It was Old Goat, but she was so furtive and well hidden that we failed utterly to get any further sight of a baby. Dian was certain she had seen the pale pink of a newborn infant and added that it had looked awkward and floppy – as though dead. A better ability to move up on the adult gorillas would have allowed us to make a positive sighting, but I was really beginning to wonder if such familiarity would ever be possible.

Aiming to shoot some film of the baby, dead or alive, I returned the next day to search along the gorilla trails and examine the night nests with extra care. But nothing showed to confirm a birth. I crawled about in the under-growth until I could spot Old Goat; she was grooming her four-year-old son and there was no sign of a baby. Back at the task with Dian the following morning, hours were spent backtracking in search of a body, or at least some evidence of a birth, but without success. Another chance to add something new to the footage had passed, and a new baby born to Old Goat had to remain unconfirmed.

By mid-May it was time to say goodbye to the professor. Nick Humphrey had enjoyed himself immensely and admitted to being reluctant and sad to leave. I was sorry to see him go as he was one of the rare visitors who caused a minimum of disruption. He had adapted to the conditions with ease, and had spent a great deal of time following and watching Group 5. The gorillas had made him work hard by staying in the far eastern section of their range, miles from camp. Interestingly, while they were there he recorded that they had twice crossed the park boundary to venture out into the fields. Added to the previous excursion by Group 6, this information had caused renewed worry over the safety of gorillas close to the boundary.

A week after the professor's departure, whatever was affecting Group 4's behaviour suddenly eased. Tension simply dissipated as if it had never been there and I found myself back at the encouraging situation abandoned eight months earlier. It was a day that began with a heavy fog and visibility reduced to a few dim yards. I trudged over the top meadow and descended slowly to intersect the marks of Group 4's most recent wanderings. The trails led me deep into the nettle fields and I groaned inwardly. Now that I was crawling about so much I was more vulnerable to being stung by the potent hairs, especially at the gap between gloves and coat sleeves. In spite of thick corduroy trousers, my knees suffered continuously too, but worst of all was the occasional, unexpected slap in the face from carelessly disturbed stems.

I found the family and was greeted by a soft chest beat. A fresh breeze began to disperse the fog and I settled in a tiny clearing, aware that the apes were unusually calm. Along the crushed pathways I could see the odd gorilla eating or just sitting. When preparations for the inevitable siesta began, it became more obvious they were completely relaxed. I crawled in search of a better position, finding a tunnel through the nettles blocked by the broad back of Uncle Bert. He sat hunched over some plant not fifteen feet away, a distance that earlier would have caused him to move to cover. While I rested on my elbows and waited, he glanced casually over his shoulder with no sign of worry. I had always felt that Uncle Bert was the key to what I hoped would turn into a fine working relationship. If he remained calm, the rest of his band tended to stay calm also and his peaceful attitude on this particular morning gave some indication that the long series of poor contacts might be over.

The camp was crowded when I got back that evening – Marshall had come in from the census camp to talk to Dian, and Alyette had arrived, bringing with her Jean-Pierre von der Beck, a man connected with the wildlife parks in Zaire. Alyette brought the startling news that a white man had been badly bitten by a gorilla somewhere on the south-east face of Visoke. Dian was immediately worried that the incident must have involved Group 5, and wondered if there would be any repercussions. We learned later that the man had been lucky to get away with his life as he had been very severely mauled. While climbing with a group of friends, apparently he had approached some gorillas found near the trail to camp – almost certainly Group 5 – and seeing a baby close by had moved carelessly forward to snap a picture. Unfortunately the baby's mother had panicked and attacked, giving him a severe bite around his neck. It was a clear example of what could happen if casual visitors took unsupervised advantage of the approachability of a habituated gorilla group.

With this incident in mind, Dian and I reviewed my intention to carry the habituation process to a stage where the gorillas would surely lose most of their fear and distrust of people. The acceptance of humans within a few feet could quite easily lead to further and perhaps more serious incidents with casual visitors. The answer to the problem lay in the enforcement of national park regulations, and in ensuring that legal visitors and tourists were led by competent and knowledgeable guides. But then so few people came to climb the volcanoes and look for gorillas there was no established process to control their activities. Apart from the assistants who worked for us, there was no one qualified to act as a reliable guide. Not only did the conservator and his men know very little about gorillas, they lacked adequate funds and were neither equipped nor trained to provide any effective services. Between Dian and myself, many people had been taken to see gorillas, but we did not want to become involved in any arrangement that would actively attract tourists and disrupt the research work. My task was to film the gorillas, and I was certain that getting one or two families to accept me at close range was the only way I could do it effectively. Fortunately, two of the three groups under observation stayed mainly in Zaire, and were unlikely to be contacted by strangers. We decided research and filming work was important enough to override concerns about visitors, but knew the problem would have to be tackled in the future.

One morning I was very surprised to set eyes on Mrs X. She had been absent for close on two months and, along with Bravado, presumed dead. A recent scar showed on her left shoulder and I wondered if the wound was what had produced the blood I had seen in April. She appeared to be less active and healthy, but it was difficult to be certain. The lone silverback Dian had named Amok was much in evidence at this time. Although he had not been located near Group 4 over the relative period, it was possible he had tried to capture some females from Uncle Bert and succeeded briefly with Mrs X. It was all very confusing and we had surely missed some dramatic events.

The rains were easing off now, giving way to warmer days and increasing hours of sunshine. But all was not well with the research project. Many weeks had passed with no sign of the urgently needed funding cheques from Washington. Financial difficulties loomed and rapidly became acute. Dian was particularly angry to discover that her contingency money kept in Nairobi by Dr Leakey had been diverted to other research work. As work threatened to grind to a standstill, letters, and then urgent cables, were sent to Washington The construction of new staff quarters stopped as men were laid off. I took over the wages and food costs for our three assistants, and Dian began to doubt she could keep the census girls going. She had already borrowed money from friends and had long since come to the limit of her credit in places where she bought supplies. Although there seemed to be no question her grant had been approved, her creditors, mainly Indian shopkeepers, were not impressed and the situation became embarrassing. We wondered if the research committee had reversed their decision to support the project, but felt sure someone would have written had that been the case. However, on 11 June all our worries and difficulties were relieved when a porter arrived late in the evening with a bundle of mail. Dian, who had become increasingly irritable and depressed, burst out of her cabin and shouted the news that a cheque had arrived; I heard the high pitch in her voice and shot out of my cabin thinking something serious had happened. She was almost hysterical with relief; the money had arrived just in time to stave off a crisis over the census survey. In addition to the two girls already established, Sandy Harcourt, one of two young university undergraduates Dian had signed on in Cambridge, was about to arrive in Gisenyi. In a happier state of mind, she immediately laid plans to go to Kigali to cash the cheque. I had shipments of film to dispatch and new stock to collect, so I went along as well – a decision I was soon to regret.

With money in hand and all debts in Rwanda, Uganda and Zaire paid off, we finally met Sandy Harcourt in Gisenyi. Fair-haired, slim and youthfully handsome, Sandy exuded an open eagerness for the work ahead. For the first time I felt some confidence that a person with the right attitude and abilities had arrived, and fervently hoped he would live up the good impression he was creating. Jackie and Raine were keen enough, but a little diffident and as yet uncertain in their work; not readily able to handle the swift transition from city life to isolated fieldwork on an African volcano. Dian was already disappointed over the accuracy of the results they were producing, but it was really too early for the pair to have had time to settle down and develop the necessary skills.

Sandy Harcourt was young, enthusiastic and obviously very fit. Following an introductory phase with the study groups, he would be established where Michael Burkhart had been situated to repeat the survey of the Ngezi area. To give him a good view of the mountains, and in particular the section that would be his to cover, we drove along the narrow track running parallel to the low-lying craters between Sabinio and Visoke. It was a route neither Dian nor I had taken for a long time, and it was disconcerting to see at close range where the land was still being cleared of its natural covering. When the work was complete, only a thin corridor of predominantly bamboo-covered terrain would be left between Sabinio and Visoke. How many gorillas utilised this rapidly narrowing strip of land was unknown, but after Ngezi it would be Sandy's job to work his way east along it.

For his first sighting of gorillas, we took Sandy to our favourite area on the western slopes of Visoke. The day opened in an unpromising fashion with cold, white mist clinging to the woodlands and shutting out the views, but as we crossed the high saddle to enter the nettle fields, the sun burned the mists away and quickly brought more heat than was comfortable. Hoping to locate Rafiki, we were pleased to come upon five fresh nightbeds – only to realise on examination that they had not been made by Group 8. Lively anticipation of meeting some strangers held for a while, until the tracks led us to a silverback whose unmistakable forehead patch quickly identified Geronimo. Group 9 had not been contacted for two and a half months, and now the formerly approachable silverback was scared and intent on avoiding us. He reacted to our approach by fleeing towards the north without a sound. We saw only one other gorilla as he disappeared, but the five beds gave mute evidence that the family had been further and drastically reduced in numbers. From the base at Ngezi it was likely that Sandy would encounter Group 9; he would only have Geronimo's red forehead patch for recognition, but it would be valuable if he could confirm a reduced number and perhaps establish the northern limits of the group's range.

The discovery of Group 9's serious decline was eclipsed the next morning when I recorded events of a much more promising and exciting nature. Taking Sandy on a wide-ranging hike to sample the higher mountain slopes, I selected an easy ridge path. Keeping watch for fresh tracks and discussing the changing plant species and foliage cover, we slowly gained height. Well above eleven thousand feet, the discovery of a single, adult gorilla's bed and very fresh spoor led us further into the alpine zone. Though we came close enough to hear sounds of movement, the gorilla eluded us in the depths of a very precipitous ravine. We were now so high, we continued to the summit so that Sandy could enjoy the breathtaking views and look at the lake contained by Visoke's crater.

The descent from the peak took us down what was known as Honeyman's Ridge, and here we encountered more fresh gorilla signs. With Sandy clearly enjoying his introduction to simple tracking, we closed on our quarry, catching up in a thicket of lobelias high above the 'meeting place'. The identity of the group was established as Rafiki showed himself, but the old man was skittish and difficult to observe, breaking away after twenty minutes. I saw Peanuts very briefly, but long enough to become aware there was something odd about his appearance. A better sighting minutes later confirmed the right side of his head and face was swollen and his right eye firmly closed. Suddenly the reason for Rafiki's behaviour became apparent as I caught glimpses of two animals that were too small to be anything to do with Group 8 – and they looked like females! But I could not be absolutely sure and we were not allowed close enough for a better look. Geezer was located some distance away, but there was no sign of Pug or Samson. Clearly something very dramatic had happened during the four days Dian and I had been off the mountain. Rafiki had acquired two new members, and perhaps this explained the reduction in the size of Group 9. Dian was excited by our news and we arranged to go out together early the following morning.

We had to climb back to the heights to intersect the group's tracks, and although I paused frequently to allow Dian time to rest and catch her breath, Sandy could not avoid noticing how taxing the climb was for her. We found a solitary nightbed, then intersected fresh trails that led all the way down to the base of Visoke again. At last we came upon five night nests, two of which by their small size and droppings confirmed the presence of strangers. When we caught up, the gorillas were evasive but did not move away. Rafiki was spotted, then Geezer and Peanuts, but the two strangers kept shyly out of sight, forcing us to sit patiently until they moved and could be seen clearly. Levelling binoculars when the moment arrived, it came as a shock to see the distinctive features of Maisie and Macho from Group 4!

Now I deeply regretted having left the mountain. There must have been a meeting between 4 and 8 – where Uncle Bert had lost two and possibly more of his females. With no sighting of Pug or Samson, it had to be considered likely that the single night nest seen earlier belonged to one of them, but then where was the other, and would he be alone or with others from Uncle Bert's family? Here was a highly significant development and all sorts of possibilities existed. If Rafiki could hold on to the two females, at long last he had a chance to breed; but would they stay with him? What would happen the next time he met Uncle Bert – and how did the two nearly mature males, Pug and Samson, fit into the picture? It was urgent now to find Uncle Bert and make a full count of his group.

Accompanied by a fascinated Sandy, for the next two days I tried to unravel clues to determine what had happened. Having by good fortune arrived at a prime moment to follow exciting developments in gorilla behaviour, Sandy was delighted by such good luck during his introduction to the great apes and was exhibiting an encouraging curiosity about everything to do with them and their habitat.

Group 4 took many hours to track down. We climbed high above the 'meeting place' and picked up old signs, then followed meandering trails until we came upon evidence that showed there had been several inter-group contacts. Large areas of crushed and shredded plants, broken branches and gouges in the soft earth at different places gave mute indication of intense activity. Remembering the confrontation I had witnessed between Rafiki and Uncle Bert in 1968, I would have given anything to have seen and filmed this latest action. Again I cursed my luck at missing what must have been a fabulous series of encounters. It was impossible to decipher from the fading, days-old evidence on the ground what had actually happened, but the engagements must have been very active and had radically altered the structure of two families.

In search of fresher tracks, we moved on to traverse some of the most difficult terrain on Visoke's western face. In ages past a huge section of the mountain had slumped down, leaving steep drops below the summit that gorillas negotiated easily enough, but which gave considerable trouble to their human observers. Because of her difficulty with heights, Dian hated and avoided the section if possible. It was an area where giant senecios dominated the vegetation cover. I liked it because the lack of heavy undergrowth often gave better than average chances of seeing the gorillas fully exposed. As we crossed the lip of the giant slump, the sun shone brightly through towering banks of cumulus, illuminating the clumps of senecios and making their broad, dark leaves shine like patent leather.

Fresh spoor did not appear until we had descended to another and smaller slumped area. Here we found a sleeping site with only six beds. The gorillas were sighted minutes later, thoroughly hidden in foliage on the far side of a ravine. Though we waited patiently, a head count could not be achieved. Final confirmation of numbers had to wait until the next morning. This time, after much circuitous tracking we made a good contact and were given a rare chance to see the animals beautifully exposed. They crossed over the bare ground of a washout caused by the March deluge, making an accurate count easy. There were now only nine gorillas. Missing were Mrs X, Macho, Maisie, Flossie's baby – Simba II – and of course Bravado, who had not been seen for months.

Already resigned to the fact there had been no quick and easy photographic successes with my chosen family, this count depressed me further. It was upsetting enough to have missed discovering what had caused the earlier disappearance of Bravado and Mrs X, but losing out on the most recent events was particularly exasperating. It still had to be conceded that Dian's research had so far added little to what was already known from Schaller's work. The missed interactions would have provided the first visual evidence on the transfer of females from one group to another. To have observed and documented what had actually happened would have been a wonderful first. But we had been otherwise occupied, and now there were numerous unanswered questions. How did Rafiki acquire the two females? Were they simply herded away like a pair of captives or did they follow him of their own free will? Why had Pug and Samson detached themselves? How had Peanuts been wounded? Where were the baby, Simba II, and Mrs X? Although they were too distant and shy to be considered as friendly, I had become strongly attached to the apes and to some degree caught up in the happenings of their daily lives, though not to the same emotional degree as Dian. Sometimes I still wished I was only working to study them; it would be so pleasant not to have to adopt the set positions and awkward postures demanded by camerawork. But I knew in my heart I was dedicated to recording what I saw on film.

While I mulled over problems and difficulties in the mountains, sad news was coming in from the outside world. I learned that Armand Denis had died at his home on the outskirts of Nairobi. The man who had so many pioneer filming achievements to his credit, including the first feature film in colour of gorillas, was gone, leaving me sorry we would not meet again. Then Joanne Hess wrote to tell me Dr Leakey had suffered a bad fall while on his latest lecture tour, and had undergone a serious operation to have a clot removed from his brain. One way and another, Louis had been having a hard time since his hip operation in 1968. Apart from a difficulty in walking, which virtually brought to an end any active work in the field, he had been struck down by a serious heart attack early in 1970. A year later he had been savagely attacked by a swarm of bees, receiving an extraordinary number of stings and falling heavily during the attack. In spite of his heart condition he had survived this onslaught, but had taken weeks to recover and was left partly paralysed on his right side.

In giving me details of the latest disaster, Joanne mentioned that when Louis's clot was removed, the surgeons had discovered a second one of long standing, which they reasoned must have formed at the time of his fall during the bee attack. The second clot had also been removed, and as he recuperated, amazingly, Louis found that much of his original paralysis had gone.

In more ways than one, June had been a stressful month for Dian too, but it was ending on a much better note – and a surge of highly interesting gorilla behavioural activity. The arrival of cheques for the balance of her long-delayed research funds eased the last of her anxiety. For the moment only one event gave cause for worry; while Sandy and I were busy with Group 4, something drastic had happened to Brahms, the silverback in Group 5 who had now moved to a peripheral existence away from the family. Detailed to locate the group, two of Dian's trackers had come across Brahms's night nest. Later they had heard a series of violent screams and roars that indicated the silverback had run into some sort of trouble. Following up this report next morning, Dian and Sandy were dismayed to find blood on Brahms's trail; also some human footprints in the immediate vicinity that strongly suggested he may have been wounded by a poacher. They followed the bloodstains, but the nervous animal had headed swiftly for Karisimbi and they failed to catch up with him. On returning to camp they encountered the park conservator with his team of guards and three captured cattle herders. The conservator's spurt of patrol work had come about because he and his men had been invited to come and accept a gift of uniforms, boots and hats that Dian had purchased for them in America. Expecting a good reception and congratulations for his arrests, the conservator was taken aback to receive the full brunt of her anger over the wounding of Brahms.

While Sandy went out with a tracker to look for Brahms again, an early patrol by the guards netted Mutarukwa, the tall Tutsi cattleman who had helped Dian recover Cindy when she had been abducted by poachers in 1969. Unfortunately, Sandy and the tracker lost the silverback's trail on the lower slopes of Karisimbi, so the location of his wound and the assumption that it was the work of a poacher could not be confirmed. I had wanted to help trail and see Brahms for myself, but felt obliged to stay in camp to film the ceremony as Dian handed out the new uniforms.

Jackie and Marshall were coming to the end of their allotted four months of work, but with Sandy Harcourt exhibiting all the right qualities, Dian felt confident the census work was well in hand. The girls had managed to cover far less ground than had been hoped, and sadly, uncertainty over some their findings left the number of gorillas they had recorded open to question. Dian was increasingly looking to Sandy as the man to match Alyette with accurate results. Early in August he would be joined by his friend Graeme Groom, and between the two it seemed certain the census would quickly gain momentum.

On 1 July I returned home for a short period, and eight days later President Idi Amin closed the Ugandan borders between Tanzania and Rwanda. Milton Obote, Uganda's deposed president, had been given sanctuary by President Nyerere of Tanzania, since when relations between the two nations had steadily deteriorated. Now Idi Amin was threatening to invade Tanzania. As supply lines were cut, landlocked Rwanda was suddenly placed in a serious economic squeeze, with no telling how long it would last or what the results would be. I returned at the end of July to find the country's gasoline, diesel and kerosene stocks virtually exhausted and various other essential commodities in short supply. On the way I had to pass through several very tense Ugandan army roadblocks, and with the border post at Cyanika firmly closed, was forced to drive on into Zaire and enter Rwanda by the back door at Goma.

It was interesting to see Mikeno and Karisimbi from a different angle, and to get a closer look at the active volcanoes of Nyamuragira and Nyiragongo, but the sightseeing was rendered less pleasant by one of the worst roads I had seen in years. At the Visoke base camp, apart from concern over shortages of food and fuel, all appeared to be running smoothly. Alyette was continuing with her survey work, and by all accounts Sandy Harcourt was doing extremely well and enjoying himself in the process. He had already covered a great deal of ground, finding scattered silverbacks with one or two companions, but as yet no substantial groups. Jackie and Marshall had left during my absence, and considering their background I thought they had done a reasonable job. Dian, however, was less happy; the scope of their survey had been limited to a rather small area, from which they had come up with a figure of approximately fifty gorillas. This was an unexpectedly large number and Dian felt positive they had confused group identifications. By examining and analysing their reports in fine detail she felt sure the count should have been nearer to twenty-three.

For my first day back in the field, I joined Dian and Nemeye to find Group 4 and adjust once more to the routines of gorilla watching. On the way down from the crest of the saddle we halted a few minutes to listen for give-away gorilla sounds, but instead detected muted human voices coming from the direction of Poacher's Hill. Curious, we diverted to investigate and found the hill was living up to its name. I always seemed to return from Kenya in time to catch the poachers spreading through the Visoke–Karisimbi saddle, and on this occasion we disturbed a large gang of men who quickly fled. Before the morning was out we had found and destroyed over thirty freshly set snares. Moving on later, my heart sank as we found Group 4's tracks heading firmly towards Mikeno and the Bishitsi bluff. By three in the afternoon we had still not caught up with them and had to turn back.

Early the next morning our regular supply porters brought up a gory sack containing the mutilated body of a silverback and an old skeleton of a female. Alyette had stumbled across the fresh remains by Mount Sabinio, close to the Ugandan border. A note from her suggested the gorilla had been killed and cut up for some ritual purpose by men from Zaire. I could see, however, that all the flesh had been removed from the body, and felt it more likely the poor animal had been killed for meat. For the record I photographed the gruesome corpse, then, leaving Dian to attend to the unpleasant task of dealing with the remains, I went out to find Group 4.

A bright and warming sun bathed the forest, burning off the last of the night's dew and soon leaving all the foliage pleasantly dry. Already late, I hastened down the main game path into Zaire, determined to catch up with my friends. Two hours later I had passed through two nest sites and the spoor led me discouragingly onwards towards Bishitsi. Focusing on increasingly fresh tracks I became aware of a confused intermingling of many more than there should have been. Unless my quarry had circled, here was evidence of another group. Curious now, I followed up the westerly trails. With Mikeno looming ever closer, at last I was halted by a harsh and threatening roar of alarm, followed by long moments of expectant silence, gently broken by several 'questing' chest beats.

Dropping to the ground, I crawled to a large hypericum tree that offered good cover. Two gorillas had climbed a tree some forty yards away and were staring hard in my direction. Staying carefully obscured, I took out binoculars and saw two females who were total strangers. This made me anxious to see as many of this new group as possible, so I began a deliberate game which involved making mock feeding noises and using my limited range of gorilla sounds in the hope of keeping them interested. Unable to see what they evidently took to be a strange gorilla, they became very curious. Hesitantly, several climbed above the undergrowth for a better view, while others moved forward cautiously through it in small increments of a few feet. Keeping behind shielding foliage, I continued the deception.

It was both amusing and pleasing that my imitations were having the desired effect. I had long ago experimented to try to perfect some of their vocal and chest-beating sounds – and any stranger watching my antics would probably have collapsed laughing. To produce the noise closest to the rapid and resounding chest beat of a big male, I had to open up my jacket, cup my hands and whack my distended stomach in just the right place – I couldn't find anywhere else on my chest or body that worked as well. Gorilla chest beats varied enormously – from faint slappings to deep resonant thumps, and from a gentle clop-clop to the incredibly loud and distinctive tattoo of a mature male. There were slow double beats, rapid regular beats, one-handed beats and the soft thumps produced by juveniles at play. Sometimes a big male would bang his chest with closed fists, and often hit the ground with a tremendous thump. Each style of chest beat and a variety of vocal sounds conveyed a fine degree of meaning, and at this stage I felt able to interpret most reasonably well. In deceiving this new group I tried the more subtle and softer, non-aggressive sounds, and they were definitely succeeding in drawing the animals closer.

I saw the silverback pushing his way gingerly through some thick foliage, straining to see who was behaving in such an odd manner close to his family. He had a reddish tinge to his forehead, but was certainly not Geronimo. I tried a playful chest beat vaguely similar to those given most often by the juveniles, and this elicited a response from two gorillas I could not see. But the silverback remained silent and watchful. I added more of my best renditions of the contentment rumble, and could tell from shifting foliage that unseen animals were still closing on my position. The male remained static for a while, lifting and turning his great head, then with an annoyed swipe at the vegetation turned away and disappeared. While I hugged the cover by the tree, twisting and shredding leaves to simulate sounds of feeding, one by one nine gorillas revealed themselves. One of the adults climbed awkwardly up a small tree and I noticed it was not using its right hand. Minutes passed before it was possible to get a clear sighting – then I saw the hand, dangling from the wrist, atrophied and useless. The gorilla was just too distant for me to be absolutely certain, but an indentation at the wrist and a protruding object that looked suspiciously like a spike of wire suggested the injury had been inflicted by a wire snare.

Many times I had followed tracks of gorillas that passed within inches of freshly set poachers' snares, and had wondered what would happen if one of the apes were caught. A gorilla's great strength would enable it to rip out the bamboo springs of the snare with ease. But that effort would draw the noose very tight, and what would happen next? What if the victim were an infant or juvenile? Fibre nooses could be chewed away, I felt sure, but a great many were made of steel wire that would draw in and lock dangerously tight. The image of a gorilla thrashing about and trying to deal with a snare was ugly to contemplate; but I reasoned that their fingers were strong and dextrous and they would have sufficient intelligence to dig at the tightened loop – and possibly release themselves. But what of the youngsters? Would the adults be able to help them? I could not believe that they would, and that scenario could only lead to something I was seeing now.

This was the first time either Dian or I had seen any gorilla with an injury that could be attributed to a snare. Leaving my observation post, I crawled towards the maimed gorilla, but in my undue haste to close in, was too careless. I heard the animal drop into the undergrowth and retreat noisily. When I surfaced to scan across the foliage, all the gorillas had slipped away and I was alone in a still forest. By now five or six miles from camp and almost on the Bishitsi bluff, I had the choice of searching for Group 4 or trying to locate the sleeping site of the new group. Knowing it would be valuable to have a more accurate count, I decided on the latter. It took time to sort out the multiple signs and backtrack to the right place, and all the while I wished I knew what Uncle Bert was doing so very far from his normal range. If he intended to stay for any length of time in this far-off area I would definitely have to give him up.

There was no obvious evidence to show that Group 4 had interacted with the strangers. I had certainly heard no noises of any kind to indicate a confrontation, but felt the two families must surely have been aware of each other close to where their tracks intermingled. I came at last to the sleeping site and located nine beds: three with the dung of infants that lifted the total to twelve. Remembering the dearth of gorillas in the vicinity of Kabara during the short survey in 1969, it was good to know that at least one group of a reasonable size was still intact and breeding well.

Not until mid-August, almost a full year since first beginning to crawl along behind gorillas, did I finally start to make the sort of contacts I had hoped for. Discouraged that Uncle Bert's family had been so severely reduced in numbers, when the month began with him wandering so far away, the decision to switch to Group 5 was almost made. The long walk north-west toward the Bishitsi bluff meant a round trip of some five to six hours. It was quite impracticable to operate so far from the Visoke base, especially when one took into account the additional time needed for careful tracking. In many ways I knew Group 5 was the better family to concentrate on: it remained larger and more representative perhaps of a typical mountain gorilla family unit. I had made many contacts with the group, particularly during mid-1970, but very seldom with Dian, and as a result was much less familiar with the names she had allotted. Fortunately Uncle Bert did not stay long in the Bishitsi region. To my great relief he slowly worked his way south. Within two weeks he was ranging across the ridges above the camp – at times only a few hundred yards from my cabin.

Half a year had passed since my rash prediction that some dramatic material would be coming up, but all at *National Geographic* appeared to be happy enough with the film I was sending over. Seemingly confident I would eventually live up to my prediction, it was arranged my assignment would extend seamlessly beyond the six months recently agreed upon in Washington. This extension made me doubly anxious to prove intimate scenes of gorilla life could be put on film. The many distractions and disruptions caused by visitors and census workers had combined with frustrating field situations to sap my confidence. Only the mild successes of a few peaceful contacts shored up a resolution to be patient. When Sandy's co-worker, Graeme Groom, arrived I took him over to the Ngezi camp and was at last free to concentrate entirely on the gorillas.

It was the appearance of a new infant that marked the last step in my habituation of Group 4 – the breakthrough to real intimacy. Much to everyone's surprise, as we had no idea she was even pregnant, Flossie produced a baby on the night of 19 August. On the morning of that day, Dian and I followed the group along a ridge above the camp, on the way shooting some delightful scenes of the juveniles using a tree to watch Dian observing from below. Unaware of Flossie's condition, let alone that she was about to give birth, Dian asked me to set aside the following morning to look for Group 8. But for that I might have seen Flossie on her bed at the dawn of her infant's first day. Instead, I accompanied Dian on a pleasant walk all the way to the valley known as Leopard Ravine, and saw nothing of interest. When we returned, Munya, one of our assistants detailed to keep an eye on Group 4, reported seeing traces of blood in a female's nightbed.

Upset I had not been there to follow up immediately, I spent the next day keeping as close as I dared to the group. If the blood meant there was a new baby, I desperately wanted footage of it. But throughout the long hours I was unable to get a good view of either Old Goat or Flossie. Not until the next contact did I establish that Flossie was the new mother. Even then, I had to be patient and wait another forty-eight hours before an unobstructed view and reasonable weather allowed me shoot some film of it. Anticipating that the baby was a male, I suggested it should be named Leo. But later, when it became apparent Leo was a female, a C was added to make the name sound more feminine.

August gave way to September and by degrees a new level of familiarity developed. Continuing to project a submissive attitude at all times, I was now being allowed much closer. The camera was less an object of suspicion and its noise no longer caused anxiety. Success was so close it was tantalising. Each week brought small improvements in visibility that added to the content and quality of the footage. Even Digit was losing his shyness, making regular and purposeful moves to find a position where he could watch me – particularly during the early part of the day.

The daily dose of thrills was addictive, leading me to hasten through the early morning tracking in heady anticipation of new, stimulating contacts. But there were no short cuts to acceptance. As always, the distribution of the individual members, the location, the weather and many other factors created infinitely variable situations. No one day matched another. Uncle Bert and the adult females could not be rushed. In the end it was their collective mood that dictated the quality of any particular contact. A quiet, rewarding day could be followed by many where the results were entirely discouraging. But overall, progress was good and the telephoto lenses less frequently in use.

The nerve-tingling tension brought on by being allowed so close had increased too. I had to exercise considerable restraint to stop attempting to speed up this last stage of habituation. I wanted to be able to film normal behaviour and it was self-evident pressing in too strongly quickly inhibited it. I could now hold a position less than fifteen feet from Uncle Bert, but this short distance was having an effect on the distribution of the rest of the family. The females – Flossie, Petula and Papoose in particular – liked to follow and stay close to Uncle Bert, but my presence often caused them to move laterally away from the path he left. By backing off slightly I could lessen the tendency for this to happen – and occasionally reaped the reward of seeing several gorillas in the narrow field of vision.

Shipments of film sent out each week began to draw letters with enthusiastic comments from Joanne Hess. While I struggled to cope with exposure problems, she could not see why I was worrying so much over the results. On viewing the shipment with the first scenes of Flossie's new infant she wrote: 'The footage on Flossie and the baby is quite wonderful – exposure, focus are fine. Again, where you note dull light, I think: "Who cares, with footage like that?"' Knowing that I was beginning to deliver on the promise of sensational footage was a great boost; I felt sure a few more weeks would see me sitting nearer the centre of Uncle Bert's family – and perhaps would then be allowed to see things happening from his point of view.

Concerned as always for the welfare of the gorillas, Dian was not yet convinced I should try to eliminate the last few feet. Every time I brought back descriptions of some particularly exciting contact, she repeated her worry that my ultimate objective would be a definite intrusion and seriously affect normal behaviour. Of this there seemed little doubt; to the gorillas, the presence of an alien creature in their midst, especially a human, would always be disruptive to some degree, no matter how well one was accepted. But there was no denying that the content of the material I was getting surpassed everything obtained before. I had all along respected Dian's concerns, and as a result had carried out the process of habituation with almost excessive care over a very long period. The motive for moving in so close was governed by the need to defeat the foliage barriers, and I was happy in my own mind that the gorillas were not showing any signs of undue anxiety.

Busier with paperwork than ever before, Dian found less time to spare for fieldwork. In addition to continuing detailed analysis of her research notes and closely following the surveys being done by Alyette, Sandy and Graeme, she was working on two manuscripts. To add to the load, important visitors were still passing through – the latest being Professor Colin Groves from Cambridge. Preparation for their stays, combined with collection and delivery at distant airports, consumed much valuable time. There was one undeniable fact though; since April, visitors and assistants seemed to have arrived at times when something particularly interesting was going on. Colin Groves's stay was no exception and coincided with further discoveries and significant events. To begin with, on the day Dian brought him up to the camp I found the long-lost Bravado. Bravado had disappeared at some time during Alan Goodall's residence and after so long we had not expected to see her again.

So as to have Group 5 nicely located before Colin and Dian arrived, I sent Nemeye out to track them down. Completely absorbed by the progress with Group 4, I had no desire to spend time away from them, but since Nemeye reported Group 5 to be only a short distance away I opted to pay them a quick visit. I had not made contact with the family for over a year and was partly curious to know how the members would respond to my crawling approach.

They were indeed close. Within thirty minutes of leaving camp I had found and counted their night nests, and, on hearing faint sounds ahead, was soon making steady progress on hands and knees. Thinking Groves was lucky not to have to travel as far as Nick Humphrey for his contacts, I concentrated on a stealthy approach. The vegetation was extremely thick, limiting visibility to a few feet, but the bulky, contorted trunk of a hagenia tree loomed ahead, promising a good vantage point. Then a deep 'contentment' growl came from a thicket nearby, eliciting responses from at least three other animals only yards away. To my surprise I was already amongst the tail-enders. They had obviously been sitting and feeding quietly, listening to my movements and apparently interpreting them as one of their companions. Unintentionally I had almost penetrated the group and immediately felt a rush of tension. The result of startling several gorillas unused to contacts at such close range, particularly if feisty old Beethoven was one of them, was quite unpredictable. I froze and hunched down to await developments.

Minutes passed slowly. It was remarkable how little noise came from the dozen or so gorillas spread out all around. Listening intently to the scrape of leaves and the small, distinctive sounds of chewing, I tried to gain some indication where individuals were placed. Still ignorant of my presence, they were intent on filling their bellies. Taking the risk one might see me and cause a commotion, I crept towards the tree ahead – but a juvenile beat me to it, climbing up to the low bough I had selected for my platform. The position allowed the youngster a perfect view across the foliage between us and her eyes soon picked me out. It was Puck, Effie's daughter, at this time thought to be a male. She regarded me calmly at first, as though I were part of the normal scenery, but then decided to mount a demonstration. Thumping out a soft tattoo on her chest, she strutted along the branch. These antics drew her mother and an old female called Marchessa out of the undergrowth – then three others. The five gorillas clustered about the base of the tree, all looking my way with wide eyes but no signs of alarm. Then a sixth gorilla surfaced and I focused on a face that looked familiar. With a heavy overcast starting to cut down the light, hastily I shot a few stills, very pleased the little gathering was taking my sudden appearance so peacefully,

Soon the cloud pressed down, enveloping the crowns of the trees and shutting off all photography. In the misty gloom I tried again to see details of the face that intrigued me – the shape of the nostrils and the wrinkles above were so familiar. Then it dawned: it was Bravado, last seen when she had come so very close after my fall from a tree over a year ago. She looked different: a little larger and more mature perhaps. Bravado was still on record as being a male, but, watching the face, certain of the identification, I had my first positive doubt about the classification. Male or female, Bravado was now the third gorilla known to have transferred from one group to another. Macho and Maisie were certainly females, but Bravado, who all along had acted like a male blackback, made it apparent such events were perhaps more common-place than previously thought.

Dian was overjoyed to hear the news, going out the next day with Colin to introduce him to the gorillas and verify my identification. Unfortunately, Bravado failed to appear during any of the contacts she made over the next three weeks. Not surprisingly she became sceptical of my sighting. Then one Sunday morning, long after Colin had left, the woodman reported hearing sounds from gorillas on the slope above the cabins. Together we climbed to have a look and found Group 5 in residence. This time Bravado did appear, coming to within a few feet of Dian, so there could no longer be any doubt about her transfer.

As had Humphrey before him, Colin Groves enjoyed his time in the volcanoes and was greatly impressed by the gorillas. Group 5 remained conveniently close to base throughout his stay, at times only a ten-minute walk away. Early on I took him out for an introduction to Group 4 – first climbing to the peak of Visoke to show off the alpine vegetation and the mountain scenery, as I had done with Sandy Harcourt. Mists screened out the views unfortunately, but on the way down we crossed fresh tracks I reckoned would be worth checking the next morning. It proved to be a rewarding decision for the spoor led us to Rafiki, Peanuts and Geezer, and one female I recognised as Macho. There was no sign of Maisie, but as other tracks led on up the mountain we followed to see who had made them. High on the difficult ridges above Leopard Ravine we caught up with Samson and Maisie. Because I had chosen to give Colin a quick mountain tour, yet another intriguing development had been discovered. Samson, though not yet fully mature, was apparently intent on separating Maisie from Rafiki. In situations like this I wished it were possible to take more time to follow the fortunes of Rafiki's small group. From the behavioural aspect, what was happening was of special interest, tempting me to spend some days with them, but from the filming standpoint the drive to penetrate Group 4 remained more important and I gave up the idea. It was now doubly unfortunate Alan Goodall had not settled in as planned. There was a definite need for at least enough people to keep track of each family in the study area. To record lesser-known aspects of gorilla behaviour some really persistent and continuous observation was needed. For one reason or another, we had missed seeing anything of the first known transfers of several females – an intriguing addition to the data on gorilla social behaviour.

Colin spent his last night in camp on 14 September, and as if to underline the interesting events that had coincided with his visit, the mountains were shaken at midnight by an earthquake. I awoke to the sensation that someone was rocking my bed; the cabin creaked as the earth swayed and long moments passed before I realised what was happening. Somewhere along the Rift Valley's massive faults, tension was being released. Sleepily, I wondered if the quake would cause fresh eruptions of lava in the active zone around Mounts Nyiragongo and Nyamuragira.

After returning from seeing Colin off, though at first frustrated, I spent a very satisfying time in the company of Group 4. It was an uncommon day where the sun shone brilliantly from dawn to dusk, making it a real pleasure to be out in the woodlands. Having been away for five days, I had no idea where the group was located. Walking along the path skirting the base of Visoke, unknowingly I passed very close to the gorillas, but not the slightest sound or movement gave away their presence. An hour later, having sweated halfway up Visoke and found their sleeping site, I was thoroughly exasperated to discover them almost within sight of the camp.

My friends were feeding on a stand of succulent thistles, with the young-sters up in the vernonia trees enjoying the small purple flowers – all so busy satisfying their appetites that my arrival was barely acknowledged. Bright sunlight streaming from a cloudless sky reflected strongly from the foliage leaves, creating harsh shadows and terrible conditions for good photography. I did not attempt to shoot anything until young Papoose appeared at an opening ahead of me. Crouched behind the camera, I watched her approach and saw her catch her reflection in the lens filter. Each time she looked her own eyes stared back – causing her to avert her face in true primate fashion to avoid the stare. From four feet away I zoomed in until her brown eyes filled the frame, sunlight glinting from a few tactile hairs sprouting from her brow. Then she swung away, swatting at some leaves to relieve the unease at being so close.

Uncle Bert began to move to the west and his family slowly followed the lead. I tagged on behind, waiting for the right moment to set up again. Ahead lay a narrow gully with plants struggling to grow where waters from the deluge had torn away the previous cover. Digit appeared, followed by Papoose, Simba and Tiger. A trickle of water ran over a bare ledge and the juveniles moved towards it and bent down. They appeared to be smelling the water, but as they continued to bend with faces to the water I realised they were actually drinking. This was the first time ever I had seen a gorilla take water. With a profuse abundance of succulent plants on which to feed there was no need for them to drink, but on a hot day such as this Simba and Tiger obviously felt the need for a thirst-quenching sip. I filmed the brief action, pleased to have seen something so rare and unusual.

The whole tone of my encounters with Group 4 was now quite different. All uneasiness had gone from the initial phase of our early morning meetings. Once the gorillas were aware of my arrival they remained watchful, but showed no outward signs of concern. Careful of their social etiquette, I took care not to displace anyone, particularly when they were eating. The generally peaceful atmosphere allowed me to crawl about with a great deal more freedom, especially near the prime central area occupied by the Uncle Bert. The optimum time for a calm situation was as always just before and during the daily siesta. Appetites satisfied, the adults relaxed contentedly and the youngsters reverted to bouts of gentle play. Digit was much more in evidence, plainly curious and regularly seeking out my position. I saw him frequently now, but he still lacked the courage to make more direct advances as Bravado had once done. He usually chose to watch from a respectable distance from behind good cover, but on the last day of September he overcame his hesitant shyness and together with others assured me my goal was in sight.

It was a day that would remain fixed in memory: the first of many that more swiftly than ever expected opened the way to less restricted views of my cautious subjects. Having spent three days with Dian in pursuit of Group 5, then another dealing with a backlog of correspondence, film reports and the recharging of batteries, I was keen to return to my favourites. A lapse of several days between contacts usually meant spending extra hours following up old trails, but on this day the welcome sight of freshly disturbed foliage lay at my feet only minutes after descending from the top meadow.

The family was in the thick of the nettles at the base of Visoke, drifting slowly back towards the mountain. I located Uncle Bert and waited for the right opportunity to break out the camera. The morning was fine and warm: great columns of cumulus bulged overhead, helping to scatter the bright light and soften the dark shadows. Several times the silverback gave a contented growl, and from the responses I could roughly gauge the positions of others nearby. Flossie and Petula appeared on the trail behind, halting to contemplate the obstruction I formed. Clutching baby Cleo to her chest, Flossie pushed into the nettles and passed several feet away, but Petula merely sat to watch, her infant Augustus squeezing in by her side. I turned away, going through the motions of obtaining something to eat. Seconds later Petula moved; she came up and brushed past with only inches between us – and perhaps a suggestion of a spurt as she came abreast. Taken by surprise and elated by what was essentially the very first genuine show of complete trust from an adult female, I watched as she disappeared to follow Uncle Bert. Left in the lurch, Augustus made to follow, but was not so brave as his mother. With a worried whimper he diverted to pass quickly along the trail opened up by Flossie.

Following along the crushed pathway, I felt immensely pleased about Petula; she was the least shy of the three adult females, but the nonchalance with which she had passed so close was astounding – as was her lack of concern for the safety of Augustus. I crept on until a movement revealed a gorilla behind some leafy senecio plants. It was Digit, craning his neck to watch me pass. When I stopped and hunched down, he left his cover and strutted forward to a bright patch of sunlight. While I waited, trying to look deferential, he plucked at a few leaves, then calmly sat to face me. Back lighting outlined his head with a shiny halo of hair, producing an image that looked so good, I slid my pack forward and with great care began to set up. Digit followed every move. I avoided looking directly at him lest it break the spell and cause him to leave. When I rose slightly to look through the view-finder, for an instant he seemed poised to go – but the moment passed. Through the lens I saw him react to the first sight of his face reflected in the lens, then flinch as the camera whirred. Almost disbelieving what was happening, I watched him come hesitantly forward until it was no longer possible to keep him in focus. My gloves lay by the tripod and he reached out to pick one up. Slowly he raised it to his nose, backed away and sat down. Delicately turning the glove in long fingers he examined his prize, lifting it now and then to give a long sniff. It was impossible even to guess what the object meant to him, but he surely was aware it was shaped exactly like a hand. Apart from the smell of my sweat from the interior, he would have smelt the strong odour of the dubbin (leather soap) and boot polish I used to keep the heavily-used gloves supple and waterproof. He let the glove fall, then, with a playful head shake, pressed through the vegetation and disappeared.

The two very satisfactory events had already made my day, but there was much more to come. Following the trail again, I interrupted Tiger and Papoose at play on a fallen tree trunk a mere ten feet away. Barely acknowledging my appearance they resumed their grappling. Then Digit moved silently out of cover and sat to watch. The situation was unbelievable – the contact was already the best ever achieved – but for the moment there was no time to savour the pleasure of it. Old Goat's face appeared twenty feet up the slope, her expression showing anxiety, but the juveniles continued to play. Except for sly glances I was almost ignored. Digit, obviously feeling frisky himself, moved to join in and the three rapidly become almost indifferent to what I was doing.

Trying to avoid any move that might destroy the carefree mood, I struggled to film the wonderful scene, cursing each time a hundred-foot load of film ran out. Breathy pants and grunts came from the wrestling juveniles, and it was noticeable they were hesitant to grapple too strongly with Digit. Immersed in unconcerned play, Papoose and Tiger came tumbling towards me with a rush. Releasing her grip on Tiger, Papoose transferred her full attention to the camera. Slowly she came towards it until her face was eighteen inches from the lens. For a few seconds she eyed her reflection, then flung herself backwards to tussle with Tiger and drag him into a tangle of plants. Digit remained on his back, chewing on a branch and giving me a fine opportunity to film close-ups of his teeth and the damaged finger on his right hand. The rest of the family appeared to be making day nests at a slightly higher level, and Digit finally moved to join them. Still amazed by the wonderfully benign mood, I climbed carefully after him – but Uncle Bert spotted me. Giving a sharp bark, he added emphasis to his annoyance by thumping a fist on the ground. I had to settle for a position that gave only a view of Papoose, spreadeagled on her back across a scrappy ledge of foliage. Continuing the act to be like a gorilla, under her casual gaze I bent down foliage and constructed my own 'nest', then sat back in it to wait.

While the family rested, I went over the morning's events and wrote notes on my film cartons. Some fully relaxed play had taken place, at times only five feet away, with the participants practically ignoring the human right amongst them. Expectations that super-close contacts would seriously disrupt natural behaviour obviously needed revision – at least where juveniles were concerned. Adults were another matter, but on the results of this latest contact I realised I had underestimated their degree of tolerance.

Having just seen to the departure of Sandy Harcourt and Graeme Groom, Dian was now free of visitors and census students. I reckoned the time had come for her to join me on a few active approaches. If she could just experience a contact such as this one, see for herself that a few of the animals were responding with extraordinary placidity, I felt sure she would quickly change her old tactics. On the basis of just one superb contact it was perhaps early to expect too much, but time was passing and footage of Dian close to her subjects remained an urgent need.

Two more excellent days with Digit and the juveniles left me in no doubt that they had decided I could be approached with impunity: a low, deferential posture in their presence and care in keeping eye contact to a minimum was definitely giving them assurance. The more upright position required to operate the camera induced a little nervousness, but still, the swiftness with which most of their wariness had collapsed surprised me. Whether or not the adults could be persuaded I was harmless remained an open question.

Dian was enthused by my descriptions of what was happening, but partly because I discovered a group of ten strange gorillas high on Visoke, a full week passed before she joined me to sample the incredible situation. By then Group 4 had moved conveniently near to the camp, so close in fact that a mere twenty minutes of tracking brought us to the point where all fours came into play. The pair of us crawled along dew-soaked trails until we were very close to our quarry. Hardened by constant use in this method of locomotion, my knees no longer bothered me, but before we had covered fifty yards Dian complained hers were rapidly becoming tender. To show how little he reacted to being followed, I intended to keep going until Uncle Bert was sighted, but when we reached the edge of a ravine known as Skull Gully he had already disappeared over the edge. Listening to the sounds of heavy bodies forcing a way through thickets on the near-vertical descent, we halted to wait for developments.

When Tiger, Papoose and Simba appeared on the game trail along the lip of the ravine, I quickly positioned the camera, then Dian slid gingerly down towards them until I signalled she was in the frame. This was an action that would formerly have made the trio back away and hide, but this time, though irresolute, they held their ground. Lying low, Dian purposely placed a glove close to her legs. Curiosity aroused, Tiger strutted and posed, but Papoose moved up until she could bend to sniff the glove and then Dian's boot. Typically, Simba timidly held off to look on with suspicious eyes. Moments later the three backed off and went down into the ravine. Dian was thrilled by the brief encounter. By coincidence we were at the same spot where a year earlier I had first filmed Bravado coming close to her – the day we had agreed I should experiment with new habituation tactics. I was keen to find Digit, but the group remained firmly out of sight in the ravine. By midday the cloud base had dropped to envelop everything in cold fog. The combination of dull light and difficult positioning persuaded us it would be best to try again another time. At least I had been able to prove that relations with the juveniles had greatly improved.

Two days later, with Group 4 still foraging high above the cabins, we shared a fine contact that netted several hundred feet of valuable footage. This time the youngsters were more playful, tumbling about around two bare patches created by earth slides. Though Digit made several cautious appearances, he seemed to be suffering a slight return of shyness. During most of the period, Uncle Bert sat in a concealed position above us, monitoring what was going on but feeding all the while. Dian had to admit there was no evidence of undue stress in the group. As she could see, though less inhibited, the adults remained very much aware of their human observers. However, the ability to observe without having to resort so much to binoculars was a tremendous advantage. Doubts remained that the silverback and females would ever become as relaxed as the youngsters, but, having already been treated to a spontaneous walk-past by Petula, I felt sure it was only a matter of time.

A week later Dian joined me again and this time was able to experience the thrill of crawling a considerable distance practically in the midst of the family. During our initial approach, Uncle Bert responded to a faint chest beat from what could have been Rafiki. His deliberate, long move towards the sound gave me hope we might see an inter-group action. While the rest of the family kept up on close, parallel courses, we followed at a respectful distance. Unfortunately, after ambling forward for a while he seemed to give up and settled instead to feed. While we rested, Dian massaging sore knees, Digit's face appeared from behind a screen of foliage. He looked us over and moved on, but then suddenly reappeared with Papoose directly ahead. Dian hunched down and, hoping for a reaction, laid out her gloves. When nothing happened, she took a small mirror from her pack and set it in the foliage. This new object attracted Digit immediately. With Papoose following behind, he came forward to examine it, hesitating as he caught sight of his clear reflection. Bobbing his head to adjust the view, he was obviously nonplussed by a face that kept vanishing. Dian tossed him a piece of chocolate, which he picked up to smell but dropped quickly. He bent to sniff her gloves, then as if to release pent-up feelings, leaped away into the foliage below with a most satisfying crash.

Further contacts like this convinced Dian beyond all doubt that the youngsters had lost practically all shyness. But I knew they were still reacting to our combined presence, and I had not yet produced the calm encounters with the adults I most wanted to demonstrate. Dian admitted to feeling tense and uneasy while crawling so closely to the rear of Uncle Bert. She felt a little more proof that the adults were really as relaxed as I claimed would be welcome; only then would she feel comfortable about moving right in amongst them. As if to accentuate her point, I ran into trouble with Uncle Bert and was made to realise he was not to be trifled with; a few strained moments of danger forcefully brought home the need to pinpoint his position before interacting with the youngsters.

Ever since Mrs X had vanished in mid-June, her infant Simba had been taken care of by Uncle Bert. The silverback shared his nest with the diminutive orphan virtually every night. Throughout the day she followed in his shadow, withdrawn for the most part from the play periods between Tiger, Papoose and Augustus; even when she did get involved, she was not able to abandon herself to romp with the same enthusiasm as the others. Uncle Bert tolerated her close company, and many times during the day rest hours I watched him gently grooming her lustreless and unkempt fur.

Moving on a path below and parallel to the silverback one morning, I stopped at a gap that gave a clear view of Simba sitting on her own and feeding on a large stem of thistle. I had not seen Uncle Bert for a while and, giving no thought to his location, half stood to get the camera on a level with the orphan. Barely moments later, with a violent scream I had not head from him for over a year, Uncle Bert came at me, bursting out of a concealed position just yards above Simba. I dropped instinctively to the ground, an immediate chill flooding my veins and registering on the instant that momentum was certain to carry him right on top of me. But the expected impact never came. With a crashing thud his huge body landed close above my bowed head. Loose soil sprayed everywhere, followed in a split second by another high decibel scream, then a tremendous thump as a mighty fist smashed through the vegetation to dent the ground by my face.

Huddled on my knees, camera jammed painfully against a collarbone, I waited for agonised moments in expectation of a bite or at least the sort of blow I'd seen Uncle Bert deliver many times to unfortunates in his family. Nothing happened, nor did the silverback move from his position. Visions of the time old Rafiki had so thoroughly subdued me three years before flashed in my mind, but Rafiki had stopped his charge at some distance – where I could get a good look at him. Uncle Bert was inches away and I dared not move a muscle. For a good ten seconds the silence was complete – then the creak and scrape of crushed plants above my head told me he was backing off. When I lifted my head he was sitting where Simba had been, squatting with hands in lap like a benign Buddha, face bland and eyes devoid of any expression that betrayed the explosion of anger. He gave a loud 'contentment' growl that was answered immediately by the scattered members of his family – most of whom must have wondered what the outburst was all about. I felt thoroughly chastised. Anticipation of a mighty blow and maybe a bite from Uncle Bert had greatly affected my nervous system and took long minutes to wear off. There was no doubt the charge had been triggered by my standing up to get a shot of Simba; I had no idea the silverback was watching, but seeing me rise he had reacted instinctively to what he perceived as a threat to the infant. The rest of the day passed with the group behaving quite normally, Uncle Bert giving no indication whatsoever that the event had changed his attitude towards me. Later, when I saw him biting great chunks out of a rotten log, he allowed me to move in close and shoot film of the action, a nice sequence unfolding as Flossie came in after him to sample the same log, her daughter Cleo squashed uncomfortably against her chest as she bent to bite into the soft wood.

My description of the event produced a concerned 'I told you so' from Dian. But the fact the gorillas had later behaved normally encouraged me to believe their acceptance of a human in their midst was almost complete, and certainly, throughout October relations with the adults did improve very quickly. Uncle Bert and the two older females – Old Goat and Flossie – had by now watched many of the very close contacts with Digit and the juveniles. Old Goat remained vigilant and guarded, frowns and scowls directed at me giving her the distinctive look that had initially caused Dian to call her Sourpuss. But though her expressive face showed disapproval of what was going on, she no longer showed anxiety when her young son came close to me.

This last phase of the habituation process had become an especially exquisite experience. Repeated peaceful and close contacts were giving ample reward for all the long hours spent developing the friendly relations. Uncle Bert now permitted me to crawl behind him with a separation of only ten or twelve feet, his acceptance of this distance giving added confidence to Flossie and Old Goat. Although neither of the matrons would push by me on the same trail as Petula had done, they were relaxed enough to pass on parallel routes – where at times we could have reached through the undergrowth and touched one other.

My constant presence was generating a tentative familiarity, so that within a short time it became necessary to be more aware and respectful of the simple social rules the gorillas followed. To avoid inhibiting normal activities and disrupting the main focus of the family, when Uncle Bert ceased to react I gave up tailing him so persistently – either making my own path or following someone else. It was noticeable that by continuing to try to behave like a gorilla, I was becoming more directly included in their communication exchanges. As with humans, explicit body postures and movements and many distinct facial and eye expressions carried a wealth of meaning, and though limited, their eloquent range of vocalisations expressed fairly easily interpreted meanings. Whereas in earlier contacts too close an approach would displace the animals, they now tended to hold their ground, letting me know quite clearly with grunts or whacks at the foliage to stop where I was. Their faces were particularly expressive; by watching them, and especially the eyes, it was not difficult to assess intention and mood. The extended time on the assignment was leading to a very satisfactory situation, and the flow of film was pleasing everyone in Washington. I began to press Dian to give more time for the scenes to convey how she lived and worked, and more importantly, those that would cut in with the new sequences being shot amongst the gorillas.

Before long there would surely be more than enough close-up footage, but I still longed to show something of the more dramatic aspects of their behaviour. Since the confrontation between Rafiki and Uncle Bert three years earlier, no others like it had been witnessed, and events where females had transferred from one group to another had twice been missed. Although able to stay all day near the centre of Group 4, the vegetation still effectively shielded much of what went on. The fact that the group had so few adult members was a serious disadvantage too: a much larger family of twenty or more would have given many more opportunities to record finer details of behaviour. Now that the observation gap had been closed, it was obvious how the smaller number in Uncle Bert's family lessened the chances of seeing a full range of interactions. Since mid-1970, when I had first begun to operate on hands and knees, the group had lost four females and an infant, and possibly two newborn babies. The births of Augustus and Cleo had brought the number back to ten, but even with a score of gorillas in the family, when they were dispersed over an area of fifty or more square yards the luxuriant greenery kept at least half of them out of sight. Uncle Bert rarely saw his family together all at once, not even during the daily siesta periods or at the night-time sleeping sites. I may have reached the nucleus of the group, but I could see no more than the silverback. It was an unusual day that allowed more than five or six gorillas to be included in the same scene. Before long I knew I would have to transfer some attention to Group 5, where the presence of two silverbacks would surely give many interesting interactions. Drawing on experience gained during the penetration of Group 4, I knew I could shorten the habituation process.

During the last week of October, I left the mountains with Dian to buy fresh supplies and collect a shipment of urgently needed film stock. Such trips made a welcome break, but, having missed important events because of them, any period spent away from the gorillas brought on a touch of anxiety. When we returned, Basile, one of the newer camp assistants, reported that two groups were on the slopes above camp and not more than half a mile apart. Chest beating had been heard, so it was certain the groups were aware of each other. Thankful not to have missed anything, I kept in touch with Group 5, in the process discovering a new adult female with them. She had silver hairs on her neck and near her ears, as though frost had settled there, and promptly received the name 'Frosty'. Each day ended with a brief patrol to keep Uncle Bert located. With great satisfaction I monitored his slow move eastwards towards Group 5.

On 30 October, the two families finally faced each other across a gully no more than two hundred yards above the cabins. While Dian climbed to find a position near Group 5, I headed for my friends and crept about in a drawn-out, increasingly desperate search for a decent vantage point. But I was defeated by the configuration of the terrain, managing in the end to shoot only a few disjointed scenes. Beethoven appeared momentarily on a high bank and, in response to a hearty chest beat from an invisible Uncle Bert, he leaped off his perch and landed in the undergrowth with a huge crash. After this, Group 5 withdrew towards the east and Uncle Bert retired to the west. I had captured nothing of value from the rare meeting and Dian said she had been unable to see much from her position either.

But we need not have worried. Early in the morning welcome sounds of a silverback hooting and beating his chest carried down the mountain slopes, again directly above the cabins. Uncle Bert was challenging old Beethoven again, this time choosing a sharp ridge for his field of action. Although trees grew along the crest of the ridge, several gaps allowed reasonable visibility. At the first sighting only four or five gorillas were in view. Uncle Bert continued to beat his chest in regular and noisy exhibitions of power, eliciting occasional responses from Beethoven on the far side of the ridge. Hoping to get a good view of him, Dian had chosen to approach from the east again.

I remained to the west, where some seventy-five yards separated me from the gorillas, but before heading for a better position I hurriedly set up to film Uncle Bert in action. As the minutes passed, a small group collected at an open patch below the silverback and began interacting. I could see Digit, Papoose, Tiger and one other. They rolled about playfully in a manner that indicated something unusual was going on. I faced a dilemma: should I try to move closer and risk distracting the gorillas, or stay put? Close-up shots of a silverback in the full glory of his chest beating display would be spectacular – I felt sure of my ability to get in amongst Group 4 – but it would take many minutes to cross to the ridge, and once there I might not find a good position.

With the tripod fully extended I was having terrible trouble keeping the camera steady, but there was really no time to make a move. In spite of the distance, my most powerful tele-lens gave a reasonable picture. Binoculars brought into focus a familiar face: it was Bravado that Digit and Papoose were romping with! This was an extraordinary development. While I filmed the three taking obvious pleasure in their reunion, Uncle Bert rose to beat his chest, running several steps down the ridge path and scattering the play group. Bravado disappeared over the ridge, but soon reappeared to resume a lively caper with her relatives. When Uncle Bert returned, strutting stiffly up the path, Digit and Papoose and Bravado followed him. Here was clear evidence of a reverse transfer and I filmed the little gathering with acute satisfaction.

Now Beethoven appeared. He advanced slowly up the ridge, an imposing figure of strength and authority. Uncle Bert withdrew further, climbing slightly and leaving the cover of the trees. Digit, Bravado and Papoose followed him as I suffered the usual cameraman's nightmare – having to change film as the excitement mounted. Beethoven, trailed by a young blackback called Icarus, continued to move deliberately forward to where Uncle Bert had turned to face him, surrounded now by others of his family. Beethoven advanced until he reached the cowering Bravado – who made no attempt to get away. With head set at a defiant angle, Beethoven stretched out a shaggy arm and grabbed her, the action causing Uncle Bert to lunge forward as if to prevent the abduction. But he thought the better of it and subsided where he was. Beethoven literally plucked Bravado from her position, turned slowly and herded her down the ridge in front of him. Unmoving, Uncle Bert watched them go. Not until they were well away did he regain some of his former belligerence and began hooting and beating his chest once more. A truly valuable sequence of gorilla behaviour had unfolded in front of the camera, leaving me profoundly thankful I had held my position. From her position on the far side of the ridge Dian had not been able to see much and the last significant action had remained concealed from her. In a way, it was sad Bravado had failed to return to her former group – if indeed that had been her intention. She would have enlivened the family scene and provided a welcome playmate for the lonely Digit. I spent the whole of the next day shadowing Group 5, hoping for another interaction, but Beethoven moved steadily away to the east.

November arrived, bringing seasonal rains that lashed the volcanoes with increasing frequency. But no matter how much it rained or how often fog closed in, the sheer pleasure of being on such friendly terms with a few of the great apes was unbeatable. Continuing to act like a submissive pseudo-gorilla, I was now almost accepted as such – at least by the younger generation – who at times behaved much as though I were some strange overgrown juvenile who could be dominated. The lack of any aggressive actions or motions obviously helped build confidence that I was inoffensive. When the adults saw repeatedly that their youngsters came to no harm, they in turn gained confidence. Though I had become an acceptable and minor disruption in their daily wanderings, nevertheless the gorillas were fully aware I could dominate practically any situation by simply rising to my full height. Such an action during a close contact would cause extreme alarm and considerable fear, as I had found out once or twice when standing up to look around, unaware that a gorilla was very close. Following the incident with the glove, Digit had initiated several more approaches. Since he was the only subadult male in the group, and now without any family members of his own age, I undoubtedly added interest to his peripheral and somewhat lonesome existence. He had begun to make more purposeful moves to seek me out, often covering a good distance to do so.

Early in November I enjoyed yet another superb contact, and was allowed to sit within eight feet of Petula and Papoose as they fed, with Augustus playing all the while and eventually going to suckle from his mother. Later, Petula and Papoose indulged in some grooming, then prepared foliage beds and lay on them to doze. This was precisely the situation I had been after for so long – a peaceful view of daily life unspoiled by too much intervening foliage, the gorillas paying scant attention to their human observer. On this occasion, after a short rest Petula moved off, carrying Augustus away. She was replaced by Tiger, who enlivened the scene by enticing Papoose to some gentle wrestling. Later, attracted by the sounds of play and the noise of the camera, Digit appeared. When I turned to film him, Papoose moved in behind me. I felt truly in the middle of the family – virtually surrounded by gorillas. Uncle Bert squatted twenty feet away, able to see much of what was going on. Flossie came up and calmly viewed the human sitting between Digit and two juveniles. In the mellow atmosphere I soon exhausted my supply of film.

When the group began to feed again, I followed the silverback, crawling along in the usual fits and starts, pretending to be intent on filling my own stomach. Though little more than three yards separated us, Uncle Bert ignored me, casually turning his back as he selected plants to eat. The afternoon wore on and I held my position, shadowing Uncle Bert whenever he moved. When evening signalled time to leave, I lay back on the crushed foliage of his trail and watched him move on. Using the same easy path, Papoose and Digit approached me from behind. Cautiously, Papoose skirted my outstretched feet, smelling my boots as she passed. But Digit did not turn aside; he came on confidently, my prone position submissive enough to give him added courage. Halting at my legs he examined them, then reached out to touch my trousers and socks. It was the first physical contact between myself and a wild gorilla and the moment was exquisite. Carefully avoiding eye contact, we looked each other over. When he reached out to clasp the handle of the panga (machete) lying by my side, gently I pressed my glove against his hand to discourage him, but the touch had no effect. Harder pressure was resisted, then he let go and stepped over my legs. Swinging an arm to snatch a handful of foliage, he departed with a noisy rush.

Sure I would be touched at some stage, I had visualised it happening in different circumstances. Unexpectedly, the moment dreamed about had come and gone, leaving a feeling of elation and an urge to follow and see what else would happen. But the light was fading fast and discretion made me abandon the idea. There remained no doubt in my mind that I had been accepted as a tolerable invader by the group. Already a variety of scenes showing less inhibited behaviour had become possible, and more would surely follow. It was not feasible to expect that such extreme proximity contacts would ever allow an observer to be entirely forgotten, but I was more than happy to accept the constraints and be on favourable terms with the animals.

Day after day I tramped over the swampy meadow and climbed Visoke's steep sides. The gorillas reacted to my day-long company with growing indifference, soon permitting scenes to be filmed that made me wish I had an extreme wide-angle lens; in many situations I was almost too close and had to pan the camera to include all the participants. I had long been aware that in normal circumstances the infants and juveniles spent much time playing with each other, but now the play sessions increased in frequency and duration, many seemingly generated as a sort of displacement activity caused by my presence.

I began to see and film things I'd seldom seen before. Already I had caught gorillas drinking, now from a few feet away I saw them purposely selecting and eating tiny snails, chewing at the bracket fungus that sprouted from rotting tree trunks, and, astonishing to me at first, eating the occasional bolus of their own dung. This latter behaviour was intriguing. I observed it several times at resting or sleeping sites and wondered about the significance of the act. I knew nothing about gorillas' digestive systems; as herbivores they obviously carried micro-organisms in their guts that helped break down the cellulose, but I could not see where their occasional coprophagy fitted in. Perhaps to aid digestion the gorillas were instinctively reintroducing organisms expelled from their gut. Dian had reacted to my first report of the behaviour with anthropomorphic disgust, doubting what I had seen and suggesting it was perhaps a clump of soil being chewed for mineral content. But I was sure of my observation and had film to prove it.

By the end of November my flow of reports and descriptions of daily excitements had drawn Dian away from her paperwork several times. Although our combined presence still inhibited the gorillas a little, I had been able to film her near to the youngsters with increasing success. During one satisfying and remarkable contact, Digit came out of thick nettles and sat beside her, only three feet away. As she lay prone, delighted by his presence, he leaned over to touch and smell her clothing, then moved off through the narrow gap between us. But it was still proving difficult to get Dian in the same picture with Uncle Bert and the females. Although I sent her forward several times, she was not at all happy to press the silverback. Sensing her apprehension, or perhaps disliking two humans approaching, the silverback would grunt a warning and on occasion smash at the foliage to discourage her.

The latest footage was now drawing enthusiastic letters from Joanne Hess; in one she mentioned that everyone at *National Geographic* was delighted with recent progress, and felt certain there would soon be sufficient film to make a fine show. She went on to say that since each new shipment contained what she saw as fresh and marvellous material, she would leave it to me to make recommendations about how long the shooting should continue. She also passed on the news that Richard had been through Washington. He had been granted funds to mount a fifth season at Lake Turkana, and had asked if I could be made available to provide film coverage.

Once again the prospect of joining the Turkana expedition had come up, but having so recently made an extraordinary breakthrough in terms of relationships with the gorillas, this time the lure was not so great. If the television division decided to go ahead with a special there would be many fresh shooting requirements – and the need to add synchronised sound. There was a spanner in the works, however, in the shape of a *National Geographic* special called *Monkeys, Apes and Man*. Some of my gorilla footage had been utilised and I wondered how much the show had influenced production decisions. It had certainly already had a detrimental effect on Dian's second article. To help publicise *Monkeys, Apes and Man*, which had been aired on 12 October, her article had been brought forward to appear in the October issue of the magazine. But to get it slotted in, some drastic shortening had been necessary. To Dian and me this had been a great disappointment. Only ten of my pictures had been used, among them three of the important touch contact with Peanuts. We consoled ourselves with the thought that the most recent and future results would surely convince the editors to go for a third article. Looking ahead, I could see that some really spectacular stills and cine would be needed to keep the assignment going through 1972.

By applying the correct etiquette, it was now possible for me to make a nearly direct approach to everyone in Group 4 – except Old Goat. The old lady tolerated me, but always with an air of distrust. Incredibly, if conditions were right, the silverback would allow me to set up the camera only six or seven feet away. Though his eyes constantly sought me out at this distance, they betrayed little emotion. Several times he had even made up his daybed and gone to sleep at the same distance. His passive acceptance of me so close continued to work wonders with the disposition of the rest of the animals. Almost daily now, I could crawl in to sit at the edge of the central part of the midday rest sites, only dark clouds and rainy weather spoiling the wonderful situation.

It had become a regular feature of contacts to find Digit at the rear of the family, apparently waiting for me, knowing I would appear after the sleeping site had been vacated. If he was not feeding it was permissible to crawl within touching distance. He would sit for a while, eyes and face devoid of expression, as if contemplating what he should do about this human who acted like a gorilla. I wished I could communicate with more than simple body language and the 'contentment' rumble, to read what went on in his mind and better convey my peaceful intentions. If he was eating, the situation was very different and then it was necessary to stay at a respectful distance. He would not hesitate to grunt an objection if the space between us was too short. I continued my practice to locate Uncle Bert each morning, letting events develop from there. While the animals fanned out for their intensive early feeding, there were few opportunities to shoot much that was unusual. But as hunger was satisfied the level of social activity quickly increased. Mothers would sit and groom themselves and their infants; bouts of active play would begin between the juveniles and infants. The approach of noon brought on a tendency for the females to collect nearer to their leader, and for me the most valuable period of the day began. Combined with the moves of the females, the romping, wrestling games of the youngsters helped depress the vegetation. Then the further bending and breaking of foliage to make comfortable beds gave even better visibility. Digit sometimes appeared at this focal point, but though interested in whatever play group had developed, he was put off by the proximity of the silverback and adult females. He would position himself nearby and watch, sometimes flopping on his back, rolling his head from side to side and spreading his arms wide as if inviting someone to take notice.

Tiger and Papoose often made moves to visit my position, and if I was prone on the foliage, would sniff my boots or trousers. If Digit was able to see this, it would encourage him to do the same. Unlike the two juveniles, however, he had become more daring, using his fingers to investigate shiny bootlace eyes and hooks, and feel my trousers, gloves and coat sleeves. One day he pushed his investigations much further, generating for me a few sublime moments. Having sniffed my boots, he went down on his elbows to delicately probe the gap between my glove and coat sleeve where my wrist was exposed. With acute pleasure, I watched the long black nail on his forefinger scratch my skin and hook briefly under the edge of my watch. He leaned over to smell my jacket, then lifted his face to mine and sniffed it. I could hear the slow, deep intakes of breath through his nose and felt the feathery touch of the long hairs of his sideburns against my cheek. Although I had now been touched many times, never had I even dreamed of a face-to-face contact. The action was a total surprise; I kept my eyes down, watching the top of his great flat nose until he withdrew it. Papoose and Tiger sat together nearby as if entranced, their eyes taking in the scene with deep interest. When he raised himself off his elbows and squatted beside me, they broke their concentration to grapple and tumble away. Digit's forearm lay next to my hand, and with the utmost care I stretched out a finger and touched the long hairs that covered it. He tolerated this for a few seconds, then, as if embarrassed, rolled on to his back, shaking his head and beating his chest with soft resonant thumps.

We were in the woodland west of Visoke, one of the more difficult places for good light because of the thicker stands of hagenia trees. Overcast skies dulled the conditions further, but all the movement and play had broken down sufficient foliage for a good view of Uncle Bert. I lay close to the edge of the rest site and ran through several rolls of film, sorry that Dian was not present to share the unconstrained mood of the youngsters. She would have been part of this whole fabulous sequence of events, but instead had been obliged to remain in camp to have discussions with Alan Goodall.

Intent on renegotiating his future association with Dian, Alan had arrived the previous evening. Dian had wanted me to be present while she talked with Alan, but I declined to get involved in what was a delicate situation and not really my business. I took Alan down to Ruhengeri the next day, but he was not a happy man. Dian had not been prepared to let him return to operate from the Visoke base; she had offered instead to set him up in his own camp at the Ngezi waterhole, a position that would give him access to four gorilla groups and several loners: some forty-five animals, all recently located and counted by Alyette de Munck and Sandy Harcourt. A letter of agreement had been drawn up so that there would be no doubt about Alan's role in the project, but he was not at all pleased with the restrictive terms that it laid out.

Dian was thoroughly put out by what had amounted to a day-long confrontation with Alan, and particularly upset at missing the contact with Group 4. But then a meeting with them a day later almost equalled what she had missed. We discovered the family had moved back on to Visoke. They had travelled in a small loop and when we arrived were already at rest right next to their sleeping site. To show off Digit's amazingly friendly attitude, I crawled ahead as soon as he was sighted. My slow approach and the sight of Dian seemed to make him impatient. He got up to strut towards us until he faced me on the trail. Then self-consciousness appeared to displace his truculent mood. He retreated to squat behind cover, but allowed me to move up and stay by his leg. When I felt his hand touch my beret, I reached out to press a glove to his thigh and make grooming motions with my fingers.

Down a tunnel of crushed vegetation ahead, Old Goat and her son Tiger watched with studied interest. A cloudy but bright sky gave good light for filming, so I backed away to unpack cameras and let Dian move ahead. Old Goat and Tiger stared intently as she crawled forward, but Digit rolled on his back and out of view. Dian took out her notebook, also a small piece of sugar cane to place where it could be seen, whereupon Digit's curiosity immediately got the better of him. Making a direct approach, he picked it up and put it to his nose, but set it down with little interest and backed away. Dian had brought the cane with the express intention of using it to elicit a response, but as with all other previous offers of foreign food, the piece apparently held no particular attraction for Digit.

Now the light faded and it began to drizzle. Old Goat and her son stayed in front of Dian, watching her put on her rain gear. From our position high above the saddle I could see a great front of white cloud moving in from the Bishitsi bluff: like a vast tidal wave of cotton wool it rolled ponderously across the forest towards us. I filmed the scene, continuing until the mist swirled about us and blotted out all but the nearest objects. Old Goat and Tiger disappeared behind the white veil, and I ended the sequence with Dian preparing to leave. The tide of moisture had shown beautifully how observations were frequently shut down by fog or rain, adding yet another visually valuable segment to the coverage.

When the time came for me to return to Kenya for Christmas, though utterly captivated by the friendly interactions with Group 4, I was not sorry to be giving up the daily slog to find them. The wet weather had continued without break and I looked forward to a change. For what would be my last meeting with the family for at least six weeks, I made a special effort to get out early and was soon reaping the benefit of a calm mood. I spent many hours close to Digit, and was permitted for a few satisfying moments during the rest period to groom his leg. Later, Petula allowed me to place the camera a bare six feet from her daybed to capture some fine scenes of Augustus suckling as he was being groomed. At such short range it was possible to see every detail: superb, close-up shots of everything from eyes to hands and probing fingers punctuated the footage. The very satisfying session ended with an intimidating demonstration of Uncle Bert's enormous physical strength – a reminder that if ever I had the misfortune to tangle with him I would be as helpless as a kitten in his powerful hands. When I backed away from Petula and prepared to leave, Uncle Bert chose the same moment to make his own exit from the area. He moved below me – an arm's length from my outstretched feet – stopping to look up with eyes wide in an almost challenging glare. In his path stood a big vernonia tree. With deliberate, almost menacing slowness, he rose to full height to take hold of a thick branch and snapped it away from the trunk as though it were a twig. The whole tree lurched and the branch split away to fall heavily across my legs. To accentuate this alarming gesture of strength, he pressed down hard on it with both hands, momentarily pinning my feet. Then with a quick spurt, he climbed over to snatch another weighty branch from the far side of the tree, wrenching it off with a loud crack and dragging it noisily away for several yards. Flossie, Petula, Papoose and Simba paraded past in his wake, their nerves apparently frayed like mine for they hastened on their way with undignified alacrity.

Though the rush of footage taken at such short range had taken Joanne by surprise, I knew we were on the threshold of new excitements. It was high time to think objectively and make decisions about the coming year. Dian needed no further proof that I had not stressed the animals and both of us were excited by the possibilities opening up. We tried to look into the future, but could not begin to guess what decisions would be made in Washington when requirements for a lecture film had been satisfied. It seemed obvious a television show should come next, and hopefully a third article in the magazine – better still, a whole book. I was particularly pleased that Joanne had left it to me to recommend how long I should continue filming. There could be no denying that the new tactics had paid off handsomely. I was at the brink of a whole new range of filming opportunities, but how much longer I should carry on was difficult to judge. There remained the important task of getting Dian more strongly and comfortably into the picture – right amongst the gorillas. I also needed more footage of her activities and work at camp – and to add synchronised sound. After that photographic coverage would surely and quite quickly reach the stage where scenes of fresh, interesting action would become increasingly rare. In terms of pure research on behaviour, however, the situation had opened up a whole new field for Dian. If the *Geographic* remained happy to continue funding my work, we agreed I should not suggest a cut-off date until I had exploited the full value of the intimate contacts, perhaps six or seven months ahead. Dian intended to go to America in the fall of 1972, and would be able to view the material then. She felt I could and should continue, at least until that time, and suggested I plan to accompany her and help edit the lecture film. After three years, the work to be done had increased rather than diminished; the end of the assignment was not yet in sight.

As had happened so often in the past, within a week of my return home I was photographing some of Richard's hominid specimens. Then came another small assignment that added more interest to fossil matters. I was asked to record an unusual meeting at the Nairobi Museum: Professor Raymond Dart and his wife were stopping over for a brief stay in Kenya's capital and had been invited to visit the museum. Raymond Dart had not been to Kenya since 1960, at which time he had made a special journey to Tanzania to visit Olduvai Gorge and see the work in progress at the 'Zinj' excavation site, also to discuss a newly discovered skull. Much had happened since then, so Louis and Richard prepared to impress him with the numerous and spectacular finds from Lake Turkana's dusty shores.

Still spry in spite of his age, Raymond Dart was led into a small room at the museum. Sharp interest and pleasure registered on his face as he examined and discussed the display of hominid fossils. Louis beamed with gratification, launching into a long and animated conversation with the professor. Listening as best I could and wanting to pay closer attention to what was being said, I was obliged to concentrate on the photography. Used to long months of lonely work with gorillas, and in particular avoiding any disturbance, while capturing this rare meeting I felt the strong return of my aversion to photographing humans: a feeling verging on distaste for the intrusion I caused with cameras, lights and strobe flashes. My present subjects were thoroughly used to having lenses thrust at them, but the need to take multiple shots from all angles lengthened the photo session, until I began to feel familiar vibes of irritation and annoyance. I was also slowly becoming aware that the extended periods of work in the Virunga mountains were having an odd effect on my ability to converse freely. I found myself remaining quiet more frequently and prompted to speak out only when there was something of value to say. I found some difficulty recalling words I wanted quickly. From lack of use, my powers of speech appeared to be turning distinctly rusty!

Richard was soon to fly to Washington and told me he had already made a formal request for me to be made available. Far removed from the excitements of insinuating myself amongst mountain gorillas, I began to consider the possibility of a change more seriously. Thin from seven months of climbing and crawling over Mount Visoke, my skin again pale from lack of sunshine, this latest opportunity to follow the palaeontologists became irresistible. The fifth Lake Turkana expedition would not begin until the middle of 1972 – which left at least five or six months for gorilla coverage; time enough I knew to finish the lecture film, but not the show I envisaged for television. Fortunately, the timing of the expedition would not intrude on the tentative plans Dian and I had already discussed. I was pleased that for the first time a commitment to two assignments was going to work out well. The Christmas season passed pleasantly and the new year brought the usual burst of activity to make ready for another sojourn at the Visoke camp. Dian had forwarded all my mail and I was happy to learn from Joanne that she had completed another round of discussions on Lake Turkana matters. I could consider the assignment as definite – provided Dian and I agreed the gorilla requirements could be wrapped up in time.

To add pressure to my preparations, both Mary Leakey and Richard made new requests for pictures. Richard needed another series of photographs of his hominid specimens, but Mary had a more complicated task. She was in the process of uncovering some extraordinary features preserved in a prehistoric land surface at Olduvai George. She had identified four strange, bowl-like depressions that looked very much as though they had been made by hand, and if that were so, it meant they were the work of hominids or early *Homo* species. Louis badly wanted to see what she had found, and with enthusiastic speculation about the value of the discovery, easily persuaded me to charter an aircraft without delay.

It was always a pleasure to fly to Olduvai. The journey of one hundred and fifty miles crossed the Great Rift Valley at one of its most fascinating and dramatic sections. Our flight on this morning was no exception. We took off on a brilliant morning with extraordinary visibility. Snow-capped Kilimanjaro sat on the limit of the southern horizon, as always looking almost unreal and out of place in the African environment. Looking at the snowcap on the huge volcano, I thought it was no wonder the explorers who first reported it were disbelieved and laughed at. The Ngong Hills – made famous by Karen Blixen's book, *Out of Africa* – drifted past on our right, their softly rounded peaks diminished by the height of the aircraft. Then the spectacle of the Great Rift appeared as we cleared the eastern escarpment. In the early, slanting light, dark shadows accentuated the huge parallel cliffs of basalt that marked massive fault lines. Ancient, eroded volcanoes littered the semi-arid landscape, and on a smaller scale, many tiny, irregular circles defined the places where Maasai nomads had constructed their temporary settlements. Louis had explored this harsh country decades ago, and even now his eyes probed the details on the ground as if to discover something new. It was sad to know that he would never again be able to roam freely to hunt for fossils. The previous year had been a very difficult one for him; although he had recovered remarkably well from the operation to remove the blood clots from his brain, his hip continued to bother him and made walking painful.

We flew on in air slowly becoming turbulent as twisting thermals built up from the rising heat. The pink and white soda flats of Lake Magadi stood out with exceptional clarity, a plume of white dust locating the factory that day and night refined the endless supply of soda. Beyond the domed peak of Mount Shombole, Lake Natron glowed in the slanted sunlight, its dark surface covered with immense slabs of orange and pink soda that looked like coloured ice floes on a purple-black sea. Mount Gelai – huge and forbiddingly dark – crowded the eastern shore. At the southern tip of the lake, Ol Doinyo Lengai (the mountain of god), floated in the increasing heat shimmer, its steep flanks still streaked with grey-white ash from the last eruption. As we passed over the fan of green acacia outlining the delta of the Peninj River, my eyes were drawn to the patch of eroded sediments where the first assignment for *National Geographic* had locked me into the Leakey family activities. Our plane cleared the western wall of the Rift, revealing baking plains of yellowed grass leading on past the massive horst that supported a cluster of extinct volcanoes, among them the huge and famous caldera of Ngorongoro. On our right Louis pointed out several distinct parallel lines that cut across the plains to the west. Shouting above the roar of the engine, he explained how winds had created several dunes of heavy black sand. Over the ages these individual dunes had shifted imperceptibly under the thrust of the prevailing wind, leaving behind clearly visible traces of their slow progress. Still moving inch by inch as the years went by, three of these crescent-shaped dunes still existed close to the Olduvai camp. Minutes later we began to descend towards the slash in the earth that was Olduvai Gorge. I picked out the grove of acacia trees where I had camped with a large American television unit five years before. The unit had been part of an ABC television team making an unprecedented four-hour programme about Africa. Although fully occupied with other clients, Richard had landed the contract to organise their safari camps, then, with the promise of possible wildlife filming opportunities, had persuaded me to take over the whole operation. With only eleven days at our disposal, Heather and I had had to purchase from scratch literally everything required for the safari – from tents and camping equipment right through to the truck to carry it all. Looking at the grove that had shaded the last and most successful camp, with a shiver I remembered the disastrous accident with the truck at the start of the safari that had very nearly brought financial ruin to Richard's small company. The eventual success of the safari operation had indeed generated a wonderful assignment for ABC television. After several months of independent wildlife filming for them, followed by more work for *National Geographic* on Leakey expeditions, I had moved away from the rapidly declining fortunes of Armand Denis Productions to a new, freelance existence.

Sweeping on along the length of the famous gorge, we turned into wind to touch down on a new airstrip, coming to a stop a few hundred yards from Louis and Mary's permanent camp. Mary drove us to the site to see her 'pits', as she called them, and there could be no doubt the curious ridges in them did look as though they had been made by fingers. I was amazed that Mary had been able to detect there were shallow pits in the earth her men were excavating. She explained how she had noticed a slight circular colour difference as her men dug down layer by layer, hunting for artefacts and fossils associated with a previous find. With her keen archaeologist's curiosity aroused, she had carefully excavated the circles to reveal the depressions with the enigmatic marks.

The ancient land surface matching these pits had been shaved away, but in the next section her men were now digging with extreme care to expose the true level. She had high hopes of finding more evidence to decipher the meaning of the four pits, there being an exciting possibility that much more than fingermarks would come to light. Mary could not know it then, but over the next six months a complex of very odd features would be revealed; they would defy any conclusive logical explanation – and give me some photographic headaches as well.

In the Family Circle

On 20 January the familiar contours of Mount Visoke stood in front of me once more. I followed my porters up the access path, listening to their idle chatter and looking over the verdant foliage for signs of gorillas. After six weeks at lower altitudes the too swift climb produced familiar sensations of lead in the legs, but failed to dampen the pleasant anticipation of new meetings with the great apes. There was no doubt the year ahead was going to be unusually interesting. The allure of gorilla watching was as strong as ever and I was keen to get to work.

Dian welcomed me with lively affection and enthused over the things I had brought for her from Nairobi: mainly small luxury items unobtainable in Rwanda, but also two smaller replicas of the stove that was working so successfully in my cabin. But that evening, while enjoying one of the few meals we took together, discussing her recent experiences with the gorillas and my break in Kenya, Dian's voice took on a brittle edge that betrayed some inner tension. I could not decide if I was mistaken and ignored the warning sign.

I was anxious to see if the gorillas had changed their attitude towards me in any way, but on that score at least there was no cause for worry. At the very first meeting my reappearance provoked an intense, almost welcoming show that was very reassuring. I was examined by frank, open looks that made me feel a genuine warmth for my friends. It was a very satisfactory start, but I succeeded in making only one more contact before it became necessary to leave camp and go to Kigali. A new government directive required all foreigners to report immediately to the immigration department in the capital and register as foreign residents; Dian also needed to meet Stewart Halpern, a young man on his way to study chimpanzees with Jane Goodall and taking the opportunity to see gorillas first.

On the long and rough road to Kigali, in an almost casual way, Dian hinted that she had heard I might be taking up a new assignment with Richard Leakey! At last I had a clue to the subtle shift in her demeanour. My premonition that something was bothering her proved to be only too correct. She refused to reveal her source of information and very soon we became involved in heated argument. Dian was not only upset that I had even considered rejoining Richard, but seemed convinced that such a plan would bring an end to my association with her gorilla research. While I tried to concentrate on the hazards of the narrow, rutted road, she insisted she would be the one to make final judgements on a halt to gorilla work in favour of Lake Turkana. I could not persuade her that plans were not fixed, and some acrimonious exchanges between us did not resolve the issue. I knew Dian hated the idea of my going to work with Richard again, and I tried to make amends by promising I would not go if she felt so strongly about it.

Though we had discussed plans for 1972 in December, I had purposely avoided any mention of Richard's early request to have me rejoin his team. Before leaving for home I had written to Joanne Hess to say that a new spell of work with Richard was a very pleasant prospect, but acknowledged the gorillas still took precedence. Joanne had responded by saying that I could count the change of assignment as definite – if both Dian and I agreed the gorilla work could be wrapped up in time. Whatever was to happen after the Turkana season ended was still very much reliant on interest from the TV division. Expecting to exploit the ability to work right amongst the gorillas as long as possible, I was already close to acquiring some very expensive equipment: a silent Eclair 16 mm camera and a Nagra tape recorder that would set me up for synchronised sound. Knowing I could produce material that would eclipse all the previous footage I felt it would be easy to persuade the powers at *National Geographic* to fund a final spell of filming.

Racking my brains to try to think who might have told Dian I had a yen to go fossil hunting again, wishing I had broached the subject earlier at a moment of my own choosing, I was now forced to add fuel to her unhappiness by telling her that the Duke of Edinburgh was passing through Kenya at the end of March. Richard had invited him to visit Lake Turkana, and had asked Heather and myself if we would help to entertain him. As accepting this invitation would commit me to a minimum twenty-day absence from the volcanoes, I had said I could not go unless *National Geographic* gave their consent. This news did not help matters at all and the trip off the mountain was not a happy one

As February began I felt thoroughly frustrated. Days taken to help Dian entertain Stewart Halpern and show him the gorillas had prevented any serious filming. Then an urgently needed shipment of film stock went astray, and to cap everything the good weather normally expected for January and February failed to materialise. For one reason or another much of my time had been spent off the mountain. I managed to shoot a few good scenes of Dian near the gorillas, and some disjointed though useful footage of her shopping at the lakeside market in Gisenyi. Days were slipping away rapidly, and even if the break to meet Prince Philip were approved, I felt it would be unreasonable to take time off without first securing some really significant material. Group 4 had left the slopes of Visoke to go wandering again in the saddle area. As always when in this region, Uncle Bert had became more nervous and wary. Though reflecting his mood a little, fortunately the rest of the family remained unaffected.

10 February came in on a dawn dulled by heavy overcast. I had arranged to go out on my own and the dark morning did nothing to lift a cheerless frame of mind. By the time I was ready to move out, a cold drizzle was wetting the

foliage. Skirting to the west of the waterlogged meadow, I headed towards Mikeno. Soon I regretted the choice of path; it was overgrown from lack of use and sagging vegetation thoroughly wetted my already damp clothing. The previous day had been given over entirely to help Dian deal with a notorious poacher called Munyarukiko. Captured by park guards operating near Mount Gahinga, the man had been marched all the way to the Visoke camp, the guards knowing they would be well rewarded by 'Mademoiselle' for his capture. I had helped take the man to Ruhengeri to be formally charged and jailed. Now I would have to spend additional time following up Group 4's trails from the last point of contact.

I sliced and shouldered my way uncomfortably through the overhanging foliage towards Kalele Hill, pausing now and then to listen for any give-away sounds that would allow me to dispense with the tracking. But the forest remained obstinately quiet, forcing me to walk on until I reached the last contact area and could follow trails to a sleeping site. A hasty bed count and examination of the dung confirmed ten individuals had slept there. I pushed on quickly, one more day rest and a sleeping site to find before the tracks would take me to the group. But my luck was out: within minutes I was into a truncated valley where the fresh spoor of many buffalo had all but obliterated the signs left by gorillas. Trying to apply a little logic to guess the direction the group had taken, concentrating on finding evidence of gorilla under that of buffalo, I neglected to pay full attention to my immediate surroundings. Head down and eyeing the ground for a tell-tale knuckle or footprint, I was brought to full heart-stopping alert by several explosive snorts. Beautifully merged with the dark-green of the tall foliage, several unseen buffalo sprang to life. They crashed past with a burst of noise that shattered the stillness – one missing me by a few feet and leaving my body alive with jangling nerves. It was sobering to realise the buffalo must have listened to my approach and subsequent manoeuvrings for minutes; they had remained quiet and perfectly motionless until I was almost on top of them. I had been very lucky so far to avoid any serious confrontations with buffalo. When I took to crawling around, occasionally crossing fresh buffalo tracks, I often wondered if it would be my bad luck to surprise one. Would it attack rather than retreat if it saw a human on hands and knees a few feet away? I fervently hoped there would be no occasion to discover the answer. The buffalo had browsed and trampled a wide area. Not until I made an extended circuit did the gorilla trails show again. By this time I was in a sour mood and the dripping thickets seemed to hinder me more strongly than usual. Group 4 had wandered aimlessly, leaving a mess of criss-crossing and dead-end paths that taxed my patience. In the end I found the family at the base of Poacher's Hill – only a short distance from where I had paused to listen an hour earlier.

I crawled amongst the scattered gorillas, seeing little of them in a luxuriant stand of nettles. Then I found Digit; he was sitting calmly on a roughly prepared bed of nettles, relaxed and ready for an hour or two of rest. He remained motionless as I edged towards him, his expressive eyes watching while I constructed my own nest and prepared to wait out the rest period. Trying to avoid the predominant nettles, I used the activity to move closer to him. By the time my bed was complete we were a mere two feet apart. Watching me fiddle with my pack and cameras, he reached out for a glove, smelling it as always, then put it down and gently fingered a frayed edge on my coat. He touched my corduroy trousers, picking delicately at the narrow ridges with his nails. He could not possibly know the feelings of delight he generated by doing all this. Again I wished I had the ability to read what mental processes went on in his head. When he let his hand fall away I retrieved my glove, putting it on under his intent gaze. I touched his forearm, parting the long hairs and scratching his skin in a grooming motion. For a few seconds he remained still, then, with a big sigh and playful head shake, turned and collapsed on his side. I leaned on my elbows and looked at his broad back – inches from my nose. The hair was much shorter than on his arms and tinged reddish at the ends. I could not resist parting them with my fingers, but my touch was too light, or unwelcome, and he sat up. For the next hour we rested side by side, seemingly alone in the forest, though I knew nine other quietly dozing gorillas were dispersed all around us.

The clouds above the trees began to thicken as noon passed. Squatting on my bed, clothing wet but body warm, I waited for the group to stir and start their afternoon feed. My depressed mood of the morning had lifted. I felt uncommonly pleased with the way Digit had behaved so far; this was one of the few times he had not put some extra feet between us before settling down, and in some respects our tentative interactions had surpassed some of those that had taken place before.

I must have nodded off for a few moments; the next thing I knew the faces of Papoose and Tiger were peering at me. Digit eyed the pair for a while, then went forward to grapple gently with Tiger. Papoose joined in half-heartedly and between them they broke down sufficient foliage to allow me a better view. The light was terrible, but I shot some stills before the trio tumbled out of sight. With heavy cloud dimming the light further I did not bother to follow. Lying comfortably on my stomach, I listened for others in the group, tracking movements with my ears as they stirred and pushed through the undergrowth. I wrote up brief caption notes on my pad, packed things away and began to think of the shortest route home.

Then the wind strengthened and drowned out the indistinct sounds of movement. On an impulse I decided to crawl along the trail left by Digit and his playmates: I had not seen Uncle Bert and wanted to find out where he was and determine what direction he might be taking. Seeing a dark shape move through the foliage on my left, I waited a moment. Petula ambled by on my right, followed by Flossie with baby Cleo perched precariously on her shoulder. Neither did more than glance my way. It was satisfying to see their eyes merely acknowledged me with no trace of worry. Then the shadow on the left made a move, catching me unawares. It was Digit! Pounding his chest with two resounding double thumps, with a quick rush he landed heavily on his forearms across my back. His action brought on a flush of pure pleasure, beyond description. We had touched each other many times, questing, hesitant and careful touches, but nothing like this, a hearty, unconcerned display of pure confidence, and what I immediately interpreted as an invitation to engage in play. His arms continued to press down as he supported the full weight of his upper body on my back. He swayed gently and I felt his fingers start fiddling with the collar of my jacket and then the hair on the back of my neck. When I responded with my best rendition of the 'contentment' growl, he patted my back, pounded my shoulder with his fist and rolled away on to his back. He looked up at me calmly, then extended a long arm across the gap between us.

The invitation to continue the playful moment seemed very clear, but I could not bring myself to test his innocent acceptance of myself as a playmate. This wild gorilla had suddenly abandoned caution and tentative physical contact and decided I could be trusted to accept a more vigorous approach. I could hardly believe it and remained immobile, literally spellbound by the implications of his action. When I failed to react, Digit playfully shook his head, rolled on to his feet and made a jaunty rush into the concealing foliage.

With the pleasure gained from earlier hours with Digit immeasurably reinforced by his last act of the day, I walked home that evening along muddy game trails, hardly noticing the squalls of rain riding in on winds from the east. Although the simple encounter was followed by others even more astonishing, it would remain the most memorable of all my experiences with the gorillas. I desperately wanted to return early the next morning to see if the blackback would retain his brash confidence, but I was committed to going with Dian to Ruhengeri to meet Dr Bernard Grzimek of Frankfurt Zoo and two other influential officials from the International Union for the Conservation of Nature.

Seven days passed before I caught up with Group 4 again. Though I searched the broad woodlands of the saddle between Visoke, Karisimbi and Mikeno and saw plenty of gorilla signs, the presence of many small herds of buffalo and a lone elephant helped to scramble the evidence. Rain had fallen daily, heavy rain that kept the soil and vegetation saturated, softening and obliterating the signs left on the main game paths and making tracking more difficult. Somehow, in spite of hours of work, fresh trails were missed and the gorillas eluded detection. I sent Nemeye to look over the slopes of Visoke but he could find nothing positive there either.

On 17 February, I moved out with a light pack, renewed despondency brought on by so many unsuccessful filming days weighing heavily. Unresolved plans for the future added to the load, and the continuing wet conditions were doing nothing to help. I trudged out past Poacher's Hill, then on to Kalele Hill, determined to ignore old spoor and hunt for something really fresh. Half an hour spent listening intently from the edge of Kalele Hill produced one brief moment of hope, but the sound of tearing foliage from under the tree canopy ahead was followed by a throaty bellow from a buffalo. Following the easier paths, I headed north-west towards the Bishitsi bluff, watching the ground and greenery for evidence of gorillas. When at last a beautiful knuckle print showed at my feet, sunlight was dancing through small breaks in the clouds.

The deep knuckle indentations held water from the rain of the previous day; a large gorilla had crossed the track, leaving a tell-tale swath of crushed plants to show it was moving east towards Visoke. The wet conditions had allowed the damaged foliage to wilt at a much slower rate, making it difficult to assess the true age of the track, but I pursued it anyway. It led me to three fresh nightbeds: one obviously that of a large silverback. As usual, the prospect of encountering gorillas that could be strangers quickened the blood and displaced any extraneous thoughts. Quietly, I followed the silverback's trail, the degree of dung-fly activity on fresh droppings giving clues that he was now very close. When a thumping chest beat told me my approach had been detected, and my low-key reply produced no adverse response, I dropped to all fours to complete the contact. I need not have bothered; seconds later the quiet shifting of foliage made it clear the gorilla was coming back along its own trail. Adrenalin flowed. The meeting was going to be too sudden and too close. Feeling stupid for using the wrong tactics on a strange animal, I felt trapped and vulnerable. Then the unmistakable head and shoulders of Rafiki materialised. Here was an old friend and a flood of relief replaced the nervous tension in my body.

The old gorilla halted ten feet away to give a long bland stare. My lowly, hunched-down position gave almost the same perspective as the day he had crashed to a halt in front of me nearly three and a half years earlier. He looked as regal as ever, his great sagittal crest if anything even more pronounced. While I kept my glances careful and discreet, he dropped his head and seemed to be contemplating the ground at his feet. He turned away, and in the angled light all the hair on his massive shoulders and broad back glowed a silvery white. I followed slowly in his wake, catching sight of Macho, the female stolen from Group 4, and finally Peanuts. It was sad to see that Peanuts had not fully recovered from the injury inflicted in June the previous year. His face was still a little swollen and his right eye was discharging some pale mucus. Rafiki continued on his way without pausing, turning to head north and soon followed by his two companions. I let them go, wondering where Geezer had gone and where Pug, Samson and Maisie might be. I still entertained hopes of seeing further group interactions, but for the present made few attempts to follow the fortunes of the other families; that effort could come later. I did regret so little was known about the activities of Group 8. Samson seemed to have made a permanent split, keeping the young female Maisie to himself, but nothing had been seen of Pug – and now apparently

Geezer had moved off as well.

A slow traverse of Visoke's western base brought me by pure luck to the gaunt remains of a dead hagenia tree, one of the many reference landmarks used to pinpoint locations. Close by the tree were seven day-old nightbeds and only twenty-eight hours of Group 4 wanderings remained to be traced. I followed the broken channels, groaning inwardly as they took me down into the nettle zone, past a waterhole on the main game trail and back towards Karisimbi. Widely spaced beds marked where they had last spent the night. A scant fifty yards further on, Kalele Hill almost in sight, I crawled in amongst my long-lost quarry. Outward bound I had missed them by a few hundred yards, and now, four hours later, was treated to a nonchalant welcome and a prolonged contact that wiped away all the disappointments of the past few days.

It was siesta time, but many of the gorillas were feeding still on a plentiful supply of *galium* vine. I could find no core to the group. Uncle Bert sat on his own with only Old Goat nearby. Clouds were thinning, opening and closing on patches of blue. Momentarily I regretted having left my cine-camera behind, but it was high time more stills were added to the record of the increasingly friendly contacts. I was able to secure several shots of Old Goat, some showing a large scar on her neck where she had recently suffered a severe bite. I could hear the chuckles and breathy panting of play near at hand – hidden until Papoose burst out of the thickets. Dabbing my backside as she passed, she was pursued at a shambling run by Tiger. I circled through the tangled foliage, but could find no better vantage point and returned to slide closer to the silverback. Now Papoose and Petula approached from behind, and pleased me immensely by casually pressing past like fellow-travellers in a train corridor. Digit broke cover and flopped down five feet away and Tiger reappeared.

For half an hour Digit divided his attentions between Tiger and me, wrestling gently with the juvenile, then rolling my way to lie on his back, clutching his outstretched feet above his belly with his hands. Several times he stretched out an arm by my camera, right under my face, giving me plenty of opportunity to examine the damaged finger of his right hand. Like a curved sausage it stuck out sideways towards his little finger, swollen and rigid, with the nail grown long. It obviously bent permanently to that position when he walked on his knuckles. When he eased in close to sniff the camera, he made no objection when I scratched the top of his head with my fingers. Afraid to affect the degree of confidence already attained, I could not bring myself to do more than touch him carefully and gently, but thirty minutes later all changed.

Uncle Bert broke up our little tête-à-tête by coming forward to squint over the intervening vegetation. His curious stare seemed to disturb Digit, who moved off the now thoroughly flattened mess of plants and went to squat to one side. The silverback backed away and began to eat again. I attached myself to Digit as he moved, Tiger and Papoose in close attendance, then sat near him as he fed on *galium* and nettle leaves. Uninterested in feeding, the two juveniles capered about and wrestled and their noisy romping soon infected Digit. He abandoned his meal to join in, his attempts to do so putting an immediate damper on the previously uninhibited juvenile frivolity. I crawled closer to record the action, setting Digit off on his back-rolling and head-shaking routine – actions I suspected were a displacement activity brought on by a repressed desire to fraternise with me.

When the juveniles resumed their tussling, I noticed Uncle Bert leaning back and lifting his head to watch. It was reassuring to see his bland expression registered no concern. Moments later Digit came up beside me. His earlier reserve had vanished and I received a playful bump on the head – followed an instant later by a double-handed pounding on my back. Lying prone on my elbows, I began to rise to get my knees under me, but Digit pressed down firmly and began to fiddle with my coat. When I rolled on my side, he sat back and watched. Throwing caution to the wind, I reached out to bump his thigh, then held his foot as he beat a gentle tattoo on my hip and ribs. Suddenly his boldness deserted him and he pushed away. Grabbing a bunch of leaves he made a rapid, noisy exit from the scene – leaving Papoose and Tiger stilled, Uncle Bert alarmed, and me with a repeat run of the intense feelings he had generated the week before.

Since the jailing of poacher Munyarukiko, Dian had not visited any of the gorillas. My long report of the day's work and the extraordinary interactions with Digit convinced her that she had to make an effort to take advantage of the situation. I needed her to share in the growing empathy towards humans being displayed by Digit and the juveniles. The wonderfully relaxed mood of the whole family would surely allow many chances for good filming. But first she had a date to visit a Catholic father in Ruhengeri and felt she must keep the appointment. She missed a truly extraordinary day. I went out to experience one of the finest contacts I ever made with the group, recording in the process some valuable scenes of gorilla social behaviour.

I found the gorillas ascending the north-east side of Kalele Hill, only yards from where I had left them the previous evening. For a while I tried to find a good vantage point, but until the family reached the top of the hill, the steep slope and thick foliage defeated me. I came across Digit sitting in small glade, and he watched me set up before going into a nice act of playing the fool. His rolling and head-shaking antics attracted Tiger and the two became caught up in a brief wrestling match. Flossie and Cleo passed by, moving on ahead to join Old Goat and the silverback, already settled in freshly constructed day nests. Followed by Augustus, Petula ambled past and made her way towards the little group forming ahead. But as she climbed over a big fallen log, Flossie and Old Goat grunted at her. Poor Petula was in an awkward position, facing resentment at her intrusion as she slid down from the log with nowhere safe to turn away. The older pair of females then broke into harsh screams that echoed eerily through the forest. Uncle Bert got off his day nest to intervene.

His stiff stance and deep grunts of annoyance immediately quelled the outbreak. Then he stalked off in a huff, abandoning his comfortable nest and leaving the females contemplating each other in uneasy silence. I had never before managed to film an interaction like this; it was just luck I happened to be set up in the right place. In the period that followed I shot many scenes of Flossie and her baby. Though still a little unsteady, Cleo was becoming brave enough to venture a few feet from her mother, her infant antics producing just the sort of scenes I knew audiences would love to watch.

When the rest period broke up, I paralleled the silverback's route, watching the gorillas feed. I crawled towards Petula and Papoose, and since neither moved, tested their tolerance by advancing slowly, pretending interest in some of the plants that hemmed us in. I went down on my elbows as the gap between us diminished, and although Petula leaned back with slight apprehension, Papoose sat unmoving until my face was inches from her leg. I couldn't see her face, but anyway slid my hand forward until it touched her thigh. When that produced no reaction, I parted the hairs in a gentle grooming motion. For perhaps ten seconds Papoose accepted my attentions, then a hand descended with a soft thump on my head and she rolled sideways to fetch up in a heap by Petula. Petula remained where she was, her slightly deformed jaw working as though she were trying to pick her teeth with her tongue. Digit appeared, strutting, arms akimbo, head to one side like a silverback in a dominating pose. Down on my elbows, I was unable to tell from his sideways glances if he was looking at me or Petula. I watched him take slow and deliberate steps until he was alongside. He bent to sniff loudly at my beret and sat down with an audible open-mouthed sigh.

There followed twenty minutes of interaction that remain a sublime memory. This essentially lonely blackback, perhaps somewhere between eight and ten years old, with no companions of his own age, simply wanted to play. This was his third unrestrained approach, but this time it developed into uninhibited, physical play. Taking into account his inability to express feelings other than by gestures, vocalisations and body language, it was difficult to judge who enjoyed the encounter most. He pulled me, he pushed me, he pummelled my back and literally drew me out until I responded. He rolled on his side and allowed me to groom his broad back, and to hold his arms as he put them over his head or behind his back to catch at my probing fingers. His still immature hands dwarfed mine by a ratio of a good three to one. Although he exerted no power, I could feel his latent sinewy strength. He grunted and panted softly, eyes closed and mouth open, and, following a typical pattern of gorilla play, tumbled away to rest for long moments before resuming his gentle assaults. While I tried to stay low, prone on my chest or hunched on hands and knees, he beat his hands on my back, stood on me, lay on me, or sat for long seconds simply picking at the seams of my jacket. Now and then he rolled on to his back and fiddled with his own feet, or flung away to rest in a Buddha-like pose as though meditating.

Still slouched on one side, all the while Petula looked on with a blank look that gave no sign she thought anything was unusual. I wondered how long it had been since she had played with anyone. I had seen Macho, Maisie, Bravado and Digit all wrestle with each other, but never Petula. Maturity, it seemed, saw the end to rough-and-tumble games. I had never observed any of the adults indulge in what could be called play. They sometimes reached out and captured a nearby tussling infant or juvenile, but if the captive did not escape, the action converted to a grooming session almost immediately.

The delightful games ended when Tiger reappeared. Petula had gone on her way with Papoose, and most of the group had moved off to follow Uncle Bert. Digit had relapsed once more into a contemplative posture several feet away, scratching his head and listening to the occasional quiet sounds from his departing companions. I edged carefully towards Tiger. He held his ground as I drew closer, but before I could test him further, he beat a hasty retreat as Digit came with a rush. Bumping my back with a final sweep of his arm, he chased the youngster into the foliage ahead.

I remained a while at the scene, reviewing the long encounter with feelings of intense pleasure, wondering also what contacts of this nature would lead to in the future. I now had proof that, with careful habituation and in the right circumstances, young wild gorillas would accept unrestrained physical contact with human beings. With obvious reservations, my personal status within Group 4 equated to that of a rather submissive subadult. Correct behaviour and careful observance of gorilla social etiquette had made it possible for me to move with remarkable freedom within the family, to be treated as a tolerable intruder by the adults, and by the youngsters as an odd but trustworthy creature with whom they could interact. All the crawling about trying to behave like a gorilla had produced a wonderful degree of acceptance. Although the heavy vegetation was still very restrictive, close-up observations of behaviour had become increasingly easy. My cameras, especially the cine-camera and tripod continued to cause the adults slight consternation. The clack of a shutter or whirring of the cine-camera sometimes made them flinch and was a distracting noise. In anticipation of filming with synchronised sound, I impatiently awaited delivery of the silent camera I had ordered. With it I hoped to be even less of a distraction.

Although outwardly calm and pleasant, Dian was still rankled by my desire to join the next Turkana expedition. She had earlier sent a strong letter to Joanne Hess on the subject, and Joanne had already replied to say it was up to Dian and myself to recommend whether filming should be continued after the Turkana assignment, adding that the TV division was undergoing a change of staff and not yet in a position to decide on a show. To establish her full authority in matters dealing with the gorilla project, Dian had made it clear to Joanne she had decided I should finish my work by June. Privately, to me she insisted that if I persisted in my intention of joining Richard Leakey, then as far as she was concerned that would see the end of my association with herself and the research project. It was not sufficient for me to promise to come back after Turkana was over – if I did not prove my commitment to her research work now, then I would not return.

This was a new and disturbing approach that I found hard to accept. By not keeping Dian fully informed about Turkana matters while I was in Kenya, I had upset her badly. But then I had no idea she had learned of the tentative plans before I had returned to explain things for myself. The confrontational approach she now adopted seemed at first to be merely a threat I felt sure she would modify as time passed, but in the meantime I foolishly added fuel to the situation by hardening my own attitude and insisting I would not now give up this one opportunity to return to the fossil fields.

On the morning following the great day with Digit, I came across the lone silverback, Amok, at the base of Poacher's Hill, apparently shadowing Group 4. I wished I could see him in a confrontation with Uncle Bert. I needed more shots of the dramatic events, but as a former member of the group, Amok's very occasional meetings with them never seemed to cause more than nervous tension in Uncle Bert. This morning was no exception. When I crawled amongst the family, Uncle Bert let me know his temper was frayed and I received several warnings to keep my distance. Grunting at the sight of me, he twice smashed a fist on the ground with an intimidating thump. His little band was less spread out than usual and Digit nowhere to be seen. I filmed some more sequences of play and the construction of day nests. A fine scene of Flossie settling down with her baby was spoiled by Papoose and Tiger coming to stare at their reflections in the lens – highlighting one disadvantage of their otherwise welcome show of uninhibited curiosity.

I kept Uncle Bert in sight and was rewarded with a pleasant sequence as he carefully groomed Petula, soon joined by Papoose to give the young female a double dose of attention that she obviously enjoyed. Old Goat watched the grooming with an expression that might have been disapproval. I felt very happy with the quiet peace of the moment. That I was bound to witness and film more and more of these sometimes intricate social gatherings put me in a comfortable frame of mind. Now able to watch the gorillas so closely, I had already become aware of an interesting fact that had not received mention before – not surprisingly, because no one had been able to get so near to them. Looking at Digit's feet, I had seen that there was no hair on the upper surfaces of his toes. Sightings of other gorillas' feet showed the same feature, but it was not until I followed closely enough to see clearly how they walked that I realised they turned their toes under as they moved. They were not only walking on the knuckles of their hands but on those of their feet as well.

Heavy cloud dimmed the light and rain began to fall, at first soft and gentle, but soon with the force and weight of a true tropical storm. I wanted to film the melodramatic setting, but the light from the gloomy, water-filled atmosphere barely moved the needle of my light meter. The gorillas made no attempt to seek shelter. I sat with them, back set against the pouring rain as the full fury of the storm built up and thunder grew in volume. Cleo was wrapped in Flossie's long arms, Tiger sat pressed against his mother, his head buried underneath hers. Papoose leaned forward against one side of Petula and Augustus pressed against the other. Like me, Uncle Bert had turned his back to the storm, little Simba almost concealed under his shaggy folded arms.

When a brilliant discharge of lightning lit up the forest, followed instantly by a vicious thunder clap, it shattered everybody's nerves, including mine. But Uncle Bert's reaction was totally unexpected. With a huge roar he leaped to his feet and ran forward beating his wet chest in a long, rapid tattoo that attained tremendous volume. His family cowered like a group expecting a bomb to go off. When he made a return run, Simba, Petula and Papoose scattered for their lives. He finally subsided by a tree close to me, sitting out the rest of the storm and several further cracks of thunder in still and stoic silence.

In a pleasant mood that gave me the impression she was relaxing her opposition to my plans, for two days Dian joined me to share the delights of moving within the spread of Uncle Bert's family. She had decided to fly to Nairobi for a few days and the prospect of a break seemed to make her happier and more tranquil. Although it was cloudy and dull, we enjoyed two peaceful contacts that allowed me to film her closer than usual to the gorillas – and some particularly valuable scenes of her interacting gently with Digit.

When Dian returned from her holiday, my hopes that she had changed her mind were soon dashed. She had stayed away for almost two weeks, mainly in the company of Alan and Joan Root. She had flown with them on a quick visit to the Serengeti National Park, and though her descriptions of what she had seen and done were light-hearted and amusing, she was again alternately cheerful and affectionate, then preoccupied and distant. I had been given unqualified consent to take up the invitation to be at Koobi Fora for the visit of Prince Philip, and Dian accepted the decision with good grace. Resistance to my now more certain move to the Turkana expedition had collapsed, but she still held fast to her threat to close the gate on further photographic work after June.

By the third week of March I had run through nearly ten thousand feet of film. There could be no doubt I was overachieving the aim of completing the lecture film. The remarkable contacts with Group 4 continued, Dian enjoying the benefits with the same incredulous wonder and delight that affected me, utterly convinced that an observer moving with care and respect for the animals could soon fill a mountain of data sheets. As the date for my departure approached she abandoned all her work at camp. We spent five consecutive days near the inner circle of Group 4, the series of contacts producing two more fine sequences of Dian interacting with Digit. For the first time he made an approach directly to her, staying close and allowing her to touch his stomach. On the second the situation was reversed. Dian crawled up to his day nest and was permitted to 'groom' him a little. Although he tolerated her actions, there was still a slight degree of tension and he reacted with warning, low-key grunts if she did something that displeased him. He did not attempt to indulge in any play, as I had hoped, but I felt a few more meetings that allowed familiarity to build would surely draw him out. The super-close contacts delighted Dian, infecting her with the same feelings of astonishment and pleasure that ran through me. They culminated in a superb encounter after we had enjoyed a near non-stop two and a half hours of juvenile activity at a day rest site.

We were near the 'meeting place', with the tree I had used for the famous Peanuts 'touch' scenes visible a few hundred yards below. Bulky clouds scudded above, alternately blanking and releasing the sun, causing me problems with light values that slid erratically up and down the scale. The young gorillas were in an easy-going mood. Except for occasional glances, they almost ignored the human presence and played their rough, wrestling games directly below us. Dian, scribbling longhand notes in her usual tiny notebook, found herself quite unable to keep up with all the interesting details. I persuaded her to slide forward and take over a vacant day nest in my foreground and waited. Play amongst the juveniles continued – until Flossie moved. Carrying Cleo, she climbed the short distance separating her from Dian and stopped right in front of her. Dian leaned away, taken aback by this first direct approach to her by an adult. Cleo clung to her mother's chest and the clear sight of her tiny face a few feet away showed she had a badly damaged left eye. Dian reacted instantly by nearly bursting into tears. The infant's eyelid was cut and swollen shut. Looking closely as Flossie moved to pass me, I could not tell if the eye itself was hurt. There was no time to see more; Petula and Augustus took their turn to sit for a moment in front of the now unbelieving Dian, then Papoose and Tiger moved in – only three feet from her. It was as if the animals had come to make an inspection and their complete lack of any uneasiness was wonderful to see. Dian sat still; signs of her emotional response to Cleo's wound still showed, but I could sense the intense, almost rapturous pleasure the uninhibited parade was giving her. The abrupt appearance of Uncle Bert destroyed the peaceful moment and sent the participants on up the slope. The huge silverback then made his own more dignified and impressive pass very near to her. Admitting afterwards that the contact had dissolved absolutely all her remaining reservations about close approaches and stress, Dian had to admit that it was she who felt the stress when the adults came so very close – particularly Uncle Bert. But above all, the sight of Cleo's damaged eye had upset her badly. Sadly, Digit had not appeared to complete the flow of excitement. He too was recovering from a wound. Three weeks earlier I had found him with a cut under his eye, still very fresh, and since he kept fingering the triangular flap of skin, sometimes making it bleed, for a long while it spoiled his looks.

To get a better look at her infant's eye, the next morning I made a special effort to keep close to Flossie. During a protracted day rest period, I was

permitted to push through some thick foliage and set up a few feet from her –
just in time to film a charming sequence as she lay in her daybed; Cleo playing
contentedly all the while and seemingly not bothered at all by her eye. The
lower eyelid was badly cut and still swollen, but glimpses of the eye behind
gave me hope it was undamaged.

Eight days later I stood in a strong, oven-hot wind blowing down from a
rocky hillock called Shin, waiting with Richard Leakey on the dusty surface of
an old World War II airstrip. Barren hills strewn with black lava rocks lay
behind us, and across a fifteen-mile stretch of heavily eroded country that
shimmered in the heat, Lake Turkana gleamed like a strip of pale ivory. In
anticipation of an interesting week, we watched as the Duke of Edinburgh's
small Andover aircraft circled in the turbulent air and prepared to land. For
the next seven days a small party of six would reside in Richard's lakeside base
and entertain Prince Philip; an easy, informal atmosphere ensuring everyone
could enjoy a few days of fossil hunting and birdwatching. Aubrey Buxton
(now Lord Buxton) and his daughter Lucinda accompanied Prince Philip, and
aside from the Duke's personal bodyguard, Richard, Heather and I completed
the guest list. Alan and Joan Root were to join us for the last two days.

Although several interesting and amusing events took place during the
period, for me the most significant moments came during one particularly
long talk with Aubrey Buxton. For the benefit of Prince Philip, I had
described in detail the wildlife situation in the Virunga volcanoes and the
recent, extraordinary progress in habituating some of the gorillas. Aubrey, the
president of Anglia Television and a founding director of the wildlife television unit, Survival Anglia, was deeply interested and wanted to know a lot
more – including my plans for the future. So we sat alone one evening on the
stone-walled verandah of Richard's living quarters, watching the waters of
Lake Turkana glowing red with reflections from the sunset. We talked until
the colours faded to purple and dusk fell. I had to confess that my long-term
future was a little indefinite. In June I would be back at Koobi Fora for three
or four months of filming. But after that, further work with the gorillas for a
Geographic television special was very uncertain. I literally had no idea how
things were going to turn out. Aubrey told me how several previous visits to
Lake Turkana had generated a personal interest in the harsh attractions of the
region, and went on to reveal his growing interest in Richard's search for
human ancestors. He was contemplating producing a film about it all. He
suggested that if I were to break away from *National Geographic* he would like
me to consider shooting for the Survival team. A year later that long and
pleasant conversation would be remembered and eventually bring about big
changes in my filming activities.

The short stay at Koobi Fora rekindled my own fascination with the arid
stamping ground of the hominid hunters. To give the Duke a chance to see as
much of the country as possible and satisfy his addiction to birdwatching, we
travelled widely, motoring across the trackless terrain to visit many places of

interest, particularly the few inland waterholes where a variety of birds and wild animals were more easily seen. As we daily drove long distances over familiar ground, I sidelined problems over future gorilla work and felt almost impatient to get started on the new assignment. The interlude allowed me to enjoy the many amusing events of the week. There was the incident with a young crocodile, found fifty yards from the lake's edge during an evening's birdwatching, and thought to be dead. But when approached somewhat incautiously, it proved to be very much alive by suddenly striking out with its heavy tail, hissing furiously and snapping its jaws together with astonishing rapidity. Then there was the sight of the royal guest silhouetted against the bright light bouncing off the waves of the lake; a tiny figure walking out on the Koobi Fora sand spit, entirely alone, but followed by anxious eyes behind binoculars as he made repeated diversions to splash into the sparkling water. Many crocodiles patrolled the Koobi Fora beach, some quite large; but in three years none had given the slightest indication of any aggressive tendencies towards the humans who daily bathed in the lake. Nobody wanted to go out and issue some words of caution to the Duke. Until he was seen to be safely on his way back, the potential for disaster set nerves on edge.

Then there was the boat trip to visit the attractions of North Island, a volcanic island twelve miles out from Koobi Fora. We were delayed slightly when one of the boat engines lost power, then spent more time than intended on the island, climbing to see the sulphur-coated gas vents at the peak, and looking hard for new birds. The sun was sinking and the sky already turning from gold to orange as we headed for home. We set course for Koobi Fora directly into a stiff wind that created an unpleasant head-on chop for the boat. With one engine still down on power, we decided to tackle the waves at an angle to reduce the discomfort. This manoeuvre took us out of the direct line of sight from the camp to the island – from whence we were expected to appear. As the brilliant orb of the sun sank to the horizon, at Koobi Fora the intense glare from the water made it difficult even to see the island. When the sun set and visibility improved, no trace of a boat met worried straining eyes. Meanwhile, aboard the pitching craft now turned south to head for home, tea had been brewed and was being served with great difficulty and considerable hilarity. More tea reached the floorboards than outstretched lips. At the height of everyone's antics to drink with some dignity, Cindy Buxton sat on a milk carton and squirted a jet of milk all over her father – his astonished look causing fresh peals of laughter. When we sailed into the calmer waters of Koobi Fora Bay at dusk, to the vast relief of the few waiting on shore, those on board were still weak with laughter.

The last day saw us driving over the circuitous route through prehistoric sediments to the Shin airstrip, one final event marking the Duke's departure. Halfway to our destination a huge cloud of dust rose from the direction of the strip, but we could only speculate on the cause. It transpired that in turning near the threshold of the runway, the pilot of the aircraft had locked a wheel.

It had broken through the thin earth crust into fine silty soil below and the plane was then effectively stuck in a dust hole. Only the application of full power had dragged it out of the predicament; propellers had been nicked by small stones lifted from the surface, but otherwise the aircraft was unharmed. Prince Philip said his farewells with a touch of genuine emotion. Richard had provided him with a unique opportunity to relax and enjoy a truly wild and remote part of Africa, and he professed not to have enjoyed such a carefree and interesting holiday for many years. Seated at the controls of the Andover, he lifted a hand in a final salute. Fine dust billowed in the slipstream as the plane gathered speed. We watched it go with studied interest, as high hills crowding the end of the old runway necessitated a quick turnout or plenty of power and lift to clear them. However, the Andover rose above the hills with ease and, turning north, was soon out of sight.

Only six or seven weeks of work with the gorillas remained before I would return to this scorched semi-desert. I felt unwilling to exchange the hard blue sky and blazing sun for the cold and clouded woodlands of the evergreen volcanoes. The rainy season would be at its height now, keeping the foliage drooping and dripping and the earth soaked and muddy. Still, there was no denying the thrill of holding a unique position at the core of a gorilla family. I knew all incidental discomforts would fade away in their company. But that was really a minor factor; what weighed more heavily on my mind was the fact that Dian was evidently so distressed by my plans for the future that she had taken advantage of her friend Alan Root's presence at Koobi Fora. She had chosen him to tell me that she desperately wanted me to stay on in Rwanda, not just because of our shared interest in the gorillas, but because she really wanted a man in her life and I was that man. She had asked Alan to talk to me while he was at Koobi Fora, and to try to persuade me somehow that I should make some sort of firm commitment to stay with her.

Taking his mission seriously, Alan had asked me to walk with him along the Koobi Fora beach, and had then done his best to state Dian's case. Disconcerted that she had chosen this method to reveal what she had not been able to say directly, I had to explain that he knew as well as I that although the friendship and affection between Dian and myself had been long-lasting, it was not a basis for a permanent association. Since late in 1969 we had maintained an intimate relationship that had generated mutual respect and fondness for one another. We had kept to our independent facilities, working as amicable partners on what had become a very long-term project. But there were no illusions that my assignment could continue indefinitely. As far as I knew, there was still a good chance for many more months of filming. Though sometimes weary of the long treks and climbs to contact gorillas, I was more than willing to work towards a final television show. I was engrossed by the incredible progress already made with one family, keen also to habituate others as well. Dian, however, was apparently set on forcing me to make an impossible decision related entirely to our personal affairs.

When I arrived at the base of Visoke ten days later the weather was miserable. Knowing difficult times lay ahead, I climbed to the camp with a heavy heart. Dian welcomed me in a cheerful way that gave no clues to her inner thoughts. But she could not for long disguise the fact she was distressed and unhappy. We were both aware that the close bond that had grown between us had reached a critical stage, and that if we were not careful the affection we felt for one another could easily be destroyed. I did not doubt Alan had written to convey the result of his approach to me and to state his opinions on the matter. When the subject was broached, Dian made it clear she was not prepared to let things continue as they had in the past. She was going to stand by her earlier decision: if I did not abandon my plans to rejoin the fossil hunters, then June would see the end of my association with her. Knowing how much I wanted to take advantage of my success with Group 4 and to develop the same degree of habituation with Beethoven's family and Group 8, she held the axe firmly over my head, hoping I would perhaps capitulate and agree to stay on in the mountains. The unhappy situation cast a shadow over the camp that seemed even to affect our three staff members. The only break in the gloom came from several letters from Joanne Hess that awaited me. They contained enthusiastic reports and comments on the last shipments of film, and helped to bolster an intention to make the best of the remaining weeks.

Being able to work right in amongst the gorillas had opened up a whole new range of possibilities, from unrestricted study of behaviour to full documentation of their lifestyle on film. I argued that the assignment to work with Richard would last only four months, and that there was no reason why my work with the gorillas should not continue after that. With the research on gorillas at such an exceptionally exciting stage, it seemed obvious that the future of the whole project was infinitely more promising than it had ever been. But we had reached an impasse. I felt deep regret and increasing resentment that personal feelings were now likely to put an end to any future chance of recording the most exciting chapter in the study of the great apes. But Dian was no longer prepared to let our relationship stay at the level that amounted to close companionship. She knew that apart from a possible extension to provide specific material for television, funding for work on a purely photographic level was coming to an end. But on the other hand, the possibilities opened up for more intensive behavioural research were almost a guarantee that new funds would be made available to exploit the situation. With forty days remaining before I would have to leave, I was optimistic that our personal problems could be overcome. Dennis Kane, head of the *National Geographic* television division, had confirmed that the recent airing of the one-hour special on primates more or less precluded any immediate production of a film entirely on gorillas. But that did not mean that he would not finance the work to produce the necessary material for a future show. I could not believe Dian would hold firm if the *National Geographic* decided to complete a special.

Meanwhile I had no intention of giving up my interest in the fossil world. Rain fell throughout the long day we devoted to discussions and argument. By nightfall I was thoroughly depressed and looking forward only to making fresh contacts with the gorillas.

Nemeye guided me to Group 4 the next morning and I went on to make a fine contact – almost as though there had been no interval. It pleased me to discover baby Cleo's wound had almost healed and her eye was intact. With a sense of urgency growing as time went by, I took every opportunity to exploit the group's new attitude to their human observers. Each new day saw a further lessening of residual wariness in the females; even the highly suspicious Old Goat was yielding.

Although the desire and great temptation to enjoy further physical interactions was very strong, I had reluctantly decided I must withdraw from active contacts with Digit and the juveniles. I could not avoid being approached during some of the play sessions, but it was relatively easy to make the youngsters back away by adopting a less submissive posture – or using grunts of warning and mild threat stares. When I employed these tactics I had to be extremely careful not to draw Uncle Bert's attention. Several times he reacted to my more dominant poses with annoyed facial expressions and grunts of his own, leaving no doubt I should be careful not to usurp his authority. Now that the females were less inhibited, I began keeping close to the silverback again and was able to film more details of their social behaviour: the way they manoeuvred in each other's company and near to their leader; the varied grooming sessions; the games of the juveniles and infants. Uncle Bert had lost virtually all of his unease. During the peace of a comfortable siesta he would happily go to sleep with only a few feet between us.

Digit was frustrated by my proximity to the adults. Sometimes, as I moved to find and close on the silverback, he followed behind. He would often brush past with a short spurt to move ahead, then pause to watch me catch up. I found it exceptionally hard to ignore him on these occasions, but as he tended to initiate an interaction if I tried to pass, I had to back away and choose another route. When the weather precluded any chances of filming, we spent many quiet rest periods in adjacent nests; or when the rain streamed down, sat out the uncomfortable hours close together – at times near enough for me to feel the heat of his body. He tried frequently to draw me into a game, but if I remained hunched down, inert and unresponsive, he would soon give up.

In spite of the impasse we had reached, Dian gave time whenever she could to come out and be filmed near the gorillas. With young Papoose and Tiger responding particularly well, we were rewarded with some effective and tender scenes. But the pair were definitely overshadowed by the few performances put up by Digit. Though I longed for him to attempt some play with her, to my great disappointment the blackback behaved with extreme gentility, lightly touching or smelling her belongings or clothing, and if the mood was right, allowing himself to be touched in turn. Some footage of him interacting strongly with her would have made exciting viewing, but Dian herself was still a little apprehensive. She was hesitant to go beyond mild and cautious touches, and clearly Digit needed time to develop the unguarded, physical familiarity he displayed towards me.

On 23 May, Dian and I walked out together along the regular route to Visoke's western slopes. We skirted the top meadow, flooded with water after a week of rainstorms, stopping at the border to capture Cindy and send her back with the woodman. We moved on down the winding trail at the base of the mountain, heading for the path that would take us high above the nettle zone. Neither of us had touched on my impending departure for a long time. Unless Dian had a change of heart, this would be our final foray together and the last contact with the gorillas she would make with me. We had intended to spend the whole week in the company of Group 4, but a recent commitment to entertain Robinson Macilvaine, the American ambassador to Kenya, had forced a change of plan.

We had earlier taken a long break away from Visoke to climb up between Mount Gahinga and Mount Muhavura and camp in the saddle between them. Dian intended to place Sandy Harcourt in the area to continue the census he had so successfully carried out between Visoke and Sabinio. She wanted to conduct a quick survey and find out for herself if any gorillas utilised the region, and to be sure a good supply of water was available. I had been unhappy to lose so many days with the gorillas, but Dian was reluctant to follow through her plan without me. Unfamiliar with the lie of the land, we had been able to cover a limited section of the thickly covered slopes, finding only a few old and decaying nest sites. Luckily, on the last afternoon the sound of chest beats had allowed us to home in on a small family of five very wild gorillas. One of two silverbacks we saw roared and charged several times to show his angry disapproval of our presence.

Since my return from Lake Turkana, a fragile calm had settled in. I had the strange feeling that Dian was ignoring my imminent departure, as though by doing so it would not happen. The date was set, but we neither discussed nor referred to it. It was as if there was no deadline and gorilla work continued as before in a pleasant and normal way. Only seven days remained before I would leave for Kenya and I wanted to make the most of them. As had become usual after a break in the continuity of contacts, the gorillas reacted to our arrival with an elevated level of attention. They were in a placid mood too, obviously appreciating a sudden and pleasant change in the pattern of weather. After many days of heavy rain and accompanying spells of clinging fog, the prevailing wind had dropped and bright blue skies opened up. Clouds of cumulus built into great bulging columns above the eastern faces of the mountains at noon, but the western slopes remained bathed in welcome, warming sunshine.

For over four and a half hours we maintained a position amongst the family, taking pleasure in the casual acceptance of our presence and watching the juveniles romp and wrestle as we waited patiently for any opportunity to film a good sequence. The mild afternoon wore on and the gorillas remained wonderfully relaxed, persisting with an already unusually long siesta, quite content to lounge in the warmth and delay the filling of stomachs. Digit wandered in from an obscured position and flopped down on a ledge of foliage below the main body of the group. We watched him fold down a few leafy stems and settle into comfortable immobility. The enjoyable though unremarkable contact would soon be over and I had filmed nothing of special interest. Taking the last opportunity to obtain one more sequence of Dian in close, friendly association with a gorilla, I asked her to crawl down towards Digit.

Moving slowly and carefully breaking a few intervening plants obstructing my view, she was able to reach Digit's side with no difficulty. The blackback watched her slow approach with a calmness that held promise and we were not disappointed. There followed a unique sequence that would eventually light up the screens of uncountable television sets around the world: the record of a peaceful interaction between a human being and a gorilla; a wild creature who had become a wonderful, trusting friend.

A growing sensation of incredulity and amazement suffused my whole being as the seconds passed. After three long years, at the last possible moment, the sort of sequence I had been after for so long was unfolding in front of me. While the camera rolled, I could not help wondering if fate had suddenly stepped in to provide a very special event that would break Dian's resolve to end our long association. The soft sunlight, a clear view, and the gentle actions of this most unusual gorilla, all combined to produce a truly touching sequence; a sequence destined to become the highlight of a film that would come together two years later. Digit made the event stand out above all others by carefully taking first a pen and then a little notebook from Dian's hands, replacing them gently. I motioned that I wanted her to reach out to touch and perhaps groom him, but she misunderstood my gestures, and instead bumped him rather awkwardly on his thigh and back. Digit accepted the physical contact calmly, then concluded the scene by turning his back on Dian to slump casually on his side. The moving encounter showed perfectly the gentle empathy of this very special mountain gorilla, and would help immeasurably to counter the long-held, unjustified image of gorillas as mainly savage, aggressive beasts.

The extraordinary contact did in fact end with a brief note of violence that was also shown in the film – but which was cut out for use in an entirely different sequence. After a few minutes, Digit moved away from Dian and displaced young Tiger from a nest lower down. Flossie then demonstrated her complete faith in us by coming to within a foot of the camera, pausing to view her image in the lens filter before sitting back to watch the juveniles at play. Uncle Bert had held a position above throughout the extended contact, resting on his daybed and only sitting up to keep a wary eye on the latter part of the proceedings. But at this point he must have decided the time had come to establish his authority. He moved forward aggressively and broke up the play group, then rose up on his short legs to crash down the slope with a rush, swinging a heavy fist at me that missed by inches. He smashed on through the foliage to hammer poor Digit with a heavy blow – this final act causing Dian to react as though she herself had received it.

I spent the final days on Visoke alone, following the slow travels of Uncle Bert's family and extracting the last moments of pleasure from their company. A fast-moving ceiling of cloud had returned to dominate the weather again, bringing rain and intervals of mist. I spent much of the time with cameras packed away, simply shadowing various individuals, keeping right amongst the family as they fed and played, groomed and slept. One morning I found Papoose and Tiger pulling up and chewing the small roots of a hypericum tree, but they finished all they could effectively remove before I managed to get the camera ready. Wanting film of this particular activity, I slid forward to dig more soil away. But there was little left of the small roots and I exposed only a short length of a large one. I tried to break it, but no matter how hard I strained it would not shift. I retreated to my camera and waited to see what the gorillas would do. Papoose came back, but did no better than me. Digit, who had been feeding nearby, watching us struggle in vain, now came over to displace the young female. He bent down to sniff the root, then, squatting on his haunches, gripped it firmly with both hands. A single, apparently effortless heave ripped the root straight out! Still far from maturity, Digit probably weighed little more than me; but this brief demonstration revealed a physical strength that exceeded mine in no small measure.

26 May found me following the tracks of the group out of the nettle zone and across the path where I had first seen a gorilla. The snaking trails led me through dripping foliage and heavy, matted thickets, then up and across Visoke's lower slopes to a sleeping site. I examined and counted the scattered beds, then climbed along a ridge above the big meadow. I came upon the gorillas high above the open patch, where eleven months earlier Sandy Harcourt and I had made a full count of Uncle Bert's family, confirming the loss of three females and an infant.

It was early but the gorillas had already ceased feeding. The few I could see were motionless, backs turned against shredded grey clouds that were releasing squalls of ice-cold rain. The dark, bulky shape of Uncle Bert loomed above me, Flossie and Petula close to him. Old Goat sat apart, her maturing son pressed hard against her side. Of the others there was no sign, and since swirling fog soon obscured all but the closest objects, there was no point in even trying to locate them. I found a low bush of giant heath to protect me from the biting wind, and prepared to wait out the rest period in the faint hope of a break in the bleak conditions. In spite of the wind, I could hear occasional, faint sounds of wood being chopped; to the south and over a thousand feet below, the camp woodcutter was still hard at his job. The ambassador was due any time now. Dian would be working to ensure everything was ready to cater to the comfort of his party. It would be my task to take the ambassador out the following morning. I wondered how he would enjoy the climb to this altitude in the cold and wet.

I fell to contemplating the remaining packing I had to do. Each evening I had been sorting through all the gear that had accumulated over the years, trying to guess if the growing pile of cartons and boxes would fit into my Land Rover. The work had a disturbing 'end of assignment' finality about it. Inevitably my thoughts turned to plans and preparations yet to be made for the new assignment. I still had no idea what would happen after the Turkana season was over. The blank in my mental calendar made me wonder yet again about the now very uncertain future of photography on gorillas.

I had fulfilled the requirements for a good lecture show, but knew it would take many more months, possibly even years, to record all aspects of gorilla behaviour. Although I had shot several miles of film, most of it covered a limited range of their social activities. Some really dedicated work would be required to complete the picture. I knew now that gorillas could be habituated to accept close contact with humans in a relatively short period of time – certainly in a matter of months and much quicker than the time I had been obliged to take. Other groups would have to be fully habituated, and then perhaps it would be possible to record the more dramatic interactions that occasionally took place between families. Since there were not too many mountain gorillas left on these isolated volcanoes, to me there seemed to be good justification for such a long-term operation. If the governments of Rwanda, Zaire and Uganda ever deemed it necessary to excise more land from their national parks, the great apes would quickly approach extinction. Full visual documentation of their secluded lifestyle would be a valuable record, but to attain that goal would be an expensive operation. I could not see *National Geographic* television financing more than a short-term project to complete a special. However, the research committee might be persuaded to make a specific grant to cover such work; but then, for the time being at least, Dian had shut the door on my future involvement.

Hunched against the freezing drifts of rain and fog, my mind churning fruitlessly, I waited for two hours before deciding that time could be better spent in my cabin. With visibility cut to a few foggy feet, on the way down the steep incline of the ridge I shoved carelessly through the dripping foliage and inadvertently displaced Papoose. Digit was nearby. With his head down and back to the rain, he was just a dark, shaggy, egg-like shape in the grey fog. I crawled up to him and stopped briefly by his side, a yard away. Droplets of rain ran off his head and down the long hairs of his coat. His soft brown eyes followed my movements, but he did not stir. I slid on past his motionless form to search for the ridge path that would lead me to the meadow below.

I never saw Digit again. Four and a half years later, the gentle, friendly creature who had so firmly captured my affection died violently – speared to death by poachers on the last day of 1977, his mutilated body left for the researchers from Karisoke to find on New Year's Day.

Early one day in June 1970 we were surprised to encounter a well-armed ranger patrol from Zaire. Standing to the left of the patrol leader in the light trousers is Sanweckwe – Dian's first tracker at Kabara in Zaire.

Then it dawned. It was Bravado (top), last seen when she had come so very close after my fall from a tree over a year ago. The sighting confirmed that Bravado was now the third gorilla known to have transferred from one group to another.

Uncle Bert lazily slumped on a slope where he was feeding earlier. At this stage of the habituation process the silverback was now content to go to sleep within six feet of me.

After their morning feed the gorillas make a rough bed or 'nest' of foliage, then spend anything from one to four hours dozing contentedly. Here Digit relaxes next to me and enjoys some weak sunshine.

In September 1971, for the first time Digit overcame his shy reserve, making a direct approach to come forward and pick up one of my gloves. This action set the tone for a fabulously successful contact with his family.

As he grew bolder Digit spent much of his time close to me, sometimes reaching out to make physical contact. Later, he overcame his shyness and enticed me to accept uninhibited sessions of gentle play.

With her baby daughter Cleo playing on her stomach, Flossie snoozes on her daybed.

Uncle Bert monitored my movements, and kept a sharp eye on the juveniles and subadults who were starting to fraternise with their human observer. His eventual acceptance of a human in the midst of his family gave confidence to the wary females.

Flossie (*left*) watches me calmly, but Old Goat's expression shows she is not convinced this human should be allowed so close.

The gorillas now reacted to my day-long company with growing indifference, soon permitting scenes to be filmed that made me wish I had an extreme wide-angle lens.

Professor Raymond Dart with Louis, Richard and Mary Leakey at the Nairobi National Museum, w he came to see an impressive array of the fossil hominid specimens collected from the east side of Turkana.

With their long, powerful arms, gorillas can climb up large trees with relative ease. Though I had observed that the gorillas had no hair on the tops of their toes, for a long time I failed to realise that for some unknown reason this was because they turn their toes under when they walk. So, not only do they walk on the knuckles of their hands, but on those of their feet also! In this photo one can see the toes turned under.

A close-up of Digit's foot, showing the long, thumb-like big toe, and his other toes tightly curled in the normal walking position.

Hominid and human reference specimens litter a table at the Nairobi National Museum as Richard and Meave work to reconstruct the 1470 fossil hominid skull with greater accuracy.

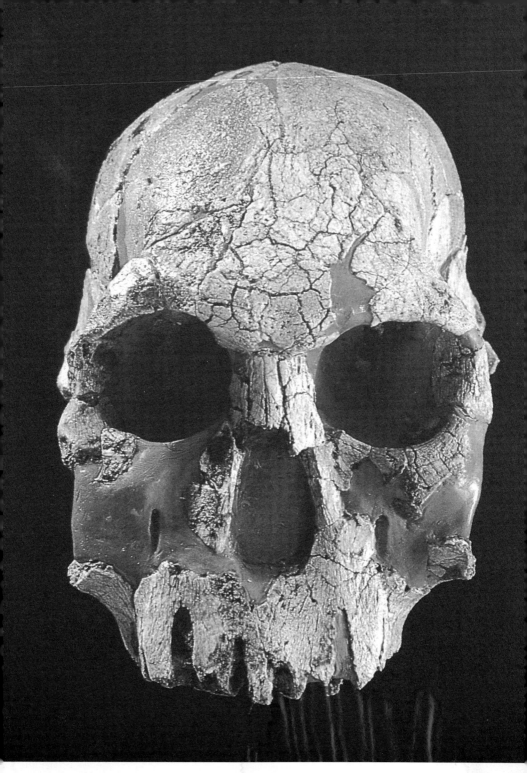

Nearly two million years old, and with a brain capacity of close to eight hundred cubic centimetres, the 1470 skull created a great stir in the field of palaeoanthropology. By good fortune I had chosen a prime time to break from gorilla work and rejoin Richard at Lake Turkana.

1470

Glowing with muted power through high cirrus and layers of superfine dust, the rising sun scattered a brassy light. Air streamed out of the east in a warm, powerful flow, buffeting my body and making it difficult to hold binoculars steady. Across a waterless expanse of semi-desert I could just make out the sharp peak of N'derati Hill, the location of a tiny oasis with some old water wells. Further south and barely visible through the dusty haze stood the rounded outline of Koobi Algi Hill, marker for a tiny spring of fresh water. Behind me, the wind rippled the alkaline waters of Lake Turkana, driving dull-green waves towards distant hills that merged with the dust-laden atmosphere.

Barely three weeks had passed since the day I had huddled on a mountain ridge, a bitterly cold wind at my back and thick fog obscuring alpine foliage in a blanket of dull grey. Now I was perched on a ridge of eroded prehistoric sediments no more than thirty feet high. Every time I moved the hot wind scoured fine grains of dust and sand from the desiccated earth. Preparations for the Turkana expedition and the long journey to the lake had put gorilla matters to the back of my mind, but at unexpected moments images of the lush mountains still surfaced. Before leaving Nairobi I had written to Dian to tell of efforts to prevent an unauthorised camera team from poaching shots of her study groups – but she had not replied.

As I scanned the harsh landscape and the hazy length of shoreline stretching towards Allia Bay, thoughts about the photo coverage of this fifth season of exploration occupied my mind. I would continue to cover the progress of fieldwork – the digs at the prime archaeological sites and the ongoing search for new fossils – but it was the shooting for a different style of lecture film for Richard that concerned me most. Building on ideas formulated during Prince Philip's visit, Richard had been negotiating with Aubrey Buxton and Melvin Payne for a new documentary on early man and his work. A commitment for a film in 1973 was going to be made on the basis of the material I shot during the present season, so I needed to produce material that would convince everyone the project was worthwhile. I could still not believe work among the gorillas had really ended, but if Dian refused to change her mind, the arrangement gave me something positive to look forward to.

I was modifying previous thoughts on the way I would handle the coverage; material much more exciting than a record of another field expedition was required and fresh ideas were still forming. I intended to relate the present with the prehistoric past by showing how existing animals lived and died; how their bones were scattered by predators, scavengers and the action of the elements; and how, if circumstances were favourable, the skeletal remains could be covered by water, sand and silt – entombed and ripe for fossilisation as the ages passed.

Earlier in the morning I had made a small start; right at the edge of the lake I had come across the broken carcass of a topi calf being finished off by a crowd of noisy vultures, and later found the bleached skull of an old topi male settling nicely into sandy mud at the water's edge. Having established how fresh bones were dispersed and buried, I would show palaeontologists finding ancient animal bones scattered and fossilised by the same processes. I would also need to show how the geologists analysed all the visual and chemical evidence in the layers of sediments; how they determined the age of the fossils and made assessments about the environments in which the creatures had lived.

The same approach would be applied to some modern humans who existed on the fringes of this old lake, humans who followed a very primitive way of life: hunting for fish, foraging for wild plant food and sometimes scavenging from predators. These were people called Shangila molo – the word molo denoting they lived off fish. Because they were poor, the molo followed a separate existence outside the main social units of the Shangila nomads who roamed the delta region of the Omo River and the eastern side of the lake. I hoped to make friends with some of the wandering fish hunters and record significant details of their way of life. They would be my modern equivalent of the pre-human creatures the scientists were searching for. I particularly wanted to show how their rudimentary campsites along the edge of the lake could be easily swamped by rising levels, or be covered by water-borne silt and sand eroded by rain from inland; sites that might be sealed away under layers of deposits in the same way as the bones of dead creatures. It would be relatively easy to relate this material to the work of the archaeologists as they sifted through the debris of prehistoric living sites.

The skeleton staff looking after the base camp had told me a small group of Shangila molo with canoes had passed the Koobi Fora spit a few days earlier, but from my perch on the ridge I could see no sign of them. Over a mile away, several dark shapes along the shoreline wavered in the turbulent heat shimmer, but I knew they were solitary topi antelopes. Beyond them the land vanished behind a curtain of dusty brown haze. Below me, near the edge of the lake, stood a solitary outcrop of rocks large enough to provide good shelter from the blasting wind. In the lee of the rocks were signs of a recent stopover: the remains of a small fire and a few fresh fish bones. In the vicinity of the rocks, ample evidence that this place had been used consistently over a long period of time lay scattered on the ground: simple fireplaces, the bleached and cracked bones of various land animals, fishes and small crocodiles, a number showing faint cuts from sharp implements. Several pieces of wood and some oryx horns bore the marks of knives, and a rotting length of plaited reeds displayed the work of dextrous human hands – all the unmistakable litter of a truly primitive human campsite.

Three or four months of work in this harsh, exciting land stretched ahead. The Koobi Fora base was at present empty, but over the next week fifteen to twenty scientists and undergraduates would be arriving. Intense excavation work would soon be under way and I hoped fresh searches would produce some really newsworthy fossils. But for the moment I was content to have the whole region almost to myself, spending the days travelling across the broken terrain, refreshing my memory of the lie of the land, visiting all the prime fossil sites and checking on the preciously few watering points.

When I returned to Koobi Fora a week later, the camp was full. Richard had flown in with his wife, Meave, and Dr Paul Abell, an old expedition friend of long standing. A day later, unaware she was destined in the near future to go to work on gorillas with Dian, Kelly Stewart came up on another plane. Glynn Isaac, now a professor and deputy leader of the expedition, headed the team of archaeologists that would be excavating deeper into the volcanic tuff that held the stone tools found by Kay Behrensmeyer in 1969. He would also deal with another promising site where stone artefacts had been found in association with the remains of a fossil hippo skeleton. New camps were already being established in the field. Paul Abell moved out to set up in a particularly windy and stony area south-east of Koobi Fora. Together with Kelly and a small team of Kenyans, his task was to excavate the complete remains of a huge fossil elephant found the previous year.

In the mail Richard brought for me were letters from Joanne reporting on rushes from my last shipments of film and advising of the good chance for a visit to Washington to view and help edit the footage. Her comments on the rushes took me straight back to the last days on the slopes of the Visoke volcano; the sequence of Digit and Dian interacting with such amazing gentleness had turned out beautifully – in every way a fitting climax to the assignment – and yet perhaps only an introduction to what was bound to follow. Having pioneered an exciting method of working amongst the gorillas, I knew significant advances lay in the future. I wondered yet again if Dian would remain determined I should not return to handle the next stage. Whatever happened, the implications of the ability to observe and work from within the family groups gave cause for serious thought.

With care, and a suitably detached approach to inhibit physical interactions, marvellous opportunities to watch uninhibited gorilla behaviour would surely become more frequent. In the ultra-close contacts required to defeat the heavy foliage, it would always be a problem to avoid being included in some gorilla activities. I had discovered how completely trusting the apes could be if properly approached, and in the pure enjoyment of being on level, friendly terms with the powerful creatures, had found it very hard to withdraw from the pleasures of the physical interactions that had so quickly developed. Initially, from different points of view, both Dian and Joanne had questioned the need to habituate the gorillas to such a close human presence; Joanne had long ago expressed her concern, wondering how the high degree of habituation would affect the gorillas' reaction to strangers – particularly those whose motives for getting close might not be so clearly defined as mine. I had assured her that strangers were not accorded the same degree of trust. Our regular African assistants were still treated with fear and apprehension, so I felt confident normal reactions to poachers and other potentially aggressive intruders would not change. However, one worrying aspect of the new situation was the distinct possibility of human diseases being transmitted to the apes; obviously people suffering from any sort of illness should not be allowed near the vulnerable creatures.

If Dian kept up my techniques, she would surely amass a great deal more accurate behavioural data; but she would at the same time lay herself open to some criticism from those who had no conception of the difficulties involved in observing shy, elusive creatures in dense vegetation, or of the recently redefined, basically passive nature of the gorillas.

Joanne's report on her communications with Dian seemed to indicate that, from *National Geographic*'s point of view, there was little chance I would be going back in the near future. She also mentioned that the film I had shot now amounted to seventy thousand feet – about thirty-three hours in viewing time. I calculated I had spent well over a thousand hours on contacts where cine took precedence – which in raw statistical terms worked out at a rough average of five or six minutes of film per contact. Joanne still had her sights on a lecture film, but Dian was for the present being very uncooperative and resistant about the project. There was a movement afoot to get me over to Washington, not just to help edit the footage but to sit down and produce a behavioural analysis of the material while my memory of events and their significance was still fresh in my mind, but in the prevailing circumstances I doubted anything would come of it. I had made a choice that seemed to guarantee a complete cut-off from the creatures that had dominated my life for so long. There was nothing to be gained by thinking about it. It was time to concentrate on the job in hand and put thoughts raised by Joanne's letters aside.

The skills I had used to track gorillas through wet and luxuriant vegetation were now redundant. The animals I would be filming were thinly scattered over five hundred square miles of arid land and were every bit as nervous and wary of human beings as the gorillas had once been. An entirely different set of skills was needed to obtain good footage of them. I had also to show the natural results of wind and water erosion, the effects of earth movements, volcanic eruptions and other events that shifted, covered and re-sorted surface layers – occasionally burying and preserving bones and man-made artefacts.

Out in the huge spread of sediments east of the lake, there were many stratified layers of sand, silt, clay, gravel and volcanic ash, each recording some particular condition or occurrence before being overlaid by deposits of subsequent events. There were numerous fine sections that showed where immense forces had fractured the earth, faulting and often tilting the sediments. Many of the layers contained fossils, and one particularly fine band was formed almost entirely of gastropod shells. Inches thick, this layer of beautifully preserved shells could be traced through the exposures for miles. Uncountable billions of shells had for some reason accumulated in still waters over a very short period. While examining and filming them I felt the repeated desire to journey back through time and find out exactly what circumstances had caused the band to be formed. In many areas, great slabs of sandstone lay exposed, their upper surfaces occasionally recording an identifiable imprint made before the material had solidified: the tracks of some animal or the delicate footprints of birds. In a few areas, huge sheets of sandstone formed the upper surface of the land, resisting the abrasive actions of the elements, but nevertheless breaking up gradually as softer sediments supporting them slowly eroded away. I scoured acres of the dark stone, hoping to come across a clearly defined and recognisable trail of some unusual prehistoric animal – perhaps even that of a hominid.

I had recently received a letter from Mary Leakey, asking if I could find time to fly down to Olduvai and photograph the 'pits and channels', as she now called them. The work carried out since my last visit had done nothing to solve the mystery of the strange formations: in fact the surface now laid bare had only added a new mass of indecipherable marks that defied interpretation by anybody. Mary mentioned that one particular indent could possibly be a footprint and she hoped I could come soon to photograph it. Hoping nothing exceptional would happen up at Turkana, I arranged to visit Olduvai after filming progress at Paul and Kelly's elephant site.

Huge tusks eight feet long now lay fully exposed at their dig, and Kelly was working to match up fractured sections of the massive leg bones. A powerful wind swept the hot and stony site, making digging a dusty business, but this time it also inflicted a disaster on me. Part way through the filming I went forward to shout instructions above the noise of the wind; at that moment a particularly violent gust blew over my tripod on which was mounted my brand new Eclair – the silent camera specially purchased to enable me to film the gorillas with synchronised sound. Several thousand pounds' worth of camera crashed down amongst the unyielding remains of the prehistoric elephant, snapping off the expensive and delicate Angenieux zoom lens. I never even heard the camera hit the ground. It was fortunate that arrangements had been made to visit Mary so soon. Twenty-four hours later I was able to ship the camera and lens to London for urgent repairs.

When I flew on to Olduvai, for the first time in weeks, cloud cover floated in and effectively eliminated the shadows I needed to outline the extraordinary complex of pits and channels at the 'JK' site. Mary's men had worked back four or five yards from the curious depressions I had first seen with Louis. Now the detail of the true surface lay revealed – and nothing in my experience gave any help to determine what had created the puzzling formations. There were few sharp edges to the overall surface, much as though countless bare feet had rounded them away, but except for the one enigmatic mark that looked like a small heel print, there was nothing to indicate what had contributed to the smoothing process. Apart from the possible heel impression, and the small ridges encircling the pits that looked so very much like fingermarks, what must have been a soft, malleable surface had not captured a single imprint that could be identified. If hominids had been responsible, they had left no knee, palm or knuckle prints, no foot or toe prints. No animal hooves, paws, or the distinctive prints of birds had marked the surface. A staggered network of near-straight grooves and narrow furrows criss-crossed the area, and there were many large pits and little pockmarks of varying sizes. The grooves in the concave pits were all horizontal, and if they were not finger marks I could not think of any explanation for their size and shape. Whichever way one looked at it, the surface did not appear to have been the work of nature; Mary's men had several feet to go before being halted by the solid wall of the gorge, but so far each additional foot uncovered stubbornly refused to present any clues to help solve the mystery. Clouds still blanketed the sky on the next day. As it was not possible to keep my pilot for a second night at Olduvai, I arranged to come back a few days later.

Richard had just returned from a quick visit to Zambia, so both of us were in Nairobi when he received exciting news over the radio link with Koobi Fora. Bernard Ngeneo, a young and new member of the fossil-hunting team, had come across several pieces of a fossil skull. Committed to photographing Mary's pits and channels, I could not accompany Richard to check out the find, and so missed the first phase of a sensational hominid discovery. When Richard visited the site a few days later, excitement began to grow. An initial collection recovered some three dozen weathered fragments of a shattered skull. Many were very small, but from their thin cross-section it was already doubtful this was another australopithecine. Work to clear the surface stones and excavate the slope from top to bottom began immediately. When I finally reached Koobi Fora, nearly a hundred fragments had been collected. Some of the larger ones had been joined in a preliminary assembly that showed by its curvature that the brain case might be quite large.

Seasonal rains in the Ethiopian highlands were now pouring vast amounts of water down the Omo River and slowly raising the level of Lake Turkana. This gave me the opportunity to take scenes of my skeletal specimens being submerged. For several days I remained unaware of growing excitement at Koobi Fora. Under the leadership of Richard's right-hand man, Kamoya Kimeu, the fossil-hunting team had worked their way down a portion of the slope at the discovery site, the painstaking excavation and sieving work producing literally scores of assorted fragments. The specimen now had a reference number: KNM-ER 1470, and to Richard, Meave and anatomist Bernard Wood, who were working long hours to sort and match the pieces, it had become very evident the skull was highly unusual in shape.

My initial visit to the hominid site came four weeks after Bernard Ngeneo had sighted the first fragment. I flew there with Richard, Meave and Bernard and we landed on a small, rough strip the hominid gang had hacked out on some level ground near their Spartan camp. We walked over stony, eroded terrain to a golden-coloured wedge of earth on the side of a gully: a small cleared patch in a wilderness of dark sandstone, stunted thorny acacia trees, aloes and yellowed clumps of spiny grass. With the whole area now a harsh, windswept environment that supported a few wild animals, and occasionally the hardy livestock of the Shangila nomads, I found it difficult to imagine the prehistoric setting that had witnessed the death of a hominid. The fragile skull taking shape at Koobi Fora could give no hint as to how it had escaped the attentions of large scavengers: perhaps the creature had been caught in a flood or drowned in the lake, or had lain down to die in some obscured position before being preserved in protective sediments. The skull had been exposed by slow erosion millions of years later, only to be broken up and scattered down this lonely slope in front of us. The geologists were still busy trying to corre-late the widespread Turkana sediments, but had already determined that the deposits in this area had been laid down before those at the tool site, several miles to the south. The skull was therefore a remnant of a hominid who had been living early in the Pleistocene epoch, approximately two million years ago.

We examined the site briefly, noting that there was still a large area to be dug up and sieved, then walked on a short distance to where palaeontologist John Harris had found some beautifully preserved hominid leg bones: a complete femur and parts of a fibula and tibia that were amazingly similar to those of modern humans. He had found them a fair distance from the skull site, but the possibility that they came from the same, or a similar, creature could not be ignored.

All of a sudden the Turkana expedition had a fabulous discovery on its hands. A creature, apparently very much closer in form to *Homo sapiens* than the australopithecines, had been living in this region at the same time as those small-brained and low-browed hominids. Over the years to come the date applied to the tool site and the 1470 skull would be continuously contested and eventually adjusted, losing several thousand years in the process. But for the present, for Richard and all the members of his team, the discovery of the skull and leg bones had enormous significance, mounting evidence that the origins of the human line probably extended much further back in time than anyone had thought, thereby adding considerable fuel to Louis Leakey's long established theories on the subject. From my point of view, the new fossils altered priorities and changed the outlook for the material I was shooting. The new discovery would undoubtedly make headlines in the presses of the world and bring fame to members of the East Turkana expedition: it would also guarantee future funding for the now very extensive operation.

I was sorry to have missed the opening moments – the first sight of the bits of skull in their original setting; the leg bones lying as they were when John Harris came across them. There was a gap in the true sequence of events, but the slow unfolding of the rest of the story was thrilling enough to cover the missing segment. The wonderful finds made me feel happier about the decision to take up the Turkana assignment. I was at last covering one of Richard's expeditions where successes exceeded all expectations; now there would surely be plenty to do for a film about Richard in 1973. I felt less troubled about the uncertainty of future work with gorillas, but remained sorry that a prime period in their habituation was slipping away.

I was finding it difficult to keep up with the filming commitments: photography at the widespread camps and digs, attempts to locate the elusive Shangila fishermen, and work with my specimens vanishing under rising lake waters entailed much travelling. I rushed to shoot scenes of my skeletons, this time finding fresh evidence of a recent Shangila visit south of Koobi Fora – but no sign of the people who had left it. Returning inland to catch action at the 1470 site, I shot another sequence of the team at work. Tons of soil had already been processed. The excavators had almost completed their task and were gently prying away the final section of desiccated earth. I was fortunate to be on hand as a very large flake of bone came to light. Surprisingly, because they generally survived the fossilising process in good condition, not a single tooth had been found.

By the end of August, due mainly to Meave Leakey's dogged persistence, the fossil puzzle was coming together. One by one, pieces were being matched and joined and the main assembly was now fully recognisable as a skull. Masses of small fragments remained in little wooden trays, but because the majority were badly weathered and abraded, more difficult work lay ahead. To shoot a sequence as he was first shown the 1470 skull, I hurried back to base to be present when Professor Michael Day arrived on a visit to Koobi Fora. My Eclair camera was doing wonders in reducing some of the problems inherent in the filming sessions. The lack of any detectable noise allowed me to shoot scenes that were considerably more relaxed, a factor I knew would be a great help amongst the gorillas. With the minimum of direction I could let the sequences unfold much as they actually happened, so avoiding some of the acting that was difficult for untrained people to carry off in an unforced way.

The scenes of Michael Day viewing the new discovery were the first to include Richard in my filming for several years, and he quickly commented on the lack of camera noise. In some ways he found the silence disconcerting, now and then remaining poised for action, instinctively waiting for the whirr of the camera. As I moved position to develop new angles, he called out several times to ask if I was filming or not. But he soon adapted, almost forgetting my presence and concentrating on Michael Day, enjoying immensely his reactions to the intriguing specimen on the table.

With time running short I motored north to find the archaeologists in a new camp by the lake. Here I learned that some Shangila molo had recently appeared and were heading south. I drove slowly along the shore and was pleased to find that the small group had settled in a patch of reeds less than a mile away. A few men and young boys were grouped at the lake's edge: three simple dugout canoes drawn up to a sandy beach in reed-choked water. I was met with casual indifference at first and was unable to convey more than a formal greeting in Kiswahili. My heart sank at the prospect of trying to organise permission to film without a common language. These were the people who I hoped would allow me to depict a natural hunting and foraging way of life, and I would need some fairly specific scenes to allow the links between the past and present to be made.

A few fish lay in sand on the beach and a man and boy were gathering dry wood for a fire. Soon, one of the men approached and made the motions of striking a match; I would rather have watched the group use the wooden fire sticks I could see lying nearby, but quickly took the chance to foster more friendly relations. I fetched a box of matches and subsequent sign language made it clear the men wanted to keep it. At this point, an apparent desire to improve communications caused one of the boys to beckon and lead me to a man lying in the sand a few yards away. Wrapped in a dirty brown length of calico, his head supported on a wooden neck rest, the man appeared to be asleep, but the sound of my shoes crunching the sand caused him to roll over and sit up. I saw at once from the overall pale and scarred appearance of irises of his eyes that he was blind. To my great relief he spoke good Kiswahili, and following the formal exchange of greetings we fell into conversation.

His name was Sha-re; he had in the past been sent to a distant hospital at Marsabit to receive treatment for what was probably trachoma. It was while there that had learned to speak Kiswahili. Unfortunately the treatment had failed, and now, totally blind, dependent entirely on others for his subsistence, he was attached to the poorest members of his tribe. He wandered with them up and down the shores of the lake, allowed to share the food they obtained on their fishing forays. When I introduced the purpose of my visit and explained what I wanted to do, Sha-re's astute mind quickly grasped the significance of his position; acting as an interpreter and negotiator he would become, for a while at least, a useful member of his group – and was not slow in figuring out how he could personally benefit from any filming arrangements.

Anxious to get back to Koobi Fora and monitor progress with the skull, I struck a deal to begin work immediately. I had various items specially brought to barter for filming permission: tobacco, coffee beans, knives, coloured beads, cloth – even some thick brass welding rods eminently suitable for making the heavy bracelets so many of Kenya's nomads love to wear. Sha-re's friends readily agreed to let me film, although it was quite obvious they were not really sure what it was all about. The sequence that came together was disjointed, but at least depicted a few facets of the group's simple way of life. I hoped to follow them for longer periods, but for the present Sha-re assured me his companions would be remaining in the locality. When payment for his part in the deal fell due, he insisted I guide him some distance from his sharp-eyed companions so that they could not see the cash that changed hands. I asked Sha-re to try to persuade his friends to travel towards Koobi Fora and long discussions followed. The men were reluctant to make such a move as the fishing to the south was poor at this time – but then the anticipation of further gifts seemed to tip the balance.

I will always remember the occasion. We stood in a group near the Land Rover, Sha-re translating, and with the prospect of further personal gain, no doubt inserting his own point of view. At one stage I took a drink of water – clear drinking water that had come from the N'derati Wells – and offered some around to Sha-re and the others. Used to the alkaline lake water, Sha-re remarked how sweet the drink was – and so cold! It struck me then that these simple men would have no knowledge of ice. To impress them, I took out the ice tray from the small refrigerator in my Land Rover and placed a cube in an outstretched hand. The reaction was instantaneous: the man yelled in alarm and threw the ice to the ground. In the gabble of conversation that followed Sha-re translated the complaint that I had burned the man's hand. It took only a moment to demonstrate that the hand was intact and that the ice was simply very cold and melting quickly in the heat. Although they accepted the fact, the men remained suspicious, finding it impossible to comprehend that ice was merely solid water. To them, ice produced the sensation of burning and they could not readily understand why their skin showed no damage.

I left, trusting the group would move as promised. Koobi Fora lay only fifteen miles directly down the lake shore and I would have followed them on their journey had it been possible. Unfortunately a huge hill called Kokoi – the solid remains of an ancient lava flow – blocked any passage by vehicle, necessitating a diversion inland of over fifty miles.

At Koobi Fora remarkable progress had been made with the 1470 fossil. The cranium was now almost sixty per cent complete, and with a shape that left no doubt the brain it had once contained was impressively large. Part of the upper jaw had been found, but sadly the all-important teeth were still missing. In spite of being worn down by his workload and almost continuous flying, Richard, was in a jubilant mood. Combined with the astonishingly human-like limb bones John Harris had found, the impact this new skull was going to have on palaeoanthropologists worldwide would obviously be profound – and definitely lead to revisions of the current perception of human origins.

The skull was naturally the subject of frequent and animated discussion; anyone coming in from the outlying camps invariably paid a visit to Richard's building to keep up with any headway on reconstruction and feast their eyes on the extraordinary fossil. Brain capacity was argued over and estimated, until finally, one afternoon the matter was settled by carefully sealing the gaps in the skull and filling the delicate assembly with fine sand. There was some difficulty in deciding how to establish the inner dimensions of a brain without the nasal bones and eye sockets in position, but eventually a consensus was reached. The quantity of sand was then measured with the only large calibrated container available – a rain gauge. After further argument over how to convert the inches of a rain gauge to cubic centimetres, the body of a large hypodermic syringe was used to confirm the final figure obtained: in round figures, 1470's brain capacity was estimated to be approximately eight hundred cubic centimetres – a figure that was later proved to be remarkably accurate.

I went in search of my little band of fishermen, who by now should have passed Kokoi Hill and be approaching Koobi Fora. With binoculars I finally picked out distant figures, distorted and broken by the shimmering waves of heated air flowing over the earth. When the gap closed I was able to see that several dugouts were drawn up to the beach. The group had grown considerably in numbers; obviously the word had spread that I was offering gifts in exchange for pictures. Sha-re told me he had walked most of the way because the canoe owners would not always give him space. I was impressed by his ability to cope with the situation; occasionally he was led by a boy, but apparently was often left to find his own way, sometimes covering ten or more miles in a day.

The enlarged band gave me many more opportunities to record their daily activities: fishing methods, making fire for cooking, the erection of simple reed shelters to give shade from the intense sunlight. Several of the six-inch nails that were part of my barter stock were soon put to use. Using dried zebra dung for his fire, and beating the metal into shape with large basalt pebbles, the expert blacksmith of the gang hammered them out to make simple but effective harpoon heads. I stayed with the group as they fished their way south, stopping at various preferred campsites that gave opportunities to show how material signs of their present and past occupations were scattered all about.

Meanwhile the reconstruction of the 1470 skull continued. Well over two hundred fragments had been recovered, but it was going to be a difficult task to match and fit those with abraded edges. Weeks if not months of patient assembly lay ahead. Richard decided that he must take the skull to show Louis before he departed from Nairobi on a long lecture tour. I wished I could be present to see Louis's reaction and hear his comments when he first laid eyes on the extraordinary specimen. As a safety measure I shot some formal pictures before it was packed away.

Four days later Richard was able to tell everyone just how delighted Louis had been with the fossil. He was immensely pleased from his first assessment that it backed his personal belief that australopithecines were not directly ancestral to *Homo sapiens* – clear vindication of his claim that the *Homo* line extended deeper into the past than anyone currently thought possible. Over seven years had passed since Louis and Raymond Dart had established a new species for the genus *Homo* by naming a new and delicate fossil skull from Olduvai. Calling it *Homo habilis*, Louis had landed himself in an ongoing controversy: first over the slender basis for establishing a new species, and secondly for the use of the word *habilis*. In creating the new species, Louis had abandoned previous firmly stated beliefs that australopithecines were ancestral to modern man, and had also been obliged to redefine the meaning of the word *Homo*. Few of his peers and critics in the academic world allowed him to forget earlier statements, and had not accepted his later reasoning.

The field season was now ending and Koobi Fora became crowded as the outlying camps closed down. On 1 November I took Glynn Isaac and some of his team to see various Shangila molo campsites. Glynn was keen to view the concentrated debris of these primitive hunters and foragers, especially at one sheltered place where an extraordinary quantity of bone and interesting artefacts had accumulated. None of us could know that while we examined the bleached and scattered bones of mammals, reptiles and fish – noting how wind-driven sand had already buried some of them – Louis had suffered a serious heart attack and was dying in a London hospital. The news that he had died came to Koobi Fora over a little transistor radio late the next day; one of the African excavating assistants heard it and rushed to spread the word. The sad news immediately cast a shadow of sorrow over the camp. In recent years Louis had suffered many physical setbacks that had slowed him down enormously, but it was hard to accept we would not see him again. Richard had flown out that morning, unaware his father had died, but he would have received the information soon enough on arrival at Nairobi.

In the latest batch of mail to come up was a letter from Joanne. Her news was also depressing. Taking advantage of a three-man camera crew already in Botswana, Dennis Kane had decided to send the team on to Rwanda to film some sound sequences with Dian at her camp – an arrangement that diminished even further the slim chance of a return to the volcanoes for television work. Joanne also mentioned she was concerned Dian still did not want to have any part in a lecture show on the gorillas. She went on to say that after all the effort and money put into the project, the lecture division was under obligation to present the material to the members of the society; she felt something would surely be worked out. Four months in the windy deserts of Turkana had almost obliterated thoughts of the gorillas, but this letter brought them to the fore again in a less than pleasant way. All the trials and tribulations plaguing the project were starting to overshadow the excitements and successes so recently attained.

The Turkana field season had ended, but there was much to do before Richard flew to London to present the 1470 fossil to the Royal Zoological Society. Plans for 1973 were beginning to fall into place too. Although uncertainty over gorilla matters remained, the possibility I would be able to view all the film was good. Back in Nairobi, I learned that the *Geographic* film crew had not gone to Rwanda after all. Joanne wrote of her worry that Dian would be bitter about the cancellation of the crew's visit. To accommodate their changing schedules she had twice postponed arrangements to fly home to America. The situation raised the faint chance of an opening to return to the volcanoes after all, but it was too remote to arouse any enthusiasm.

A gulf of silence lay between Dian and me. I tried to breach it with a letter discussing matters relevant to gorillas that kept coming my way – particularly the attempt by Professor Weis-Fogh from Cambridge to persuade me to describe and analyse behavioural aspects of the film material. There had been was no reply to this, but late in November, at eleven o'clock at night, the phone rang: Dian was in the Nairobi Hilton Hotel and wanted to see me. I could tell by her clipped words and the tone of her voice that she was emotionally upset, but in answer to my questions she simply repeated, 'I've just got to see you.'

I drove in to the empty city and met Dian in her room high in the lofty Hilton tower. In spite of the midnight hour she was dressed in a smart, long dress, as if ready to depart for a dinner party. She looked darkly attractive – the sophisticated Dian Fossey, far removed from the booted, jeans-clad scientist stressed by the rigours of high-altitude research on gorillas. I had seen her work the transformation on many occasions, but this time shadows darkened her eyes and in the subdued room lighting she looked drawn and weary. Items of luggage were strewn about the room. The pungent smell of cigarette smoke hung in the air, and an ashtray with many stubs spoke of a strong return to smoking. She had finally agreed to give a lecture to society members and was on her way to Washington to help edit the film. Stilted small talk about what we had done over the past half year occupied our initial conversation. She was sad about Louis Leakey's death, but my descriptions of the highly successful season with his son met with little response. She told me that Sandy Harcourt had returned shortly after my departure, and that the work was going well; but in my absence the gorillas had become more wary and she was having a little difficulty following my techniques. The animals were apparently not yet treating Sandy with anything like the level of trust that had been accorded to me. To improve the situation he had even tried wearing a beret and clothing similar to mine.

The small talk dwindled; suddenly Dian blurted out a plea for me to give up the pursuit of fossil bones and return to help her with the gorilla study. She was desperately unhappy with the way things had come to an end between us. If I would come back we could get married and continue with the research on a new basis. Tears marred her careful make-up, and overwhelmed by the depth of her distress I could not find the words to ease it. Yes, I wanted to go back and finish what should be a definitive visual record of the mountain gorilla's way of life. I had opened the door to a new level of habituation, but had only stepped inside. What lay beyond was fascinating to contemplate – but I could not accept the terms Dian expected to be fulfilled in return. As gently as I could I reiterated what had been the gist of many past conversations: the intimate friendship that had developed between us was not a foundation for a permanent relationship. I could not transform my fondness and respect for her as a person into love and marriage. Giving up my life in Kenya and marriage to Heather had never been a consideration. Even if it had been, the funding for photographic work with the gorillas was not unlimited. I was prepared and more than willing to take the gorillas' amazingly calm acceptance of close human contact to a logical conclusion – if the support were there – but beyond that, for a photographer an indefinite future loomed. Dian dried her eyes and seemed almost to change a mental gear. She suggested that perhaps we could still work together as before if the opportunity arose. She would soon be able to find out what the people at *National Geographic* had in mind. Unaware I would never see Dian again, feeling the same disconcerting mixture of regret and sadness that matched our last parting, I left her standing in the sterile hotel room, tall and shadowed in the dim lighting.

Richard returned from his visit to London and Paris in a buoyant mood. In spite of strained moments when he and Lord Zuckerman, the secretary of the Zoological Society, came face to face with a large contingent of the press clamouring for an interview, the official presentation of the 1470 fossil had gone off very well indeed. The news media had given the skull almost unprecedented publicity, elevating Richard in a matter of days to a prominent position in the world of palaeoanthropology. The large-brained creature represented by 1470 was being tentatively accepted as directly ancestral to the genus *Homo*, shunting aside the robust australopithecines which had formerly been considered the main candidate for that position.

Richard had been pressed to give a lecture to National Geographic Society members before the end of the year, but this plan had been cancelled and a new date set for March 1973. The whole concept of a fast-moving, thirty-minute film on which I had been working had to be changed, and I set about expanding the material for a one-hour showing. Joanne advised me that some senior members of staff at the *Geographic* had suggested I should attend the lecture also, so a combination of this idea and the tenuous arrangements for me to see my gorilla footage made it more certain I would go to Washington. I tried hard to look beyond the immediate future, quite unable to guess whether gorillas or bones and stones would dominate in the coming year. I was unaware that, contrary to all expectations, 1973 was destined to be a year of complete change, one that would see the slow breaking of ties with the National Geographic Society and the beginnings of a long run making wildlife documentaries for Survival Anglia.

Though a return to the Virunga volcanoes still seemed possible, I sensed that the opportunity had been lost. Joanne reported on Dian's recent meetings with Dennis Kane, which had gone well. But as Wolper Productions had already used some of my material in the *Monkeys, Apes and Man* show; in their opinion, a full-length film on gorillas was for the present not a good idea. I found the attitude astonishing, but then I was heavily biased. The decision to break away at a crucial point had perhaps not been wise; it had led to a confrontation with Dian which had closed down photographic coverage at the wrong moment. With hindsight, it was obvious I should have moved in on the gorillas very much sooner. I had spent nearly a year and a half following a restrictive style of non-intrusive contacts, initially approving the approach and accepting the limitations it placed on photography. A much earlier discovery that the apes would accept humans so passively would surely have altered the whole course of Dian's study – and the impact of my work.

A formal invitation for me to be present at Richard's lecture soon arrived. In mid-March I flew to Washington and for three weeks remained heavily occupied viewing the gorilla footage. Dian had spent a long time at the *Geographic* offices also. Beyond being made nervous by the thought of facing a large audience of society members, she was now fully resigned to the ordeal and thinking positively about the publicity it would generate for her work. I learned that the magazine was not considering a third article, instead, the book division was seriously contemplating publishing a whole book on gorillas, a project that interested me a great deal. Early in 1972, Louis Leakey had told his English publishers, Collins, about the exciting developments with gorillas. As a result, Sir William Collins had written to try to persuade me to write up my experiences. But I had already given Dian a solemn promise I would wait until she had published her own adventures before attempting anything myself; now it seemed the chance would come sooner than expected.

With a television show pushed to some unknown time in the future, it was frustrating yet still satisfying to view all the film – especially the footage that followed my descent to hands and knees and attempts to behave like a gorilla. I spent hours in the cramped screening room, reliving the thrills and tensions that had accompanied so many of the extraordinary encounters. In spite of the noise and heated air blowing from the projector, I was easily transported to the mountain environment and almost able to feel the atmosphere: the chilled, misty air that flowed over the steep slopes; the frequent icy showers; the rare days of sun that marked the wild scenery with harsh brilliance; the sometimes fierce storms that often left the peak of Karisimbi capped in white. Again, I wished I could extend the wonderful experience: but having talked to every-one concerned it was obvious the assignment had definitely ended.

The taming of a whole family of wild gorillas had in the end been un-expectedly easy. Their almost docile acceptance of the alien creature who had joined their family had been unexpected also. Being allowed to move freely amongst them had been exciting enough, but to be touched and examined, and finally played with so trustingly, had moved me beyond words. In spite of the very successful season at Lake Turkana, the decision I had made to follow the fossil hunters now came back to haunt me. I knew the visual record of gorilla behaviour was very incomplete. Given a few months with reasonable weather, I could practically guarantee to produce some spectacular footage that wildlife film producers would give their eye-teeth to have.

Fifteen years were to pass before I saw a mountain gorilla again, the opportunity arising only because Warner Brothers and Universal Studios wanted to use my name in their production of *Gorillas in the Mist* – and then, the circumstances of the eagerly awaited contact were such that I almost regretted that the creatures had become so amenable to the presence of human beings.

Gorillas in the Mist

'Silence!' 'Quiet!' The stentorian voice of the assistant director, Patrick Clayton, rang out across the thickly wooded slopes, echoed moments later in Rwandese and French by a Rwandan production assistant. Conversation between crew members died and the noisy chatter from lounging porters faded away. In the hushed silence a few natural sounds from the mountain wilderness broke through again: the distant call of a turaco echoing eerily in the misty air; the twitter of sunbirds seeking nectar from lobelia flowers; the low buzz of a few bees at work. At a murmured command, camera and tape recorder rolled noiselessly. 'Aaaaaaand... action!' The soft voice of director Michael Apted set actors in motion and another carefully composed scene played out.

For three weeks I had followed the activities of the film crew in the moody scenery of the Virunga volcanoes. Engaged by Warner Brothers and Universal Studios to advise and assist the directors during the shooting, and designated a 'special photographer', I had spent the time taking photographs of the unit at work and of actors Sigourney Weaver and, later, Bryan Brown playing the parts of Dian and myself. Constantly revived memories of past events, most far removed from those being portrayed for the filming, had at first made the work a bizarre experience, but as the days passed I had gradually come to terms with the situation.

With only the major features of her compelling story in mind and drawing strongly on their own visions of her African adventure, the film-makers were busy condensing eighteen years of Dian's life into a few hours of screen time. I was part of a team creating an epic designed to enthral the public with action and romance, all filmed in beautiful or harsh African settings as the script demanded. From my point of view, the screenplay had such a tenuous connection with historical accuracy that I had to keep reminding myself the production was a commercial venture aiming for box-office success. I knew the high-cost enterprise would surely thrive on the fictional settings and elevated drama, and in so doing would give immense publicity to the precarious state of the remnant population of mountain gorillas.

I was expected to provide pictures of the gorillas too, a factor that had given me added incentive to join the production team. Impatiently, I waited for the chance to meet them again. But Rwanda's national park authorities were sticking very firmly to the regulations covering the gorilla groups that could be visited. Even for this high-paying major production, nothing could persuade them to relax their insistence on compliance. The number of people allowed to contact the two groups open to filming were severely restricted, and the study groups that ranged in the vicinity of Karisoke were initially ruled out of bounds. Knowing full well that in many other African countries the offer of money would have cut through all regulations and made a mockery of the rules, I had to admire and respect their stand. The crew of the second unit shooting all the gorilla sequences was forced to cut their numbers to a bare minimum; they also took preference for the contacts, so I had to wait my turn.

My chance came when the main unit took a break while their camp was being transferred from the base of Mount Sabinio to Karisoke. By good fortune, the day set for us to climb and settle in at Karisoke coincided with a rest period for the second unit; my first opportunity to satisfy a deep longing to see the great apes again had at last arrived. Because no advance arrangements could be made I had to gamble on a park ranger being available to lead me to the gorillas. Though I left the hotel in Gisenyi well before dawn to make the three-hour journey to the second unit's camp, on arrival no rangers were anywhere to be seen. The two whose duty it was to keep track of the gorillas had already set out to do their work. It seemed I had been thwarted and my spirits sank. At this moment of despair, a man from the camp appeared and said that the rangers had gone off a matter of minutes earlier; I could catch up with them if I hurried. I set off at a trot immediately, finding that the rangers were indeed not far ahead. Relayed shouts by other people on the path halted them until I could draw level.

The men were at first reluctant to let me accompany them. As far as they were concerned, no arrangement had been made for any film people to be taken to the gorillas on this day – rules were rules and prior permission was needed. But then the younger of the two suddenly relaxed his official attitude and said he knew me perfectly well. He asked if I remembered him, but I could not place his face. He had been a boy when I was here last, he said, and because older men always took the portering jobs, apparently I had only chosen him once to take a box up to Karisoke. He laughed when he recalled that his father had taken the wage he had earned anyway. He had been sixteen then: now he was a man of thirty with a large family. Our conversation melted the official ice; I was invited to join the pair and without more ado we moved off.

Like all the men who lived in this region, the rangers were wiry, tireless walkers, conditioned from childhood to contend with the hilly, high altitude and often carrying heavy loads on their heads. We moved at a fast walk, heading west and following the distant line of bamboo forest covering the long, cratered saddle separating Mount Sabinio from Visoke. I was thankful for the benefit of two weeks' walking and climbing that had allowed me to acclimatise and improve my physical fitness.

We strode on for a full hour at a merciless pace, until at last my companions turned to head directly towards the bamboo fringe. Along the way, the younger ranger told me that many of the people near Visoke were still wondering why I had come back to Rwanda. The word had spread that I was likely to bring down more trouble on the heads of those who had worked for Dian Fossey. There was still a good deal of speculation and uncertainty about the activities of the film crew too – in particular some scenes set up to depict a funeral procession following Dian's coffin into the mountains. A large number of the local men and women who had watched the decidedly strange antics with the dummy coffin were apparently convinced some sort of strange magic was being practised. This led the conversation down another channel; I asked the men what they thought about the murder. 'Did they believe that the *M'sungu*, the American student Wayne McGuire, had been responsible?' Shrugs and shaking heads answered that one. 'What about the *wawindagi*, the hunters, or possibly the poachers?' I persisted, but this produced more shrugs and negative head shakes. It was obvious the pair were not at all keen to pursue the subject, so I let it rest. By the time we entered the bamboo thickets an hour and a half had passed. Hazy sun had already heated the atmosphere and I was grateful to enter the deep shade of the bamboo.

Now the pace slowed. The rangers knew where the gorillas had been the previous day and fresh signs were soon located. As the tracking process began, I cooled off and at last began to enjoy myself. I kept close behind the leading man, watching the signs he was following, remembering the countless days spent following gorilla trails through the thickets and woodlands of Visoke. My tracking skills had deteriorated from lack of use, but gorillas leave too many obvious marks for their passage to be difficult to follow. I let my eyes absorb the evidence unfolding ahead of us: the foliage displaced by heavy bodies, pale undersides of leaves signalling the freshness of the damage; the foot and knuckle prints in the open patches of soil; plants shredded and eaten; the occasional, distinctive bolus of dung.

It was near noon before the snapping of twigs and the sound of vegetation being pressed aside gave away the presence of gorillas. The animals had moved in a great half circle, leading us back close to the point where we had entered the bamboo. We were soon well beyond the position where in the past I would have taken to my hands and knees, but the lead man moved ahead with no attempt to be silent or to conceal himself. My conditioned instincts were battling with the knowledge that the gorillas we were shortly to see had been visited almost daily for years. They would have seen park rangers constantly and literally hundreds of tourists in that time. I knew perfectly well visitors were regularly brought to within a few yards of the animals. I followed the ranger's lead, accepting with a touch of sadness that my crawling technique had become outdated long ago.

A loud though constrained vibrato hoot came from the bamboo thicket on our right, followed immediately by a tremendous thump on the ground. My guide crouched to see better through the shadowed stems, motioning me to do the same. In dappled shade not twelve feet away, a massive head turned and I looked straight into the eyes of a big silverback. He stared balefully back with what in human terms could only be described as disdainful arrogance. My guide spoke in a normal voice to tell me this was Mrithi, the leader of the group. He then made the deep, rumbling 'contentment' sound I had used so often myself and the gorilla looked away; beyond him, soft sunlight glowed from a grassy glade so that his dark bulk was beautifully outlined against the pale background. I levelled a camera to capture the imposing image, feeling a touch from the man behind as I focused the lens – but it was not the ranger! As I glanced back, the small furry body of a gorilla juvenile brushed by; it went on past the man crouching ahead, thrusting out a rear foot to kick his boot with contemptuous familiarity. I watched the little body ambling away, distracted by this show of complete nonchalance – and lost my shot of the silverback. He got to his feet, swinging a great arm to catch a bamboo stem, breaking it with a vicious crack that clearly served to relieve a little of his annoyance at being disturbed.

We followed Mrithi closely, moving through the bamboo to the edge of the glade. Now I could see a few of the rest of the family. Several females were squatting in the open, stripping short thistle plants of their upper leaves, turning them deftly to avoid the sharp spines as they stuffed them into their mouths. Many other gorillas were in the thick vegetation on the periphery of the glade, but without hesitation my two guides walked forward, upright and with no concern for the positions of the animals. One or two had to give way as we approached, but were obviously not in the least perturbed by our presence: they simply shifted a few feet to another feeding place. I was dumbfounded by the casualness with which the contact had been made and was now being followed through without any consideration for the gorillas. We halted for a moment as the silverback stopped briefly and surveyed the field. The older ranger sat down and pulled out a pipe, which he then pro-ceeded to light. My young friend motioned me forward and we followed a few paces behind the big male as he moved again. Mrithi glanced back at us momentarily, headed for a patch of thistles, sat down and began to eat.

I asked the ranger what he would have done in normal circumstances when leading a group of tourists. He explained that tourists were obliged to follow instructions very carefully. He would have kept everyone together, then halted on the fringes of the group and not moved out into the middle as we had just done. He considered me an old gorilla hand and therefore privileged to move right in amongst the animals. If I had not been with him he would have simply located the group, maybe stayed for a while to see where the animals might be heading and then left. Now he told me he wanted to go soon because he needed to visit someone. If I would, please, take my pictures quickly, we would depart as soon as I had finished. Leaving me to do as I pleased, he walked off to a grassy mound and sat down beside it.

I turned and contemplated the scene. Gorillas were scattered all about, some static and eating, others moving to seek out fresh plants. In the company of a female, two small juveniles tumbled in gentle play. The family patriarch sat fifteen feet away, chewing slowly, now and then glancing up to watch me.

Still feeling the compulsion to follow my old tactics and conform to gorilla etiquette – to get down to their level and mind my manners – I began taking the portraits I needed, shifting position frequently, virtually ignored unless I made too direct an approach. Knowing how impossibly restrictive it would have been under normal circumstances with a group of other people and a strict guide, I was thankful to be working alone with such complete freedom. But in my heart I felt increasingly unhappy. As I shot my pictures the situation began to feel unreal. The two rangers were now all but invisible, both having lain back in the grass and apparently gone to sleep. Time was slipping away, but as neither stirred I took advantage, continuing to manoeuvre and take pictures until I had more than enough.

The initial excitement I had always felt when meeting gorillas had rapidly dissipated. Being able to stand tall and look down on these magnificent creatures from such short range had somehow diminished their stature – they seemed smaller than I remembered. All the thrill and tension of what I knew as a normal contact was missing. The gorillas scattered all around me now were almost contemptuous of my presence; I was merely another of the humans they saw every day. With sly glances they kept track of my move-ments, but unless I came uncomfortably close, they went on feeding. Silverback Mrithi was a fine specimen; weighing anywhere between three and four hundred pounds he looked to be in prime condition. He reminded me slightly of Geronimo, leader of the Visoke Group 9: the first silverback I had laid eyes on nearly two decades ago. With a twinge of guilt, it struck me I could in some measure be partly to blame for the gorillas' casual acceptance of humans so close. If I had not insisted on closing in on them, in all probability Dian would have maintained her policy of static, non-interference with the groups, continuing to let the gorillas dictate the outcome of a contact. But then I knew that unless actively restrained, others who had come to join her study would eventually have initiated a condition similar to the one I had created; and anyway, the high level of habituation that allowed tourists to visit and see gorillas with such ease was one of the main reasons the creatures still survived on these mountains.

As I watched Mrithi, mulling over the complex issues surrounding the conservation of wild places and the protection of wild animals, my young guide suddenly sat up, blinking. An hour and a quarter had passed while he dozed. Now he realised he had stayed far longer than intended. He rose quickly, calling loudly to his companion, who did not answer. Beyond glancing his way, the few gorillas still visible ignored his raised voice, taking little notice as he strode across the glade to rouse the sleeping man. Walking through the gorillas, most now obscured again by bamboo thickets, we hurried away from the place and back across the cultivated fields. Preoccupied with whatever meeting lay ahead of him, my friend left me to return to camp with the older man and headed towards a distant cluster of huts.

By mid-afternoon I was climbing the old path to Karisoke, expecting to see it trampled to a broad path by the thousands of feet that had pounded up and down with gear to set up our new camp. To my surprise, the old trail showed remarkably little evidence of the heavy traffic it had carried. I caught up with members of the first unit, still shooting some scenes at the little stream marking the traditional porter resting point. At Karisoke, the open glade south of the cabins had been transformed, the sounds of frenetic activity ringing out as the last jobs to be done were rushed to completion. A mass of large tents crowded the narrow stretch of grass that had once been the view from my flimsy tent. Here the passage of hundreds of boots and bare feet had turned the water-saturated area to a quagmire – but the camp was ready.

During the course of the filming around Karisoke I met the current director of the establishment, David Watts, and also, at last, Vatiri and Nemeye, the two assistants who had shared with me many of the early excitements of working with the gorillas. Both of them had been employed on gorilla work since mid-1969. They, more than any of the other men who had come to work at the Visoke camp, knew how I had influenced Dian and had eventually transformed the contacts with gorillas. Through thick and thin they had remained loyal to her, and were now the longest-serving members on Karisoke's staff lists.

I talked with David Watts about the groups that remained restricted to research workers, our conversations serving to highlight the passing of time. Most of the mature animals I had known had long since died, and sadly many of the infants and juveniles also. I talked again with Kanyarugano about the mystery of Dian's murder, and then at some length with Nemeye and Vatiri. These men had suffered at the hands of those investigating the brutal act, and the pain of their experiences showed in their faces and manner as they talked. Listening to their comments and theories about what might have happened that fatal night, I, like all others who had voiced or written opinions, did not believe that Wayne McGuire, the student researcher condemned to death *in absentia* by a Rwandan court, had anything to do with the murder; a motive was lacking, and unless he had become enraged for some inexplicable reason, hacking Dian to death with a panga would have been hard for him to do. Everything I had heard or read about, and what I now learned from my old employees, gave little in the way of strong evidence to form an opinion on what had actually happened. Both poachers and government officials who were in conflict with or opposed to Dian and her activities had the strongest motives, but I reasoned that the poachers were not directly involved. In the limited area where her study groups ranged, Dian had been at odds with the animal hunters for eighteen years; I felt sure that had any particular group or individual from the poaching fraternity chosen to eliminate her, they would not have selected an approach that involved cutting a way into her house and tackling her inside. To me, the disjointed evidence available pointed to the two men whose footprints had been found on the trail the morning Dian's body had been discovered. Kanyarugano told me the fresh, bare footprints he and others had seen showed that the pair had come up the trail that night and descended the same way. But who were they? Poachers seeking revenge or in search of treasured possessions she had taken from them, or others with more sinister intentions? The unexplained disarray in her house indicated a search for something, but then apparently nothing was missing from it, and what appeared to be a ransacking could possibly have been caused by a struggle to subdue her. Aware that a Rwandan government official had got himself into serious difficulty over his harsh treatment of Dian, I was inclined to think the most plausible explanation was that the two were hired hit men sent by another, or others, specifically to murder her. Vatiri told me she had been killed with her own panga, which indicated her assailant was not armed with his own. Some time later, it was with a sudden chill that I remembered giving Dian the rather special panga I had carried and used throughout my term in the mountains. I fervently hoped that it was not the one that had killed her.

I had got nowhere with my investigations, and it was a disturbing thought to know that, somewhere, there were two or three men, or perhaps many more, who knew exactly what had occurred. My memories of Dian belonged to a period of time almost two decades in the past, a time being constantly revived as I revisited old haunts and followed the activities of the film-makers. The ups and downs of Dian's life in the years that followed, increasingly tempestuous and difficult, belonged to a different era; one of which I had only small knowledge and not in any way enough for me to analyse the complicated circumstances surrounding her sudden end. One thing was certain: her death and the manner of it had focused worldwide attention on the status of the mountain gorillas. She would be remembered as the one above all others who had championed a few hundred of the wonderful creatures who had come to dominate her life. Her death had been swift, and to me there was some consolation in the knowledge she had avoided a difficult period of increasing illness and old age.

By this time I was more entertained than disturbed by the screen story. Every trip we made into the mountains covered familiar ground that had witnessed a far more complex story than the one being shot, but no film could ever be expected to capture the true essence of those past times. The years of work following and studying the giant apes, the long, lonely, sometimes exciting hours spent making friends with them had no room in the script. Aside from the central figure of Dian, to give the film authenticity, the screenplay used the names of Louis Leakey, Dian's friend, Ros Carr, and mine, but all other characters were fictional. There was one true-life exception: the Reverend Wallace, the man who had actually conducted Dian's funeral service at Karisoke, had been engaged to play his own part.

Much of the filming at Karisoke involved the decrepit-looking shack built on the lower end of the top meadow – first to help recreate Dian's initial arrival at Kabara, then as part of the setting for a sequence describing her forced abduction by a very hostile group of soldiers. The shooting script blandly ignored Dian's very first visit to Kabara as a tourist in 1963, where Alan Root had somewhat reluctantly condescended to show her some gorillas; also that Alan had returned with her three years later to help set up the now novice researcher. The scenes of her violent arrest and removal by soldiers ignored even a suggestion of historical accuracy, but I had to concede they certainly had all the drama and ferocious action needed to enthral an audience.

Many of the sequences that had been devised caused me wry amusement: in particular those that involved Bryan Brown. The sequence describing my first day out in the woodlands to search for gorillas caused inward smiles: Sigourney Weaver was hoisted up on to a large limb of a hagenia tree, where she balanced in an imposing stance. Like a queen of the jungle, she watched from this lofty perch while Bryan struggled up from below, supposedly following her uninvited, and suffering badly from nettle stings. Fear of heights would never have permitted Dian to have stood in that precarious position; the scene transported my mind to the many times I had to unlock her rigid fingers and help her traverse some hazardous sections of Visoke's higher ravines. Although it was a sequence due to be shot later in English studios at Shepperton, for my first arrival at Dian's camp the screenplay had me turning up in a rainstorm – unannounced and unexpected – and finding Dian practising gorilla vocalisations. Reading this, laughing at the redesigned meeting, I thought back with some pleasure to the day of my own first arrival in 1968, the wonderful and exciting weeks working alone with the gorillas that followed; and five months later, the events that very nearly terminated the subsequent assignment before it had really begun. But again I had to admit that the film version would have much more impact.

During one of many excursions to work near Karisoke, a particular scene to be shot called for a steep slope, some pleasing mountain scenery, and one of the volcanoes standing out clearly in the background. I directed Michael Apted to a shoulder of Visoke that overlooked some fine, moss-sheathed hagenia trees and allowed a good view of Mikeno: it was a position I had used myself as a setting to film Dian climbing to search for gorillas. It also happened to be at the base of the ridge where my last meeting with Digit had taken place. Before long, while the crew ran through the drawn-out procedures before shooting could begin, an insistent urge to climb up became too strong to deny. I headed quickly up the shoulder, almost drawn upwards. Soon I broke out on to the open patch where long ago I had counted Group 4, drastically reduced by one-third after the unexplained loss of three members and the transfer of two females to the bachelor band led by old Rafiki. I climbed higher, purposely heading for the place where I had last seem my wonderful gorilla friend.

Except that the ridge path was overgrown, everything seemed curiously familiar, as though nothing had changed shape or grown much over the past fifteen years. I came to the depression where in some previous age a large section of pumice and ash had slumped to form a shallow bowl. A few yards away was the edge of the ridge where I had sat in a bitter wind, waiting fruitlessly for better conditions to grace my last day alone with Group 4. I moved across to it, searching for old markers to get my bearings. A gentle breeze wafted up from the ravine that fell steeply from the ridge, bringing sounds of activity from the film crew far below. But I found I could no longer remember the exact position of the contact, or where I had passed the hunched form of Digit. Nursing an uncomfortable sense of loss, I abandoned the sentimental journey and descended hastily to rejoin the unit.

Most of the work in the vicinity of Karisoke evoked recall of the past. I had lived here, on and off, for three and a half years, part of the exhilarating events marking the initial period of Dian's study – the years when the gorillas were still wild, ever elusive and difficult to approach, but, because of that, intensely exciting to be with. Overcoming their fear and great distrust of humans, little by little establishing a trusting and then friendly relationship, I had been able to crawl past the foliage barriers to work right in amongst them. Since leaving the mountains, nothing had come close to matching the pleasure and excitement gained from making those first intimate contacts with a family of great apes. The memories were indelible and time had not dimmed them at all.

Before I left Rwanda, a final photographic opportunity remained that I was determined not to miss. It involved climbing to the top of Mount Visoke to shoot scenes of an old DC3 'Dakota' aircraft flying between the peaks of the volcanoes. Stills of the flight were not really necessary, but I had resolved to take this last chance to visit Mount Visoke. To be fully prepared, the film crew had climbed the peak to camp for the night on top of the mountain, but I opted to get up very early and make the ascent with a companion at dawn. Unfortunately, a diversion to collect two porters delayed us. We reached the base of Visoke with less than two hours to spare before the plane was due on its first run. Reminding us of the swiftly passing minutes, the sun cleared the horizon as we began to climb. Already doubting it would be possible to climb the four thousand feet in time, we set out at a pace that brought memories of my first climb to meet Dian Fossey. This time, though I was thoroughly altitude-conditioned, I was twenty years older. I knew the test would come when we left the main trail to tackle the steep incline direct to the volcano's summit.

Haze and thin cloud were producing soft, golden light, but there was no time to enjoy the scenery. We rushed through the lower belt of hagenia and hypericum trees, then on through the zone of giant senecios and lobelias. When the wind brought the distinctive sound of radial engines powering the DC3 away from the distant Ruhengeri airstrip, several hundred feet still stretched ahead of us. Sweating and panting, we neared the edge of Visoke's crater, covering the last lap in a state approaching that of exhausted marathon runners straining for the finishing line.

When we cleared the rim, the aircraft was already cruising behind the high peak at the far side of the crater. Mount Mikeno jutted into the sky beyond, its dark outline softened by skeins of light cloud and blue haze. On the far side of the rim, silhouetted against the pale background of sky, I could just make out the tiny figures of the camera crew. We had beaten the deadline by seconds only. Following the plane as it turned and flew between Mikeno and Visoke, I struggled to hold the camera steady, then caught it again as it passed in front of Karisimbi. Luckily the aircraft made a second run, giving me time to reach a new vantage point and improve the composition; only then was I satisfied the exhausting climb had been worth the effort.

As luck would have it, the filming had been completed barely minutes ahead of increasing cloud that would have ruined the setting. I watched as the camera team began to make their way back along the narrow rim of the crater. I had used the same path uncounted times in the past, usually when the gorillas had led me high on the north-western slopes. Rather than take the long route across the grain of the mountain, it was easier to climb over the top on a direct line back to camp, and, weather permitting, I always enjoyed the superb views.

Waiting for the crew to arrive, I moved to a lava outcrop overlooking Karisoke and sat to enjoy what would surely be my last visit to this peak. The wind was beginning to sweep shredded wisps of chilly mist over the edge of the crater, curling it over like breaking surf towards the dark lake at the bottom. Soon the scenic panorama at my feet would be obscured. To the best of my knowledge, Dian had never reached the top of Visoke and seen the impressive views. I had been thinking less often of past events as the days went by, but while feasting my eyes one more time on the great sweep of territory that had been my stamping ground for so long, disjointed memories returned. From the high vantage point I could see at a glance many of the landmarks and distinctive features that had figured so strongly in my work: the swampy meadow that touched the border with Zaire; the main game trail that led north past the dark edge of the Bishitsi bluff near Mount Mikeno; the line of five hills south of Karisoke, favourite haunt of poachers and often frequented by the gorillas of Group 5. But it was Poacher's Hill I remembered best, the hill below which Digit had surprised me with his first uninhibited physical approach, and then Kalele Hill, where eight days later he had succeeded in drawing me into nearly half an hour of rough and tumble play.

As the clouds closed in, drawing a white screen over the view, the arrival of the film crew brought me back to the present. To everyone's great relief the weather had held just long enough for the shoot to be successful. The use of the ancient DC3 aircraft to portray Dian's arrival in Africa was an effective way to introduce the sequences to follow: Dr Leakey meeting her at the grass landing strip in Ruhengeri; and, later, at a wonderfully colourful and crowded market place near Gisenyi, several complicated scenes would show her engaging porters and some men to assist her work, and also meeting the man who would become her interpreter, gorilla tracker and friend. I knew Dian had really flown to Nairobi in a jet, and that after being outfitted by Dr

Leakey, aided and escorted by Alan Root she had driven herself to the Congo in an old, second-hand Land Rover. The film version of her start in Africa was going to be much more visually exciting and fast-moving. Sigourney Weaver was doing a fine job of her portrayal of Dian. I couldn't help feeling that, although she might have balked at many aspects of the storyline, Dian would have approved of the audacious, romantic image that was being created.

A week later I boarded an old Boeing 707 jet for a return to Nairobi. The hectic weeks in Rwanda had been an extraordinary period. I had come back to the country with my mind centred heavily on long past events, emotions and excitements. I was leaving with new knowledge about the status of the gorilla population; the efforts to ensure their protection, and the thriving industry based on the ability to take tourists very close to the animals. Of such value were the gorillas to Rwanda, the narrow stretch of land they inhabited was much more secure. There was no reason to doubt that numbers would increase and that they would survive to see the twenty-first century – which had not been so certain when Dian first arrived.

During the 1960s, swift human expansion and lax control of the shrinking national park had threatened extinction – until the arrival of a lone woman, poorly equipped physically, but endowed with courage and great tenacity, who had worked to stem the trend and eventually reversed it. The one, all too brief contact I had been allowed to make with the gorillas had made it obvious that human intervention and management would increasingly affect their lives. Rwanda was more densely populated than ever – hard put to sustain a viable economy and in desperate need of the foreign exchange earned from tourists.

My short stay was over. Watching the remodelling of the life of a person I had grown to like and respect had given rise to some very strange feelings, but had also revived wonderful memories of an unmatched wildlife experience. I was leaving Rwanda with many unsatisfied desires and no expectation of another return. Except for a few brief forays after work at the Karisoke camp, I had found few chances to enjoy walking alone in the gorillas' lush habitat. I had been particularly disappointed at not being able to visit any of the research groups, especially the Group 5 family, whose numbers now included old Flossie and Petula. I would have loved to have met the two and observed their reactions; I knew I could recognise them – but would they have remembered me?

Leaving behind the mountains where the real-life events had occurred placed the remaining filming to be done outside the country on a different, less personally felt level. From what I had already seen evolving under the careful direction of Michael Apted, I knew for certain the completed film would sharply affect many people's perception of Dian's work and achievements. Although history was being remoulded to suit an entertainment medium, I couldn't help feeling that had Dian been able to see what was being made of her eighteen tempestuous years in Africa, she would have been astonished but, deep down, secretly flattered by her screen image.

Sitting in the noisy 707, thinking the gorillas were better protected than ever before, I could not know that three years later things would go drastically wrong in Rwanda, once more putting them at risk. By October 1990 Rwanda would begin to be enmeshed in a civil war that would bring the country to its knees. The research station at Karisoke would be abandoned and looted several times, and smouldering tribal hatreds would eventually flare into genocide on a horrifying scale.

Epilogue

When I left the Karisoke research camp in May 1972, I knew that a new and productive association between humans and the giant apes was developing. In the work to infiltrate their hidden world, I had discovered that the wary, almost reclusive creatures could be exceptionally amenable and tolerant of intrusion. Indeed, twenty years on, virtually all of the gorillas living on the volcanoes had become used to regular and peaceful contact with large numbers of people. National park boundaries were being maintained, and an acceptable balance between the basic needs of the gorillas and those of the people surrounding them had been established. The future for the gorillas seemed secure. Sadly, a change in the human factor, one more dangerous to the gorillas than ever before, altered this very favourable situation.

In October 1990, Tutsi exiles intent on overthrowing the predominantly Hutu-led government of Rwanda invaded the land. Highly-organised forces under the name of the Rwandan Patriotic Front confronted the Rwandan army, quickly destroying the stability of the region. The ensuing civil war and horrific genocidal massacres that followed soon brought the nation of Rwanda to its knees. For several years, efforts by the Dian Fossey Gorilla Fund and other organisations to repair and maintain the repeatedly looted and damaged Karisoke research station, and to fund anti-poaching patrols, continued – until the risk to life forced withdrawal. With the gorillas' habitat providing exceptionally suitable terrain from which to launch guerrilla warfare, for a long time the misty forests of the volcanoes helped conceal men bent on keeping the country destabilised.

The century in which the formidable primates of the Virunga mountains were first discovered by a European explorer has closed. The mountain gorillas, *Gorilla gorilla beringei*, so named in honour of Captain Oscar von Beringe who encountered them on Mount Sabinio in 1902, have survived to see the new century, but only time will tell if the people who surround the volcanoes can calm their ethnic animosities, and will permit the gorillas to maintain their tentative hold on the fragile and desirable mountain habitat. Now confined to the higher slopes of the volcanoes, many gorillas were killed during the years of civil war; some were even learning that it was best to flee at the sight of humans. However, with the Volcanoes National Park open again, the year 2000 has brought the cautious promise of more peaceful times. Researchers are being allowed to enter the forest to continue their work, and they will bolster the efforts to see that the volcanoes remain protected. The trustful relationship between humans and the forest giants that began thirty years ago may yet help them survive deep into the future.

17